EXCHANGE RATE CRISES IN DEVELOPING COUNTRIES

The International Political Economy of New Regionalisms Series

The International Political Economy of New Regionalisms Series presents innovative analyses of a range of novel regional relations and institutions. Going beyond established, formal, interstate economic organizations, this essential series provides informed interdisciplinary and international research and debate about myriad heterogeneous intermediate level interactions.

Reflective of its cosmopolitan and creative orientation, this series is developed by an international editorial team of established and emerging scholars in both the South and North. It reinforces ongoing networks of analysts in both academia and think-tanks as well as international agencies concerned with micro-, meso- and macro-level regionalisms.

Recent Titles in the Series

Globalization and Antiglobalization
Dynamics of Change in the New World Order
Edited by Henry Veltmeyer

Latin America's Quest for Globalisation
The Role of Spanish Firms
Edited by Félix E. Martín and Pablo Toral

Twisting Arms and Flexing Muscles
Humanitarian Intervention and Peacebuilding in Perspective
Edited by Natalie Mychajlyszyn and Timothy M. Shaw

Asia Pacific and Human Rights
A Global Political Economy Perspective
Paul Close and David Askew

Exchange Rate Crises in Developing Countries

The Political Role of the Banking Sector

MICHAEL G. HALL
University of Northern Iowa, USA

Routledge
Taylor & Francis Group
LONDON AND NEW YORK

First published 2005 by Ashgate Publishing

Reissued 2018 by Routledge
2 Park Square, Milton Park, Abingdon, Oxon, OX14 4RN
711 Third Avenue, New York, NY 10017, USA

Routledge is an imprint of the Taylor & Francis Group, an informa business

First issued in paperback 2018

A Library of Congress record exists under LC control number: 2005018437

ISBN 13: 978-0-815-38896-8 (hbk)
ISBN 13: 978-1-138-61964-7 (pbk)
ISBN 13: 978-1-351-15844-2 (ebk)

Contents

List of Figures and Tables

Figures

Tables

List of Acronyms

APRA	American Popular Revolutionary Alliance (Peru)
BBC	Bangkok Bank of Commerce (Thailand)
BIBF	Bangkok International Banking Facilities (Thailand)
BIS	Bank for International Settlements
BOT	Bank of Thailand
CBI	Central bank independence
CFA	African Financial Community
CNBV	National Bank and Equities Commission (Mexico)
CPI	Consumer price index
DNP	National Planning Department (Colombia)
EAER	*Exchange Arrangements and Exchange Restrictions*
EMU	European Monetary Union
ERR	Exchange-rate regime
FDI	Foreign direct investment
FDN	National Democratic Front (Mexico)
FIDF	Financial Institutions Development Fund (Thailand)
GDP	Gross domestic product
HOT	Hollowing-out thesis
IBM	International Business Machines
IFC	International Finance Corporation
IFS	*International Financial Statistics*
IMF	International Monetary Fund
LIBOR	London Interbank Offered Rate
NAFTA	North American Free Trade Agreement
NIC	Newly industrializing countries
NPL	Non-performing loans
OCA	Optimum currency area
OECD	Organization for Economic Cooperation and Development
PAN	National Action Party (Mexico)
PRD	Democratic Revolutionary Party (Mexico)
PRI	Institutional Revolutionary Party (Mexico)
SDR	Special drawing rights
SET	Stock Exchange of Thailand
SOE	State-owned enterprises
TBA	Thai Bankers' Association
TED	Total external debt
UIP	Uncovered interest parity
WDI	*World Development Indicators*

Preface and Acknowledgements

The 1990s saw a number of exchange-rate crises in developing countries, ranging from Mexico to East Asia, to Brazil, to Russia. The puzzling aspect of so many of these crises was that they struck developing states that were growing rapidly or had significantly reformed their economies. The crises renewed a long-running debate among economists concerning who or what was responsible for the crises. Some economists argued that the governments of these countries were to blame for pursuing inflationary economic policies or failing to provide the proper regulation of domestic financial institutions. Other economists argued that free financial markets are inherently unstable and the herd mentality of investors produced panics over the exchange rates of particular countries. But the rash of exchange rate crises in the 1990s also provided the backdrop for a new idea, that "pegging" the exchange rate in an environment of high "capital mobility" increased the risks of an exchange rate crisis. With a pegged exchange rate, a government promises to exchange its currency for other currencies at a specified rate, but it may not have enough foreign currency on hand to satisfy everyone who wants to buy foreign currency. In most cases this may not be a problem, just as a bank does not have the cash on hand equal to all of the deposits of its customers, since the chance that all bank customers will withdraw their money from their accounts simultaneously is so unlikely. Some economists, however, have argued that in today's world of international finance, where investors can transfer and exchange huge sums of money across national borders with electronic speed, a government promise to exchange currency, if not given solid backing, risks a situation in which the government cannot sell foreign currency to all of those that demand it. These situations are crises and the government's credibility in setting exchange rates collapses. Many of the states listed above had some form of pegged exchange rates before they experienced a crisis. Economists thus focused more attention on how exchange-rate policy affects the likelihood of exchange-rate crises.

But if pegging contributes to crises, why did these governments peg their exchange rates? Some of the older answers to this question, which focused on purely economic variables such as the size of the state's economy or its degree of exposure to international trade, no longer seem enough to explain why governments choose to peg. Newer scholarship on political economy, which explains economic policy as the result of political forces, has drawn attention to a whole new set of explanations. Different scholars have argued that states peg in order to please manufacturers, or in order to maintain public confidence before an election, or because dictatorships have few alternatives in combating inflation. If true, these explanations may give us clues as to what has to change to alter exchange rate policies and to prevent further exchange-rate crises. This book examines the validity of all of these explanations, both economic and political, in the light of evidence from statistical tests and case studies.

The book also examines (and makes a case for) one other explanation that scholars have only recently developed, that governments may also peg to satisfy strong, active banking sectors in their country. Research on the role of the banking sector on exchange-rate policy has been underdeveloped until recently. Some economists have noted a connection between banking crises and exchange-rate crises, the role of lax banking regulation on undermining economic performance, and one scholar, David Shambaugh, has made the case that different forms of international finance are correlated with different exchange-rate policies. This book ties some of this research together, and argues that active banking sectors encourage pegging in part because these banking sectors are often concentrated groups with a small number of large firms, with a critical role in financing economic development, which gives them advantages in lobbying for pegged exchange rates.

I would like to thank Timothy Shaw for including this book in the *International Political Economy of New Regionalisms* series by Ashgate Publishing. I would also like to thank Kirstin Howgate for all of her patient help in shepherding me through the publication process. Thanks are also due to Donna Hamer, Carolyn Court, and Halima Fradley for their efficient editorial administration.

Considerable thanks go to Benjamin J. Cohen for his guidance and advice. He went through early drafts of this work with a well-used set of red pens. Through books, conferences, and classes he has taught a generation of scholars in many settings about international monetary relations and I have been blessed to learn so much from him. Without his sage advice on several points this book would have been much poorer. I thank Kate Bruhn for discussing case selection strategies with me, giving me perspective on the case of Mexico, and for bringing Sydney Weintraub's work on the Mexican peso crisis to my attention. I thank Michael Gordon for pushing me to consider the ramifications of the research for related topics in political economy and the governance of East Asia and Latin America. I also thank Nathaniel Beck, Bill Bernhard, Bill Bielby, J.J. Chwieroth, Garrett Glasgow, and David Leblang Michael Licari, and John Woolley for their help on various technical concerns of quantitative methods. I thank Cynthia Kaplan for her advice on case selection strategy. I thank Peter Montiel and Tamim Bayoumi for their advice on how to measure capital mobility. I thank Philipp Rother for his advice on measuring financial intermediation. I thank Tom Willett and Ken Shadlen for their many suggestions on a conference paper I presented at the APSA Annual Meeting in August 2000. I thank Lisa Martin for her several comments on a manuscript I sent her. I would also like to thank the many scholars, especially Nancy Auerbach, who, after I presented some of my research findings at conferences, pushed me to think longer and harder about the relationship between external debt and the preferences of banks and commercial firms in emerging markets. The role of external debt turned out to be a crucial part of the theory in this research.

Many people also assisted me in the collection of data for the book. For this, I must particularly thank Lia Roberts, Shu Fan and Feng Tao. I would also like to thank Stephen Haggard for allowing me to use some of the resources at the

Graduate School for International Relations and Pacific Studies at the University of California, San Diego.

I would like to thank the University of Northern Iowa for its financial support and the resources that allowed me to gather data from the International Monetary Fund. I must also thank the Institute on Global Conflict and Cooperation (IGCC) at the University of California at San Diego for their generous financial support. The contributions of all of the above have improved my work, but of course I alone am responsible for any and all errors of judgment and fact in this book.

Thanks also go to my parents, who provided me with more patience, emotional support, and financial support than I could ever repay them. Not enough people have parents as loving and supportive as they are. This book is dedicated to them.

Chapter 1

To Peg or Not to Peg, That is the Question

Exchange-rate crises are awful, harrowing spectacles, analogous to bank panics and stock market crashes, with terrible consequences of their own. The past decade has witnessed numerous currency crises in developing states that many had thought were making economic progress. Mexico suffered a peso crisis in 1994, numerous Asian states suffered crises in 1997, Russia devalued and defaulted on its debts in 1998, and Brazil was forced to devalue in early 1999.

The consequences of these crises are familiar to those that followed these events but are still striking when listed. If the government has agreed to exchange its currency at a given rate, governments frequently lose billions of dollars of foreign exchange reserves as investors race to sell the government's currency. In 1994, the Bank of Mexico lost $15 billion, half of its reserves, in trying to maintain its exchange rate for almost a year before the crisis (Banco de Mexico, 1995, p.41). In the end, the value of a country's currency drops suddenly, making the price of imports jump. People lose purchasing power in their wages. Banking crises erupt as banks often fail once they are unable to service the costs of increased external debt (Kaminsky and Reinhart, 1999; Eichengreen, 2003). The loss of foreign and domestic investment damages the growth of the economy. One famous study from many years back estimated that 30% of governments fell within a year after the devaluation (Cooper, 1971, p.28-29). The governments that end up in charge of cleaning up the mess must often accept the policies the International Monetary Fund (IMF) advises as conditions for a loan. In addition to all of this, the effects of the currency crisis can spread like a contagious virus and damage confidence in neighboring economies. The devaluation of the Thai baht in 1997 demonstrated this spectacularly as the crisis spread into the financial markets of Indonesia, Malaysia, and the Philippines.

The number and severity of these crises has prompted scholars to look again at the causes of currency crises. In most of the literature on speculative attacks and currency crises, speculative attacks are caused either by poor economic fundamentals or self-fulfilling prophesies and panics.[1] In some economic models, inflation and current account deficits, especially if they result from expansionary fiscal and monetary policy, will cause investors to lose confidence in the value of a currency. A currency crisis is thus a rational response by investors to the poor condition of the economy or inflationary macroeconomic policy. Others, however, argue that investors can behave like herds of cattle that can stampede at the slightest tremor. If enough investors simply believe that a currency is going to lose its value, others will follow suit, and major sell-off takes place. This could happen regardless of whether governments followed prudent macroeconomic policy or not. Economists thus debate how rational and stable investor behavior is during currency crises.

Against this backdrop of economic theory, some economists have begun to argue that exchange-rate policy is also a key culprit in producing currency crises. In this view, exchange-rate pegs have made developing states prone to speculative attacks and currency crises. Pegged exchange rates are those in which the government mandates a specific value or range of values for the exchange rate, but retains the power to alter the exchange rate at its discretion at any time. Many of the states that suffered in the crises listed above, such as Mexico, Brazil, and Thailand, had pegged exchange rates up until the crisis hit. If the government reserves the right to alter the exchange rate at any time, investors stand to gain or lose substantial amounts if they buy or sell before an alteration in the exchange rate. Investors are thus tempted to place bets on when the next devaluation or revaluation will take place. These bets could reflect either estimates of a government's macroeconomic policies or the behavior and mood of other investors. As the international capital market grows, these bets grow can larger, even to the point of overwhelming a state's ability to exchange currency. When a state does not have the reserves of foreign currency to exchange currency at its announced rate, that is a crisis. Policy analysts and other observers have called upon developing states to avoid pegged exchange rates in order to reduce the risk of speculative attacks.[2]

Many economists now argue that the growth of international capital mobility has made it prohibitively costly to maintain exchange-rate pegs. By 1997, investors owned a total of $6 trillion of tradable securities across borders (IMF, 1999a, p. 142). The amount keeps growing, and most of these assets are highly liquid. The growth in electronic computing and telecommunications, the innovation of new financial instruments, and deregulation of financial markets have combined to expand the flow of capital across borders dramatically. A number of economists have argued that the current international environment of mobile capital has made the option of pegging simply unworkable (Eichengreen, 1994; Goldstein, 1995; Obstfeld and Kenneth Rogoff, 1995; and Fischer, 2001). One, Barry Eichengreen, even predicts that in the future, capital mobility will leave states with no choices but monetary union (in which a country shares a currency with another country) or floating (in which currency markets determine the value of the exchange rate) (Eichengreen, 1994, p. 4-7). Different forms of pegging which lie between the "corner solutions" (Goldstein, 1995, p.9) of monetary union and floating will be "hollowed out" (Eichengreen, 1994, p.6). This contention that high capital mobility will prevent states from pegging their exchange rates is referred to in this book as the "hollowing-out thesis" (HOT).

But some states insisted on pegging their exchange rates in spite of the risks and costs of growing capital mobility. Thailand, Mexico, and Brazil each maintained a pegged exchange rate for years while its exposure to capital flows grew and kept on pegging until a crisis erupted. Meanwhile, other states such as Peru and the Philippines had abandoned pegs many years before. Why should some countries persist in pegging while others were quick to abandon it? Why would some state take longer to abandon pegs than others if the risks are the same for each? Why did some states tempt fate while others did not? These are the central questions for this book. This book will attempt to explain differences in exchange-rate policies and the use of pegging among developing countries.

The interests and lobbying of domestic banks, I contend, explain much of the drive behind maintaining a peg until a crisis erupts. The choice of an exchange-rate regime is thus rooted in politics as much as economics. Banks and commercial firms[3] often borrow more from abroad when bank financing is active. If the exchange rate should fall and foreign currency becomes more expensive, external debt becomes harder to repay. An active banking sector has advantages in influencing exchange-rate policy. In countries with financial systems based on bank-credit, banks are critical engines for investment and a banking crisis could cripple the economy. Banking sectors also tend to be more concentrated in such countries, allowing bankers to organize easily to defend their interests. In countries where businesses rely on other sources of financing, private banks are weaker and governments have more opportunity to abandon pegging earlier.

Exchange-rate regimes

Before exploring the theory, what options do governments have in choosing an exchange-rate regime in the first place? The exchange-rate regime (ERR) is the rule for how an exchange rate is valued. An exchange-rate regime is defined by the extent to which either government or market forces determine a country's exchange rates. A government can choose from any one of a number of exchange-rate regime options, which can be arrayed along a spectrum (see Figure 1.1, next page). Across the spectrum, governments trade-off degrees of exchange-rate stability for control over interest rates and monetary policy. At one end of the spectrum, a government can determine the rate and devise mechanisms for rigidly maintaining that exchange-rate value into the distant future. The primary benefit of this arrangement is that the exchange rate remains stable over time. The government, however, loses control of interest rates and autonomy over monetary policy when capital is mobile. At the other end of the spectrum, a government can let currency markets determine the value of exchange rates at all times, with no government interference. Government has the most autonomy over the money supply and interest rates, but currency markets tend to make the exchange rate fluctuate. In between these polar alternatives are various mixtures of government and market determination of exchange rates, yielding different degrees of exchange-rate stability and monetary policy autonomy.

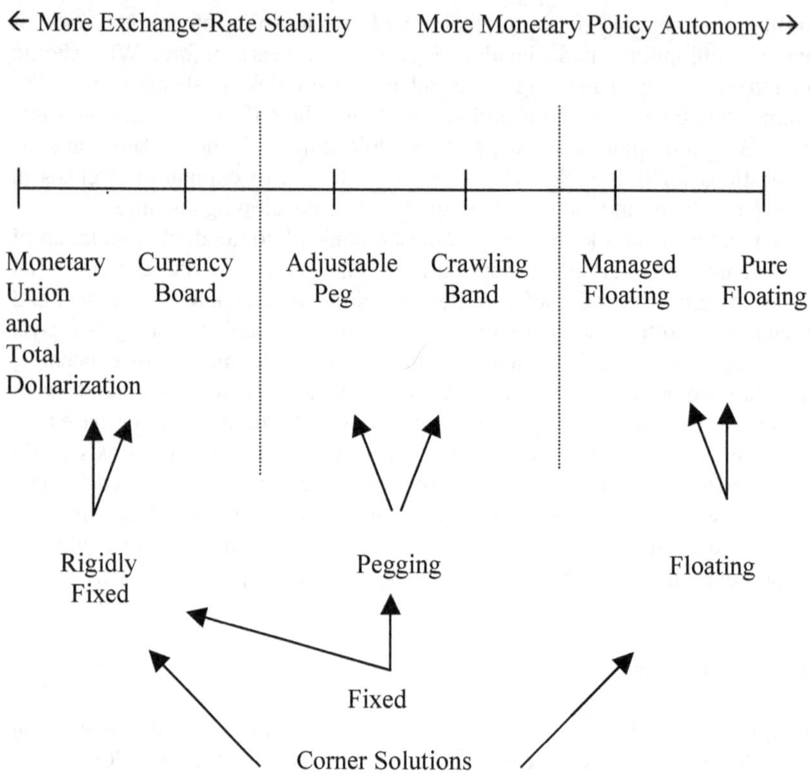

Figure 1.1 The spectrum of exchange-rate regime choices

At the fixed-rate end of the spectrum is the option of monetary union. Here, countries share a common currency because one or more of the governments involved agreed to do so. The U.S. and Panamanian governments established a monetary union in 1904, which has continued ever since with only one brief interruption (Cohen, 1998, p.174). Panamanians use the U.S. dollar in their daily domestic transactions. Thus, the people of Panama effectively have an exchange rate of one dollar to one dollar.

The next choice along the spectrum is that of a "currency board," in which a country has a separate currency, but only issues currency at a fixed ratio to reserves of a specific foreign currency that it holds. For example, in Lithuania in the early 1990s, the Bank of Lithuania was charged with the power to issue new currency, but under law it could only issue four new Lithuanian litas for every one U.S. dollar that it could acquire for its reserves (Camard, 1996). In this way, the Bank of Lithuania could guarantee that it will exchange one U.S. dollar for four litas. This choice also provides for exchange-rate stability, as in a monetary union, but government still does not have the autonomy to determine interest rates or the volume of the money supply. It is the equivalent of a monetary union, except that a government has the political symbolism of its own currency and the government can earn interest on its foreign exchange reserves. For the purposes of this book, monetary union and currency boards will together form one of three basic choices for an ERR, called "rigidly fixed exchange rates."

At the other end of the spectrum are "floating" or "flexible" exchange rates, where the market determines the value of the exchange rate. In a "managed float" currency markets are the main determinant of exchange rates, but the government, at its discretion, may influence the exchange rate by adjusting the money supply to raise or to lower interest rates or exchange rates, or by intervening in currency markets. The government does not necessarily commit itself to an announced exchange-rate target. Many emerging-market countries, such as Indonesia, the Philippines and Bolivia, engage in managed floating. Many floats in developing states seem to be managed floats (Calvo and Reinhart, 2000). In a "pure float," the government does not attempt to influence the exchange rate at all. A pure float represents the opposite extreme from monetary union. Both forms of floating are the second basic choice for exchange-rate regimes. "Floating" exchange rates in this book refer to both managed and pure floats. As rigidly fixed rates and floating rates represent opposite ends of the spectrum, they shall be referred to as the "corner solutions" to the problem of ERR choice.

"Pegged" exchange rates constitute the choice in the broad middle of the spectrum between rigidly fixed rates at one end and floating rates on the other. Pegged rates involve a claim on the part of the government that it will exchange its currency for another at a specified rate, even though the government may not have the reserves to supply all the foreign currency people might demand, as it necessarily would with a currency board. The exchange rate is an "adjustable peg" in that the government can alter the rate at its discretion at any time.[4] The peg value is thus contingent upon the government commitment to that exchange rate, its volume of foreign exchange reserves, and its foreign borrowing capacity. With discretion to alter the exchange rate, governments have more monetary autonomy than in the case of monetary union or a currency board. The more adjustments the government makes to the exchange rate, however, the less stable the rate will be.

Pegging arrangements come in a number of forms, reflecting a number of different considerations. A country may peg its currency to a single currency, as say, Jordan pegs to the U.S. dollar or Lesotho pegs to the South African rand. It could also form a composite index of two or more currencies (called a "basket") and peg the currency to a specific value of that index, as Morocco does, to accommodate its exchange rate to two or more trading partners. The government could set a specific pegged rate for its currency, or it can let currencies float within a "band" that allows exchange rates some room for maneuver. For example, Saudi Arabia allows its currency to float within plus or minus 7.25 per cent of its assigned value against the dollar. Furthermore, whether a country uses a specific peg or a band, a government may choose to alter the exchange rate at specific, unannounced instances that suit its interest or according to a pre-announced timetable (which would be an "adjustable" peg or band). However, the government may continuously alter the exchange rate according to specific economic indicators such as domestic inflation (called a "crawling" peg or band) in order to adjust the exchange rate to constantly changing economic conditions. Here, all of these variants on adjustable pegs (baskets, bands, and crawls) will be included under the umbrella term "pegging."[5] All forms of pegging are in a sense a "hybrid" or compromise form of ERR, between the polar alternatives of monetary union or currency boards at one extreme or freely floating exchange rates at the other. The composition of currencies in the peg, the amount of wiggle room for the exchange rate, and the timing of alterations in the rate are not the central focus of this book. The research here investigates why states choose pegged exchange rates instead of one of the corner solutions despite a high level of capital mobility.

Capital mobility

Capital mobility refers to the ability of capital to move across national borders. In a world of high capital mobility, currencies and other financial assets can be traded with little problem. In a world of low capital mobility, international investment may incur all sorts of transaction costs, which include brokerage fees, costs for acquiring information, and legal restrictions on capital transactions. Foreign and domestic assets also come with different risks and taxes, which may also reduce incentives for investors to move capital across borders. In the absence of such frictions, perfect capital mobility has the effect of equalizing the price of similar financial assets in different countries. "Financial arbitrage," where investors profit from differences in prices in different markets, produces this equalizing process. Assume a case in which six-month treasury bonds in two different countries have different rates of return, even after accounting for the expected exchange rate between the two countries. Assume also that the exchange rate is just as likely to appreciate as it is to depreciate, making each investment equally risky. Investors in the country with the lower rate of return would sell their bonds to buy bonds in the country with the higher rate of return. As bonds with the higher rate of return are bought, their price increases, and their rate of return goes down. As bonds with the lower rate of return are sold, their price decreases, and their rate of return rises.

Financial arbitrage helps to explain why capital mobility, which is the *ability* to trade capital across borders, is not the same thing as capital flows, which are the *amount* of capital traded across borders (Machlup, et. al, 1972). In the example just given investors stop trading bonds when the rates of return for both bonds are equal given the expected exchange rate. Capital flows for these bonds would cease, even though capital mobility has not changed. Investors are still *able* to make international transactions, but would not be *willing* to do so because there would be no further profit in it. In practice though, higher capital mobility is associated with greater capital flows. Capital markets only reach a durable equilibrium if exchange-rate expectations and other investment risks remain constant for long periods, but they almost never do.

Capital flows have undoubtedly grown over the past few decades. In developing countries, net capital investment (both direct and portfolio) as a share of GDP rose from an average of two percent in 1987 to five percent in 1997 (IMF, 1999a, p. 3). The daily turnover in major foreign exchange markets reached $1.88 trillion in 2004, almost triple the daily turnover of $650 billion in 1989 (BIS, 2004, p. 5). As it is more difficult to measure capital mobility, economists are in less agreement as to how much that has grown, if at all. Many commentators today write as if the world has perfect capital mobility. It is probably more accurate to say that while capital mobility is not perfect, it has been growing over the past two decades. Many countries have lifted their controls or restrictions on international capital trading since the 1970s. The recent growth in capital mobility is the result of improvements in trading and settlement practices and computer technology that have lowered transaction costs, as well as efforts by governments to liberalize capital flows and the development of various financial innovations that allow investors to diversify risks more efficiently. Nevertheless, some risks, information costs and capital controls still remain.

Any ERR, such as pegging, that involves a government commitment risks the possibility that the government will not have the international liquidity to meet that commitment. International liquidity includes both the government's reserves of foreign currency and its capacity for foreign borrowing. The government's stated exchange rate may generate a demand for foreign currency that outstrips the ability of private agents and the government to supply it, which is an exchange-rate crisis. As capital mobility rises, the potential for demand to outstrip supply increases. Volatile foreign exchange markets are trading ever-larger volumes of currency, beyond the volumes of foreign exchange that governments have on reserve or can raise through borrowing. As recent events have shown, currency crises seem to be becoming more common.

Governments can manage such market pressures with capital controls, higher interest rates, or foreign borrowing (Eichengreen, 1994, pp.66-73), but these are becoming increasing costly as capital mobility increases market pressures. Investors increasingly find ways of circumventing capital controls. Higher interest rates deflate the economy and make public debt more expensive. Borrowing from the International Monetary Fund, foreign governments or international banks can come with unacceptable conditions. States have weakening costly or weakening defenses for exchange-rate commitments. Growing capital mobility, then, presents growing risks of currency crises for states that peg.

But why do states have such different attitudes to the risks of capital mobility? If pegs are more risky as capital mobility grows, why do some states peg and others not? In the late 1990s, for example, Lithuania and Estonia had currency boards, but Latvia floated its currency, despite gaining independence from the Soviet Union and integrating with the European economy at roughly the same time as the other two Baltic States. Why did Thailand peg its currency and Indonesia engage in a managed float prior to the Asian crisis, while Thailand was arguably more open to foreign capital flows than Indonesia was? In the 1990s, many South American states removed their capital controls and opened themselves to American and European investment. Why then, until a few years ago, did Brazil use a crawling peg, while Argentina used a currency board and Bolivia floated? Why did Brazil and Argentina fall into the trap of a currency crisis but Bolivia did not?

Hence two puzzles need to be explored. First, assuming similar levels of capital mobility, why should some countries try to maintain a peg while others float or pursue a rigid fix? Second, why have some countries held on to pegged rates longer than others did? Why do some states hold onto a peg for so long that it takes a crisis to force a change, while other abandon their pegs earlier and more readily? These are the central questions of the book.

The scope of this book

This book does not survey and analyze all of the causes of currency crises. It only explores an under-appreciated but key ingredient of many currency crises, the drive to maintain a pegged exchange rate. Moreover, it explores one of the main causes of a drive to peg, a strong bank-financing system for economic development.

The focus of study in this book is the ERR choices of developing states. Specifically, whether states will choose an intermediate regime, some form of pegging, as opposed to either of the corner solutions. Many scholars have studied exchange-rate regime choices, but they normally analyze the decision between fixed exchange rates (be they monetary unions, currency boards, or pegs) and floating exchange rates. At issue is whether the exchange-rate stability associated with fixed rates or the monetary policy autonomy associated with floating rates is more appropriate for the economic or political conditions of a country. But states may also choose a mix of exchange-rate stability and monetary policy autonomy rather than wholly sacrificing one or the other. Since little has been written on the choice of pegging versus not pegging apart from the literature on the HOT, a new theoretical approach is needed to address how governments frame the choice of ERRs.

Moreover, the research incorporates the dimension of time, asking why states peg for as long as they do. Only a few studies of exchange-rate policy have investigated why states choose the ERR they have for as long as they do. One study, by Blomberg, Frieden, and Stein (2002) however, examines the factors behind why states peg for certain periods, highlighting the role of the manufacturing sector and the timing of elections. By looking at timing one can examine gain perspective on the behavior of governments facing the risk of speculative attacks on their currency. At any given speculative attack, a government has the choice of defending its exchange rate or abandoning its policy (Leblang, 2003). Different factors will shape that choice, including elections, partisan affiliation of the government, and macroeconomic conditions. The more the government chooses to defend, defends successfully, and maintains confidence in the currency, the longer the peg will hold. Examining the length of time the government chooses to maintain a policy says much about its behavior towards currency crises.

The research presented here includes statistical tests of aggregate data and four qualitative case studies. The time frame for the quantitative research will be the years from 1987 to 1998. This is the period for which statistical data on capital mobility and ERRs are most available. The case studies will provide some insight on the choice of exchange-rate regimes from 1976 to the present, when states were allowed to choose ERRs freely under IMF rules.

The book will focus on the policies of middle-income countries, countries whose GDP is between the most developed and least developed nations. Many of these states are the "emerging markets" that experienced crises in the past 15 years. Developed countries either float their currencies or are participants in the European Monetary Union. Conversely, the least developed states in the world have less exposure to capital mobility. States such as those in the CFA Franc Zone, for example, have relatively little international trade or capital flows, and what there is in the way of external economic activity is mainly centered on one trading partner or commodity. Thus, it is the middle-income countries that demonstrate the most puzzling cases of ERR choice and the most variation within the possible range of options for ERRs.

The main argument

As mentioned above, I argue that when private banks provide most of the financing of commercial firms in a middle-income country, the government faces stiff opposition from domestic banks against abandoning a peg. If a state's financial system does not rely heavily on banks, banks (and often commercial firms) offer less resistance, and the government has more political opportunity to abandon a peg in difficult circumstances. I call this the financial-intermediation hypothesis. Financial intermediation refers to the role of intermediaries such as banks or capital markets in mediating how the money of those who save is allocated among those who borrow. In some developing countries, banks and commercial firms acquire unhedged dollar-denominated debt from foreign banks. Guillermo Calvo and Carmen Reinhart (2000) have dubbed this process "liability dollarization." In such cases, those who borrow have an interest in an exchange-rate peg and exchange-rate stability, which will make the repayment of dollar-denominated debt easier (Mishkin, 1996; Shambaugh, 2004). When financial intermediation is strong, as it is in Thailand, Mexico, and Brazil, liability dollarization tends to increase. In countries with less financial intermediation, such as Peru and the Philippines, liability dollarization tends to affect fewer vested interests. Different developing countries thus face different degrees of liability dollarization.

Why does bank-based financing in particular lead to more pressure on the government to keep the peg? First, in many developing states with strong banking sectors, the banking sector has a concentrated structure, with most of the assets and activity concentrated in a few large banks. The private banking sector is even more easily organized for political action if it is protected from foreign and domestic competition, organized through a banker's association, and thus operates as a cartel. The concentrated and/or cartelized structure allows banks to organize and articulate their interests and organize for political action more easily than a mass of diverse investors in capital markets or diverse business owners (Olson, 1982). Secondly, if the banks are the primary channel of finance in the economy, then problems in the banking sector have more significant effects in the rest of the economy. Increased or uncertain costs for external debt repayment could constrain future investment and economic development. If the banking sector also has a worrying amount of non-performing loans (NPLs), then a floatation or devaluation of the currency could also trigger a banking crisis. Governments would presumably be more attentive to warnings from a strong banking sector. Governments faced with a strong banking sector are more likely to maintain a peg, even as capital mobility grows.

What role does capital mobility play then? It structures the economic risks and costs of ERRs, but these risks and costs alone do not determine the political decisions over ERRs. The HOT argues that today's environment of high capital mobility has made pegging too costly to be workable, and thus states can only operate rigid fix or a float. These corner solutions, however, also have their own costs, which can be quite high (Frankel, 1999). Floating can lead to exchange-rate instability, resulting in volatile prices for imports and exports, which are especially hard on small, open economies. With rigidly fixed exchange rates lose autonomy over monetary policy, forcing states to confine economic adjustment to fiscal policy or changes in the goods market. The HOT argues that the costs of pegging are still greater than these costs as capital mobility grows. But the relative costs of pegging, floating and rigid fixes differ from state to state, and the decisions that weigh those costs become an inherently political process.

Capital mobility has an indirect effect on ERR choices. Evidence from tests presented here indicate that increases in capital mobility does not increase the likelihood of abandoning a peg. The likelihood of abandoning a peg is correlated with other variables, such as the strength of bank-based financing, trade exposure, and the size of the manufacturing sector. Capital mobility instead largely determines what the consequences of an ERR policy are. If a state pegs and capital mobility rises, a state is at a greater risk of a currency crisis. If a crisis erupts, it forces a state to abandon a peg. Once forced off a peg, a state rarely re-establishes one. Those states that do not have a peg are less likely to experience a currency crisis unless it is experiencing contagion from other states going through a crisis. Domestic politics and economic conditions thus encourages states to make a particular ERR choice, and capital mobility will shape the risks and costs of that decision, costs that may be high enough to force a state off any chosen peg.

The contributions of the book

This financial intermediation hypothesis makes six contributions to the literature on international political economy. First, this hypothesis helps to explain why so many emerging markets that achieved high rates of growth experienced currency crises. Many of these crises have struck emerging markets that have had relatively strong investment prospects, such as Mexico, Thailand, South Korea and Brazil. Strong institutions for financial intermediation (be they banks or capital markets) increase a state's long-run growth (King and Levine, 1993; Levine, 1997). But the very banking systems that contributed to rapid growth in these states also became vested interests in favor of an ultimately unsustainable exchange-rate policy.

Second, it fills some important holes in the literature on ERR policy and currency crises. Some economists have analyzed the link between banking and currency crises, discussing how losses of confidence in the currency often lead to losses of confidence in the banking system (Velasco and Cabezas, 1998; Cooper, 1999 and Kaminsky and Reinhart, 1999). The emphasis in these works, however, is on the links between economic variables, such as how a currency crisis affects a country with a high rate of non-performing loans. The research here emphasizes the political connections and demonstrates that causation also works in the other direction. Banks are treated as an interest group with some power to sway exchange-rate policy in developing countries, and the research investigates how banks have that power in some developing states and not others.

Other scholars have investigated other political sources of exchange-rate policy in developing states. Some have found that the stronger the manufacturing sector in the economy, the more a government faces pressure to abandon a peg so that the real exchange rate does not appreciate, making manufacturers less competitive (Blomberg, Frieden and Stein, 2002; Frieden and Stein, 2001). Elections can also encourage governments to maintain a peg, in that a government that devalues or abandons a peg before an election loses credibility and faces the wrath of consumers who may pay more for imports (Blomberg, Frieden and Stein, 2002; Leblang, 2003). Lawrence Broz (2002) has also argued that autocracies are more likely to maintain pegged exchange rates. Democracies, he argues have the credibility to fight inflation through an independent central bank and do not need a fixed exchange rate. Autocracies, however, do not have the credibility to establish a truly independent central bank, and so must rely on fixed exchange rates to fight inflation. Only one scholar, George Shambaugh (2004) has examined the relation between patterns of financial investment and the choice of ERR. This book refines and extends the research on the connection.

Third, it contributes to our understanding of the autonomy of the state in a globalizing economy. The first wave of writing on the subject of globalization tended to argue that states would lose their autonomy to the global marketplace and states would have to converge on the same set of economic policies to satisfy the market. The HOT could be interpreted as one strand of this position. A more nuanced view of globalization has arisen that argues that states retain some autonomy over economic policy, (Garrett and Lange, 1995; Rodrik, 1997; Garrett,

1998; Mosley, 2000) a view that explains why economic policy still differs across different countries despite advancing globalization. This research yields some implications for our understanding of this question. Globalization, in the form of international financial transactions, is powerful, but its power is primarily to shape the costs of economic policy. Once a state is hit with a successful attack over its peg, it often dumps the peg, refusing to establish a new peg anytime soon. But states may go for years tempting fate with international capital markets before a crisis hits. In which case, domestic political considerations might push a state to take risks that other states would not take. States thus have "wiggle room" in choosing ERRs that can last for years, which explains some of the diversity of ERR policy in a world of highly mobile capital.

Fourth, it expands our understanding of the workings of interest group politics in developing countries, by expanding our understanding of the resources banks have to exercise power. When banks are the primary source of financing in a developing country, the banks are often a concentrated sector, with most of the assets in a few firms. This makes it easier for the domestic banks to cartelize their operations, organize to articulate their interests, and lobby to keep foreign banks from operating in their country. This book explores the structure of banking systems in different states, and how different structures lead to the presence or absence of bankers in the constellation of interests lobbying on questions of ERR policy, and how in some cases the bankers can use their cartelized organization and role in the economy to pressure the government.

Fifth, it helps illuminate the effects of different systems of finance in developing countries. Most studies of financial intermediation examine its effects on economic growth (King and Levine, 1993; Levine, 1997). Only a few studies have examined their effects on economic policy (Zysman, 1983; Henning, 1994; Shambaugh 2004). While banks in bank-financed systems often develop strong coalitions with commercial firms, capital markets do not develop such coalitions, since investors are more atomized and less organized. The system of finance in a country shapes the political organization of financial interests.

Sixth, the hypothesis allows us to identify developing states with strong banking sectors, dollar-denominated debts, and a pegged exchange rate as states with the warning signs of a currency crisis. The analysis allows us to add to the list of warning signs that observers of international monetary relations use to identify states at risk of a crisis (see Eichengreen, 2003). As will be discussed in the conclusion, however, few states today exhibit this combination of conditions.

The plan of the book

Chapter 2 examines the theories of ERR choice. Included in this survey of theory are economic theories of ERR choice such as optimal currency area theory and the HOT. More recent theories from political economy are then examined, such as theories that highlight the role of the manufacturing sector, elections, and democratic transparency in governing. Finally, I explore the assumptions and reasoning behind the financial intermediation hypothesis.

Chapter 3 reports on the methods and results of the statistical tests. It begins with details on the research design and the indicators used in the tests. I perform a number of cross-section, time-series hazard tests that attempt to predict the likelihood of pegging as a function of political and economic variables. These tests find no correlation between the level of capital mobility and the likelihood of pegging. These tests also show that countries in which banks are heavily involved in the financing of industry are more likely to choose to peg, and to persist in maintaining pegs as an official policy of the government, even when controlling for other variables. The subsequent case studies thus examine the connection between financial systems and ERR choice in more depth.

Chapters 4-7 report on the evidence from case studies. Chapter 4 illustrates the connection between financial systems and exchange rates with the experience of Thailand. Chapter 5 illustrates the connection in the more complex case of Mexico. Chapter 6 illustrates the different path that Peru took. Chapter 7 on Colombia examines a case in which a country maintained a peg for reasons that had nothing to do with financial intermediaiton. The purpose of the case studies is to weigh evidence for the financial intermediation hypothesis using methods that avoid the problems of statistical testing, by putting each country in its proper context. The case studies also provide comparisons for how the well the financial intermediation hypothesis performs against rival hypotheses in the same context.

Different cases are selected for examination according to their banking systems and exchange-rate policies. Instead of testing for causation, the cases are selected so that they can check the validity of the measures used in the statistical tests and investigate why certain cases deviate from the theory. Thailand is the first case because it is a good example of a country with a strong bank-credit system that pegged up until 1997, longer than most middle-income countries. Since the case fits the theory well, it provides an opportunity to trace out the causal processes posited in the theory.

Mexico is a country with a relatively strong bank-credit system that did not formally peg during the late 1980s and 1990s. On closer inspection, though, Mexico's "managed float" was highly managed, involving a crawling band from 1991 to 1994. Extensive dollar-denominated debts throughout the economy also provided an incentive against devaluation until the combination of foreign investment inflows, current account deficits and an overvalued peso became unsustainable.

The case of Peru demonstrates the financial intermediation through a negative example. Peru has a relatively weak banking sector. It also abandoned its pegged exchange rate much earlier than any other case in the book. President Alberto Fujimori, who floated the Peruvian currency in 1990, faced little domestic opposition to the abandonment of a peg, in contrast to the leaders of Thailand and Mexico.

Colombia is a case of a country that maintained various forms of pegged exchange rates, but has no strong financial intermediation, either through bank credit or through capital markets. A rigid political system that encourages policy inertia, a commitment to relatively low inflation, and an economy dependent on (often illegal) foreign trade have given Colombia an interest in maintaining some form of pegging for some time. The examination of the Colombian case demonstrates that deviations from the theory do occur, but under circumstances that are unlikely to repeat themselves in other countries.

Little data is available to the public concerning the lobbying of interest groups in developing countries. The case studies rely on what data is available to the public, such as central bank data on economic conditions or the operations of banks. These case studies often draw on the exchange-rate policy-making process from journalistic accounts of sudden adjustments of exchange-rate policy, whether they are significant changes in the value of the exchange rate or changes in the exchange-rate regime. Journalists are more likely to report what various interest groups would like to see the exchange rate do and what governments concerns are in times of pressure and crisis. The narratives, then, combine central bank data, studies by economists, and journalistic accounts.

Chapter 8 explores the implications of this research for theory and policy concerning the international monetary system. The chapter summarizes how well the evidence in this and other empirical investigations support the hypotheses discussed in chapter 2. It also details the implications of the financial intermediation hypothesis for current literature on ERR policy and makes predictions concerning exchange-rate crises in the future.

Notes

[1] Ozkan and Sutherland (1994) develop the most significant model incorporating economic fundamentals. On self-fulfilling crises in foreign exchange markets, see Obstfeld, 1994. For a good overview of the causes of speculative attacks, see Eichengreen, et. al, 2003, pp. 103-113.

[2] For examples of this view in policy analysis or popular literature, see Goldstein, 1995; Council on Foreign Relations, 1999 and Economist Survey, 2003.

[3] In this book, the phrase "commercial firms" refers to all business firms primarily engaged in production or trade but not in banking or other financial activities. Commercial firms include both manufacturers and producers of primary products and both the tradables and non-tradables sectors.

[4] This adjustment though, may require the agreement of other governments, as it did in the special case of the European Monetary System.

[5] Eichengreen (1994) argues that currency boards, as well as pegs, will be hollowed out as capital mobility grows. The recent crisis in Argentina would seem to bear him out. Properly administered currency boards, however, have the liquidity to deal with currency exchanges while pegs do not. Since this lack of reserves makes pegs particularly prone to crises, they are treated separately here.

Chapter 2

Theories of Exchange-Rate Regime Determination

This chapter surveys literature on ERR choice and examines the causal logic behind the theories examined in this book. Researchers have developed three main bodies of theory to explain the choice of ERRs: optimal currency area theory (OCA), the hollowing-out thesis, and political economy approaches. OCA theory discusses how various characteristics of an economy determine its ERR. The hollowing-out thesis (HOT) argues that as the capital mobility rises, fewer states will peg. Economists developed both OCA theory and the HOT and unsurprisingly they analyze ERRs in terms of economic variables. In order to make specific, falsifiable hypotheses with these theories, one normally has to assume that states are unitary actors run by governments primarily interested in increasing output or price stability. This assumption, however, is probably responsible for much of discrepancies between these theories and actual ERR choices. By contrast, a new approach based on theories of political economy treats the state as a collection of diverse political actors. Political economy approaches explain ERR choices in terms of the domestic politics of a state and the financial intermediation hypothesis described here is part of this approach. The chapter examines the role of three political economy variables (elections, transparency, and the size of the manufacturing sector) that have potential for explaining the persistence of pegging before examining the role of financial intermediation in more depth.

The Mundell-Fleming model

Economists base almost all of their theorizing on ERR choice on the Mundell-Fleming model of exchange rates. This section briefly describes the Mundell-Fleming model to provide a foundation for the review of the literature on ERR choice.

The Mundell-Fleming model states that, given rigid prices in the short-run, states cannot sustain the conditions of high capital mobility, exchange-rate stability, and monetary-policy autonomy simultaneously (Mundell, 1962; Mundell, 1968; Fleming, 1962). To follow this analysis, it helps to group monetary union, currency boards, and pegged exchange rates under the umbrella term "fixed" exchange rates, as all of these choices involve some level of state-determined exchange-rates. The analysis assumes that prices are rigid in the short-run, and thus increases in the money supply produce increases in the nation's output, and decreases in the money supply produce decreases in output. Increasing the money supply lowers interest rates and reducing the money supply raises interest rates, all other things being equal. When a state can raise or lower interest rates without corrections from financial markets, that states has "autonomy" or control over its monetary policy.

The analysis also assumes securities in different countries are perfect substitutes. If securities different countries have similar properties then investors will seek to engage in financial arbitrage, selling securities with lower interest rates to buy securities with higher interest rates, looking for the maximum profit. As investors buy up securities with higher interest rates, the price of those securities increases and the return or interest rate on those securities falls (The prices and interest rates of securities are inverse to one another). As investors sell securities with lower interest rates, the price of those securities falls and their interest rates rise. Thus, with financial arbitrage, interest rates will have a tendency to equalize over time. Arbitrage ceases when interest rates become equivalent given existing exchange rates and investors cannot exploit interest rate differentials. If capital is "immobile" and investors face legal or practical obstacles to financial trading however, then financial arbitrage cannot occur.

Given these assumptions, states may have only two out of the following three: capital mobility, fixed exchange rates, and monetary policy autonomy. If a state has fixed exchange rates and high capital mobility, then it has no control over its monetary policy. In such circumstances when a state lowers interest rates and increases the money supply, investors sell off the country's securities and buy foreign securities. As investors buy foreign securities, the government buys back its own currency and sells foreign currency at its specified exchange rate. Low interest rates on domestic securities rise to meet foreign interest rates. The state loses control over interest rates and the money supply as market activities counteract state policy. If capital is mobile and the exchange rate floats, however, then as investors buy or sell foreign currency to buy or sell foreign securities, then market activity alters the exchange rate, not the interest rate. The state can alter the interest rate without countervailing arbitrage pressures. If capital is immobile and the state maintains a fixed exchange rate, then any attempts to alter the interest rate will again not face countervailing market pressures, as financial arbitrage is blocked.

The dynamic described in the Mundell-Fleming model does not determine what ERR choices states will make. The model simply argues that all ERR choices come with economic costs, costs that differ along the spectrum of ERR choices. If capital is mobile, then attempts at improving exchange-rate stability come at the expense of monetary policy autonomy. Correspondingly if a state would want more monetary policy autonomy, it would have to sacrifice some exchange-rate stability. Theories of ERR determination discuss different the benefits and costs to the state under different ERR options, and specify the conditions that would determine why a state would prefer one set of cost and benefits over another.

Optimum currency area theory

OCA theory developed in response to the question of whether or not different states should share a common currency. An OCA is a group of countries for whom the benefits of price stability associated with fixed exchange rates outweigh any macroeconomic costs such as inflation, unemployment, and trade imbalances. Conditions that make an OCA worthwhile give a country an interest in maintaining some form of fixed exchange rates. Conditions that make an OCA too costly make floating preferable. Economists have developed a number of theoretical models and identified a number of different variables that would determine how feasible it would be to have a common currency or fixed exchange rates (Edison and Melvin, 1990; Tavlas, 1993). High trade exposure, a small economy, and trade dependence on one country or one economic sector make fixed exchange rates and exchange-rate stability preferable. By contrast, low trade exposure, a large economy, and diversity in foreign economic partners or domestic economic sectors would make floating preferable. Assuming that all other conditions are constant, each individual condition might have a decisive impact on the desirability of either fixed or floating exchange rates. Unfortunately, economists have had difficulty in determining how desirable an ERR might be if two or more of these conditions vary simultaneously.

Shortly after IMF rules allowed member states the freedom to choose ERRs, several economists ran a number of statistical tests to determine whether the variables cited in OCA theory correlated with actual ERR choices. Different economists employed different statistical models on datasets incorporating several developed and developing countries: Robert Heller (1978) employed discriminant analysis, Jacob Dreyer (1978) employed probit analysis, and Gordon Weil (1984) employed ordinary least squares regression and logit models. While the models yielded some minor differences in results, they largely confirmed that high trade exposure and geographic concentration of trade correlated with fixed exchange rates, and also found that high inflation differentials among states correlated with floating exchange rates. A different study by Paul Holden, Merle Holden, and Esther Suss (1979) dispensed with operationalizing ERR choice as a dichotomous variable (fixed or floating). They developed an index of exchange-rate flexibility that cast ERR choice as a continuous variable. The index measures changes in the trade-weighted exchange rate, changes in foreign reserves, and the sum of imports and exports. OCA variables, like those used in Heller's and Dreyer's studies, accounted for forty-two percent of the variation in this index.

These early studies faced two difficulties. The first was that subsequent economic theory developed a new strand of thought called "optimal exchange-rate management." Optimal exchange-rate management analyzes what ERR is best for managing different kinds of economic shocks (real or monetary, foreign or domestic) instead of emphasizing country characteristics (See Aghevli, et. al., 1991). In the face of a domestic monetary shock, such as a decrease in the money supply, a fixed exchange rate is preferable. This would encourage people to purchase less foreign currency and transfer some of the shock to the stock of foreign reserves instead of domestic consumption (Flood, 1979; Melvin, 1985). With a real domestic shock (such as a recession) a floating exchange rate would allow a depreciation of the currency, encouraging exports. A floating exchange rate is best for managing a foreign monetary shock as the exchange rate would be forced to adjust, instead of the export or import-competing sectors (Friedman, 1953; Turnovsky, 1976). Empirical studies verified these contentions (Melvin, 1985; Savvides, 1990). But measuring shocks involved sophisticated use of standard errors, data which was difficult to collect on a widespread basis.

The other basic problem with these early studies is that they were undertaken within a decade after the breakdown of the Bretton Woods system. At the time, most of the countries with floating rates were large, developed economies with diversified trade, and the vast majority of developing countries retained their exchange-rate pegs with a major currency. Since the 1970s, however, exchange-rate policies have changed markedly. During the 1980s, several of the developed economies of the European Union pegged their currencies to the D-mark and floated against the dollar and the yen, while many small and open developing countries, as noted earlier, officially adopted more flexible exchange rates.

Two more recent studies have attempted to investigate how well the evidence of recent years supports the hypothesized connections between country characteristics and ERR choices. Unfortunately, they come to different conclusions. Seppo Honkapohja and Pentti Pikkarainen (1994) employ logit and probit models to predict the ERR of countries as of December 31, 1991. They test models with both a binomial (0 or 1) and multinomial (0, 1, or 2) categorization of ERR. Of all the variables they test, (GDP, GDP per capita, openness to trade, the degree of foreign assets to the money supply, diversification of trade, and terms of trade) only the diversification of commodities traded consistently matter to ERR choice. Some evidence indicated that the size of GDP also matters. They conclude that country characteristics do not matter much for ERR choice after all. Jean-Marc Rizzo (1998) has also run binomial and multinomial probit analyses, but h e focuses only on developing countries. Rizzo incorporates data from 1977 to 1995, and breaks down this period into five subperiods of three-to-five years each, according to changing conditions in the world economy. Data are averaged for entire subperiods. A number of country characteristics, such as GDP, GDP per capita, geographic diversity of trade, and the rate of inflation consistently demonstrate statistical significance.

The hollowing-out thesis

Both OCA theory and optimal exchange-rate management theory examined the economics of choosing between fixed and floating rates. But the history of separate national currencies has few examples of ERRs that were cases of permanently fixed or purely floating exchange rates. Most ERRs have been hybrids designed to deliver some of the advantages of both arrangements. As economists become more sensitive to the subtle variations of policy along the ERR spectrum and debate the benefits and cost of monetary unions, currency boards, and pegs, more economists are emphasizing the distinction between rigid fixes and pegs (Willett, 1998; Poirson, 2001). Pegs have two features that separate them from rigid fixes. First, the adjustable nature of pegs allows states to implement relative price adjustments on some occasions, rather than force the entire burden of adjustment on employment and output. Second, pegs require more credibility in their management. Since the government may not necessarily have the foreign exchange reserves to back up every unit of domestic currency, the stability of the exchange rate depends on confidence in the currency. Lack of investor confidence could provoke a currency crisis and force the state to abandon the peg. Rigidly fixed ERRs do not suffer from such liquidity problems as often since they have automatic defense mechanisms. The theory of the HOT emphasizes how capital mobility exacerbates adjustment problems and credibility problems.

Andrew Crockett (1994) questioned how feasible adjustable pegs would be in an environment of high capital mobility by discussing how ERRs facilitate adjustment in the current account. For alternative ERR arrangements adjustments to the current account are predictable. With a rigid fix, a state does not have the option of altering the exchange rate. A current account deficit produces a loss in the government's foreign exchange reserves, the money supply decreases, the economy deflates, and the state simply imports less. With a floating exchange rate, the exchange rate can make all of the economic adjustment. With a current account deficit, the exchange rate can depreciate, which encourages more exports and fewer imports. With a peg, however, the state can adjust through either deflation or devaluation. On the one hand this gives the government some flexibility in dealing with current account deficits. On the other it raises the question of when deflation or devaluation would be the best option under different economic conditions, and how the government would choose. This would encourage currency traders to bet when the government would devalue the currency and make investors worry about how well the government makes adjustment decisions.

Maurice Obstfeld and Kenneth Rogoff (1995) focused attention on why pegged exchange rates have increasingly limited credibility. Capital mobility has forced states to choose how much monetary-policy autonomy they are willing to forgo for exchange-rate stability. Since there are limits to the amount of monetary-policy autonomy states are willing to forgo, pegs have limited credibility, which makes investors more likely to engage in occasional sell-offs. Morris Goldstein (1995) and Stanley Fischer (2001) echo this point, arguing that monetary policy is caught between competing objectives. Capital controls and sterilized intervention have increasingly limited effectiveness, and fiscal policy is too difficult to coordinate among states. This puts more pressure on monetary policy to manage the problems of price stability, exchange-rate stability and business cycles. The more that investors know that monetary policy must satisfy competing objectives, the less credibility they give to promises of maintaining exchange-rate stability (Goldstein, 1995, p. 10).

Compounding adjustment and credibility problems are increasing frustrations governments have in using policy instruments to manage financial market pressures. In making his case for the HOT, Barry Eichengreen (1994) argues that governments rely on three policy instruments to contain adverse market pressures: capital controls, interest rates, and international borrowing. Investors can increasingly circumvent capital controls, high interest rates can exacerbate unemployment, and foreign borrowing may come with intolerable conditions. The rising costs of containing market pressures means that as capital mobility grows, the maintenance of pegged exchange rates becomes more costly. Governments are increasingly caught in a dilemma. Adjusting the peg reduces its credibility, while adherence to the peg prevents its use in economic adjustment and comes with increasing pressure on reserves and interest rates. As capital mobility increases the cost of containing market pressures, the state's promise to defend the peg becomes less credible and more prone to speculative attack. Eichengreen goes so far to say that in the future, all form of exchange-rate commitment, including currency boards and pegs, will be hollowed out, and states will have only the options of monetary union and floating. Fischer (2001), however, qualifies the argument by claiming that pegs are simply "unsustainable" under capital mobility, although states will still implement them out of concern for exchange-rate movements.

What causes speculative attacks? Economists debate whether speculative attacks are the result of poor macroeconomic fundamentals or self-fulfilling prophesies and panics by investors.[1] Either cause, however, makes pegging more difficult to manage. According to studies of East Asian markets by Ramon Moreno (1995), expansionary fiscal and monetary policies are associated with speculative attacks and depreciations. To the extent that speculative attacks are due to poor fundamentals, states that peg must work harder to restrain fiscal and monetary policies to maintain credibility. But empirical research on OECD countries by Eichengreen, Rose and Wyplosz (2003) suggests that speculative attacks are often the result of self-fulfilling prophecies, and Moreno finds some evidence of this in East Asian states as well. To the extent that speculative attacks result from self-fulfilling prophecies, states that peg face increased risk of currency crises as capital mobility rises, regardless of their macroeconomic policies. While states with rigid fixes or floating exchange rates can experience currency crises, credibility problems cited by proponents of the HOT indicate why pegs may be particularly prone to panics under high capital mobility.

Given its intellectual pedigree, the HOT has become a guiding principle for some policy recommendations. The Council of Foreign Relations put together a panel of luminaries to discuss how the architecture of the international financial system should be reformed after the Asian financial crisis, a panel that included Eichengreen among many others. Its report (1999) argued that emerging market countries should avoid pegged exchange rates altogether and use limited controls on only short-term capital movements. Lawrence Summers (1999), Clinton's second-term Treasury Secretary, testified to Congress that he believed that there was "shrinking scope for countries to occupy the middle ground of fixed but adjustable pegs." Stanley Fischer (2001), the former Deputy Managing Director of the IMF, argued that almost no developed country uses a peg since the adoption of EMU, and the number of de facto pegs has declined in emerging markets since 1991.

Despite so much theoretical and policy literature favoring the HOT, however, not everyone agrees that capital mobility is making pegs obsolete. Some argue that the evidence of currency crises in the 1990s does not necessarily confirm that pegs caused the crises (Bird, 2002). Others reiterate one of the original lessons of OCA theory, that "no single currency regime is right for all countries or at all times" (Frankel, 1999; see also Corden, 2002). Jeffrey Frankel in particular argues that all ERR choices come with costs, and proponents of the HOT have emphasized the costs of pegging without considering that rigid fixes or floats may still come with higher costs at some times and places.

Unfortunately, few empirical tests have been performed on the HOT. Frankel, along with Sergio Schmukler and Luis Serven, (2000) have performed tests to determine how "verifiable" an ERR commitment is, determining how much information is needed to show that a government is keeping its exchange-rate commitments. Using Chilean data, they show that basket pegs and wide bands are more difficult to verify than single currency pegs or narrow bands. Their implication is that basket pegs and wide bands would have less credibility in the eyes of investors, but this only applies to certain kinds of pegs. Paul Masson (2001), however, has performed Markov chain models on data that classify ERRs according to different methods. While Masson found that states with rigid fixes do seem to maintain them, floating is not always maintained, and pegs remain the ERR choice of several states. The statistical tests in this book find no evidence that more exposure to capital mobility leads to less pegging in the short run. A closer look at the logic of the HOT helps to explain why this might be.

Rational vs. adaptive actors

The HOT is an example of a systemic-level argument. Systemic theories identify features of a state's external environment, the international system, as the key determinant of a state's behavior. The international system is generally regarded as composed of a structure and a set of interacting units (Waltz, 1979, p. 79). To simplify a systemic-level theory, the theory assumes that the state is a unit with no internal mechanisms, in order to focus attention on the influence of the external environment. The international system determines what the consequences of state's behavior will be, and these consequences, in turn, are assumed to condition what the state can and cannot do. In a systemic-level theory, capital mobility is a structural feature of the international system, one that constrains states by determining the benefits and costs of state policies (Andrews, 1994).

Consequently, most of the analysis of the HOT has focused on the economic outcomes of pegging rather than on the political question of how states decide policy. Eichengreen bases his argument largely on how capital mobility has raised the costs for capital controls, interest rates, and foreign borrowing (1994, pp. 60-73). While he asserts that states will find these costs politically too intolerable to pay, he does not specify how states decide what is politically intolerable and what is not. Obstfeld and Rogoff argue that while a state could theoretically resist a speculative attack of any magnitude on its pegging commitment, the state would have to subordinate all goals of monetary policy to the exchange-rate commitment in order to do it, which is unlikely (1995, pp. 78-80). They do not, however, make any generalizations about when a government will sacrifice an exchange-rate commitment to other economic goals.

Systemic-level arguments are theories of consequences, as they make causal claims that take the form "if a state does X under conditions A, B, and C, the result will be Y." Result Y could be collective outcomes for several states or the outcome for an individual state (Elman, 1996, pp. 12-13). In the case of the HOT, the claim is that if a state pegs in circumstances of high capital mobility, then it will pay more costs in lost monetary policy autonomy, investment, and/or growth. By itself, however, this claim does not allow one to determine how states assess risks or costs or when a state will abandon a pegged ERR. Theories of the consequences of behavior are not automatically theories of behavior. To make the HOT's causal claim into hypotheses of state behavior, one must specify how unitary states make choices within their systemic environment. One could assume that states are "rational" actors with forward-looking expectations, in which case states observe changes in capital mobility and reassess risk accordingly. Alternatively, one could assume that states are "adaptive" actors that alter their behavior only after the external environment has inflicted relatively heavy costs on the state.

The advantage of a rational, unitary actor assumption is that one could develop specific, falsifiable predictions about how states behave. In the case of the HOT, one could predict that states with greater exposure to capital mobility will be less likely to peg. The length of time a state maintains a peg is a function of the state's exposure to capital mobility. One could also predict that a state would abandon a pegged exchange when the level of capital mobility grows to a point where its liquidity cannot accommodate potential demand for foreign currency. This is the more stylized assumption and the one more vulnerable to falsification by the evidence.

On the other hand, one could argue that states adapt to systemic conditions over time using adaptive, trial-and-error behavior. In the case of the HOT, one assumes that states would choose a variety of options under capital mobility. The prediction would be that the states with corner solutions would experience fewer exchange-rate crises. Pegging states would face more crises and those that do would afterwards abandon pegging for other ERRs. Over several years, the number of states pegging will decrease and the number of alternative ERRs will increase. States that abandon pegs would also refuse to re-establish them. In a sense, state decision-making evolves to adapt to environmental conditions, analogous to biological adaptions in Darwinian evolution. But predictions based on the adaptive assumption are vague and neglect important questions (Elman, 1996, pgs. 42-44). This approach yields no hypotheses about how long it will take states to alter their behavior, which states will choose pegging in the first place, or which states are most likely to abandon pegging before a crisis hits. The predictions of the adaptive approach are more verifiable, but only because they are less ambitious. To make further hypotheses one would have to incorporate domestic-level variables into the analysis. Using an adaptive actor assumption, domestic politics explains why states may choose to maintain a peg or abandon a peg, and the HOT would explain the consequences of those decisions.

Domestic politics

One can classify political economy research according to three different levels of analysis. Systemic-level theories emphasize the influence of the international political and economic system. Domestic-level theories emphasize the role of domestic politics. Cognitive-level theories emphasize the conceptual frameworks of policy-makers. Domestic-level theories explain why some states would maintain pegs longer than other states more often than other theories do. Systemic-level theories of the political economy of exchange rates emphasize the role of powerful hegemonic states or the role of the IMF. The hegemonic stability theory argues that fixed exchange rates are more likely when a single large economy (the hegemon) provides a stable currency for fixed rates (Kindleberger, 1981; Gilpin, 1987). As the hegemon declines, however, it is not clear why some states would maintain fixed rates longer than others would, since the hegemon's power wanes for everyone simultaneously. The IMF does not impose consistent exchange-rate policies when offering structural loans. The IMF staff recommend different ERR policies for different countries on the basis of the country's economic characteristics, often in accordance with OCA theory. Cognitive-level theories argue that shifts in thinking among radical, Keynesian, or neo-liberal outlooks within a country's governing elite alter exchange-rate policy (McNamara, 1998). The neo-liberal economic thinking that has become more popular among developing countries, however, does not mandate a specific ERR choice for all states. Of those states that have made the shift from import-substitution to neo-liberalism, one can observe definite variation in ERR choices. As shown in later chapters, Mexico's shift to neo-liberalism incorporated a crawling band, while Peru's shift to neo-liberalism incorporated a float. Thus, I give more attention to domestic-level theories when discussing theories drawn from political economy.

According to the literature on political economy, several political variables are influences on the value of the exchange rate. Some of these variables, such as political stability (Edwards, 1996a & 1996b), central bank independence (Henning, 1994; Simmons, 1994) and the partisan character of governments (Simmons, 1994) appear to have an effect on a government's preferences for a high or low exchange rate. No one has yet made a plausible case that these variables, however, influence ERR choice. Previous statistical tests I performed could not establish evidence that political stability or central bank independence has an effect on official ERR policies (Hall, 2002). This section, then, focuses on four variables with demonstrated effects on ERR choices: elections, the transparency of the government, the size of the manufacturing sector, and patterns of financial intermediation. An emphasis on elections and transparency takes an "institutionalist" approach, where the rules and practices of the political process are assumed to influence policy. An emphasis on the manufacturing and financial sectors takes an "interest group" or "societal" approach, in which the analysis focuses on the interests of specific private groups and assumes that governments design policy to satisfy these groups.

Elections

Different features of the electoral system have generated a number of hypotheses. William Bernhard and David Leblang (1999) observe that the ERR has implications for political discretion over monetary policy. Under capital mobility, a floating exchange rate allows politicians to manipulate monetary policy for electoral or partisan advantage, while a fixed exchange rate denies that possibility to politicians. In electoral systems where the cost of losing the election is high, politicians are more likely to choose a floating exchange rate. Majoritarian electoral systems and systems in which the opposition has little input in the legislative process impose large costs on parties that lose an election, and thus are more likely to employ floating exchange rates. Furthermore, states with fixed times for elections will encourage a floating exchange rate so that politicians can stimulate the economy in the run up to the election. Bernhard and Leblang test these hypotheses with logit tests on data from twenty industrial democracies from 1974 to 1995 and find confirmation for all of their hypotheses. Unfortunately these hypotheses are difficult to apply to a broad range of developing countries where one cannot take democratic processes for granted.

In developing countries where competitive elections are held, the timing of elections seems to matter most. Politicians are loath to offend voters as an election approaches. A devaluation or a broken exchange-rate commitment can raise the cost of imports and hurt electoral chances. Upcoming elections are thus more likely to encourage the maintenance of a peg. Jeffry Frieden, Piero Ghezzi, and Ernesto Stein (2001) perform cross-sectional ordered logit tests on ERR choices on Latin American data and find that devaluations are delayed in the run-up to an election, while devaluations often occur immediately after a new government takes office. On a closely related note, Blomberg, Frieden, and Stein (2002) ran hazard models on Latin American data that indicate that fixed exchange rates are more likely to be maintained in the run-up to an election and are more likely to be abandoned in the few months after an election.

Transparency and Democracy

Some of the newest research on how domestic institutions influence ERR choice emphasizes anti-inflation credibility and the time-inconsistency problem as the central problem in the determination of ERRs. Time-inconsistency occurs when short-run interests conflict with long-run interests. In the case of inflation, the interest governments have in stimulating the economy in the short-run damages their credibility for fighting inflation in the long run. This new approach treats fixed exchange rates and central bank independence as alternative methods of credibly committing to low inflation, as both restrain governments from stimulating the economy with monetary policy. The research focuses on how domestic institutions affect the costs and benefits of choosing a fixed exchange rate or central bank independence (Bernhard et. al, 2003). Using this framework, researchers have investigated how variables such as unitary vs. federal government, the number of political parties, information asymmetries, and cabinet durability affect the choice of ERR and central bank independence in developed countries.

Two difficulties arise when trying to apply much of this new domestic institutionalist literature to developing countries. First, as with Bernard and Leblang's work on electoral systems, most of this literature assumes that the state has strong democratic institutions. It is difficult to apply hypotheses about party systems, federalism, and cabinet durability across a variety of regime types. Second, since this new approach is based on the problem of time-inconsistency, it poses ERR determination as a tradeoff between anti-inflation credibility versus output maximization or as a tradeoff between anti-inflation credibility and government durability. Anti-inflation credibility is not necessarily the only goal of exchange-rate policy. Blomberg, Frieden and Stein (2002), for example, examine ERR determination as a tradeoff between credibility and competitiveness. Moreover, while inflation is undoubtedly a problem for any country, not all governments demonstrate an interest in fighting inflation, or a capacity to fight it. Argentina, Brazil, and Peru had high inflation for years of the early 1990s before their respective governments cracked down. Many emerging-market countries have persistent moderate inflation. Governments demonstrate different levels of tolerance for inflation. The simplest way to account for this variation is to control for inflation rates when testing this hypothesis.

Lawrence Broz's research (2002) focuses on government transparency, however, and demonstrates one way that this time-inconsistency approach is applicable to developing states. Broz argues that governments with transparent decision-making are more likely to use independent central banking and floating exchange rates. "Transparency is the ease with which the public can monitor the government with respect to its commitments (Broz, 2002, p. 861)." The argument is based on four claims. First, states require some sort of monetary commitment mechanism to fight inflation credibly. Second, states select from two major options for inflation-fighting mechanisms, either central bank independence (CBI) or some form of fixed exchange rate (rigid or pegged) with a low-inflation currency. Broz treats CBI and fixed exchange rates as rival alternatives. Third, people can monitor commitments to a fixed exchange rate more easily than commitments to the independence of a central bank. Changes in a fixed exchange rate are public knowledge in any regime, while central banks normally operate behind closed doors. Fourth, central banks only have credible independence in a society with transparent decision-making. Generally only democracies have institutionalized processes to assure transparency. Truly competitive opposition parties and independent media organizations can monitor the government and inform the public of government attempts to pressure the central bank. Elections institutionalize methods of expressing public disapproval of government actions. Broz argues that since only transparent democracies can credibly grant independence to a central bank, they are less likely to fix exchange rates. Authoritarian systems lack institutional mechanisms of protecting a central bank and must rely on some form of fixed exchange rates instead.

This argument assumes that all governments have low tolerance for inflation and if a state has an independent central bank it will have no reasons to fix the exchange rate. Its advantage is that one can test it against a broad range of developing states, using standard measures of democratization.

Manufacturing

Jeffry Frieden (1991 & 1994) has put forward a theory of how interest groups form preferences for exchange-rate policy. It is a second-image-reversed analysis, analyzing the role international conditions play in determining the preferences and alignments of domestic interest groups. When considering ERR choice, Frieden begins by assuming that all sectors of the economy face a world of high capital mobility. Sectors face the choice of preferring exchange-rate stability or monetary-policy autonomy. According to Frieden, exporters and international investors have a strong interest in exchange-rate stability, as volatility in exchange rates introduces risk into their business. Furthermore, industries with a foreign focus can shift their business abroad when the domestic economy suffers, and thus they do not need to rely on macroeconomic stimulation to solve domestic recessions. Frieden argues exporters and international investors would prefer some form of fixed exchange rates. For industries that produce for domestic consumption, however, the reverse holds. Producers for the domestic market and industries that compete against imports have little interest in exchange-rate stability, but would have an interest in a monetary policy that can stimulate the economy during a recession. Thus they would prefer some form of floating exchange rates. Note that the theory attempts to explain preferences for ERR choice, not the ERR choices themselves. Using this line of thinking, it follows that the growth of exporting and importing sectors will increase the political support for fixed exchange rates, especially if hedging instruments are unavailable or prohibitively costly, as they are in most developing countries.[2] Consistent with OCA theory, Frieden's argument implies that higher levels of trade exposure would most likely lead to fixed exchange rates. Frieden, however, couches the argument in terms of what interest groups would want, rather than the preferences of a benevolent social planner.

But later Frieden, in subsequent work with Ernesto Stein (2001), introduces an important caveat to this theory. They allow that for states in which the total of exports and imports is more than 100% of GDP, such as in many

Caribbean states, economic agents are exposed to significant exchange-rate risk and fixed exchange rates are common (2001, p. 5). But in many Latin American states, the use of fixed exchange rates has resulted in an appreciation of the real exchange rate, which hurts the competitiveness of tradables producers (2001, p. 6). Consequently, they argue that the more powerful tradables producers are, the more likely the government will employ a float that can allow the exchange rate to depreciate. Cross-country, time-series tests on Latin American data by Frieden, Ghezzi, and Stein (2001) indicate that the larger the share of manufacturing in the GDP of a country, the more likely it was to use a float or a backward-looking crawling peg. Hazard models by Blomberg, Frieden, and Stein (2002) indicate that a greater share of manufacturing in GDP also make a state more likely to abandon a fixed exchange rate at any given time. The size of the manufacturing sector then, becomes a proxy for how likely the government is to use ERR choices to improve the competitiveness of the economy.

Finance

Frieden's analysis of interest group preferences does well at defining different kinds of producers and their interests in exchange-rate policy, but his analysis ignores financiers. Financial actors and financial systems also come in different types and one can identify preferences for ERR choice among these financial actors. This point has been developing in the theoretical literature of political economy for some time and has only recently been articulated as a testable theory.

First, political economists had to distinguish different financial systems and financial actors. John Zysman (1983) argued that developed countries had different systems of financial intermediation, the process of allocating saved capital to those who borrow. The process of how commercial firms receive most of their financing distinguishes different systems of financial intermediation. The U.S. and Britain were examples of financial systems based on capital markets. West Germany financed its firms largely through private banks, and France and Japan financed firms through state-directed banking systems. Zysman argued that different financial systems determine how different states adjusted to economic crisis. Barbara Stallings (1992) extended the analysis to developing countries, arguing that economic adjustment in developing countries depended in part on the extent to which the country depended on foreign direct investment, foreign portfolio investment, or foreign bank loans. C. Randall Henning (1994) applied the examination of financial systems to the analysis of exchange-rate policies of the U.S., Japan and West Germany after World War II. In his theory, a state will or will not develop a pattern of competitive devaluation or depreciation depending on the organization of the financial system. With a bank-based financial system, such as in Japan and Germany, banks and industry form close ties as banks invest loans in industrial firms. Banks and industry in such states form a coalition in favor of a competitively low exchange rate. If capital markets are the primary financiers of industry, as they are in the U.S., then no such coalition forms, as investors in capital markets are less likely to develop long-term financial interests in industrial firms. The demand for low, competitive exchange rates is thus weaker. Sylvia Maxfield (1991) detailed a similar analysis for Latin American countries such as Mexico and Brazil. She argued that alliances between private bankers and central banks and between private bankers and private industry shaped government policy on exchange controls and exchange-rate valuation, among other economic policies.

Recently, however, researchers have also been able to develop the arguments for why financial transactions can shape the choice of ERR. Guillermo Calvo and Carmen Reinhart (2000) took issue with standard classifications of ERR choice (and the HOT) by arguing that while many developing states claimed to be floating their exchange rates, analysis indicated that governments were in fact routinely intervening in the exchange-rate market. They attributed this "fear of floating" to liability dollarization, the load of debt denominated in a foreign currency, which is difficult to service with exchange-rate volatility. The problem of liability dollarization highlights one of the reasons Graciela Kaminsky and Carmen Reinhart (1999) find that currency crises often provoke banking crises, as rapid plunges in the exchange rate can provoke defaults and crippling costs to holders of dollar-denominated debt.

Based on Stallings' (1992) arguments about how dependence on international capital shapes economic policy in developing countries, George Shambaugh (2004) argues that ERR choices in developing countries depend significantly on the degree of dependence on different types of foreign capital. Shambaugh presents qualified evidence that states with greater dependence on foreign bank loans are more likely to maintain a fixed exchange rate, as devalued currencies increase the cost of loan repayment and floating currencies increase the risks of non-repayment. He provides stronger evidence that states that dependence on foreign portfolio investment is more likely to make a state choose a floating exchange rate, in order to reduce vulnerabilities to capital flight.

The financial intermediation hypothesis

Institutional and interest-based approaches have different strengths and weaknesses. Interest-based approaches answer the basic questions of who wins and who loses from particular policies. Given that different states have different constellations of interests, interest-based theories can explain why different states have incentive to choose different policies. What interest-based explanations often lack, however, is an explanation of why some groups or coalition of groups have more power to influence policy than other groups. Interest-based approaches, by focusing on private actors, tend to treat the state as a passive actor (Nordlinger, 1987). Defining the preferences manufacturing or financial firms have in ERRs does not explain how these groups get their preferred ERR policies. Institutionalist explanations, by focusing on the political process, directly answer the question of what constraints leaders face. Unfortunately, these explanations have the equal and opposite problem of the interest-based approaches, often neglecting the role private actors have with a stake in policymaking. The purpose of this section is to refine the financial intermediation theory. It elaborates on how banks form preferences for ERR policy and improves the theory by addressing the question of how the financial sector influences the government.

The hypothesis here is that the more a middle-income economy relies on bank credit for the financing of firms, the more likely the state is to maintain pegged ERRs. The hypothesis follows from three propositions. First, most commercial firms in middle-income countries have an aversion to rigidly fixed exchange rates, except in cases of hyperinflation. Second, the nature of the financial system shapes the interests of the financial sector. In systems where firms rely on bank-credit for investment and the state is open to international capital, banks often acquire dollar-denominated debt and become advocates of reducing exchange-rate risk, thus opposing devaluations and floatations. The shared interests that banks have with commercial firms also make them opponents of rigid fixes. Pegs are thus the preferred alternative. Third, banks in an active banking sector often have strong political advantages in the political system due to their small numbers, tight organization and their critical role in economic development. The government has incentive to address their interests by attempting to maintain the pegged rate for as long as it can.

This hypothesis builds on not only the work of Shambaugh but also the work of analysts who cited foreign lending and investment booms as part of the causes of the Mexican peso crisis and the Asian financial crisis (Kahler, 1998; Pomerleano, 1998; Velasco and Cabezas, 1998; Cooper, 1999). As states maintained pegged exchange rates, foreign investors felt encouraged to invest heavily due in part to the promise of reduced exchange-rate risk. Financial bubbles developed that destabilized domestic financial systems. The financial intermediation hypothesis argues that causation also worked in the other direction, and growing bank indebtedness reinforced the original desire to maintain pegged exchange rates, even though governments had increasing trouble managing their pegs. Pegs and foreign investment thus reinforced each other. This is consistent with empirical research that shows that banking sector bubbles often precede currency crises (Kaminsky and Reinhart, 1999). The financial intermediation hypothesis given here emphasizes how and why the banking sector becomes a political lobbying group in favor of an exchange-rate policy (even one with a misaligned exchange rate) that could contribute to a currency crisis.

The Aversion to Rigid Fixes

Many commercial firms within states have reason to oppose rigidly fixed exchange rates. When capital mobility is high, flexible exchange rates allow greater monetary policy autonomy, allowing a government to raise or lower the exchange rate, thereby restraining or stimulating foreign demand for domestic goods (Aghevli, et. al, 1991, p. 6). Unless they rely on imports for production, firms would prefer that the state had the option of exchange-rate flexibility in times of recession. Without exchange-rate flexibility, the pain of macroeconomic adjustment becomes confined to the domestic goods market during every recession. Recessions are often deeper and longer in economies with rigidly fixed exchange rates because they cannot use monetary policy to stimulate the economy, as Argentina and Hong Kong demonstrated. Argentine firms and other interests favored a currency board only after years of hyperinflation demonstrated that some sort of harsh medicine was necessary to cure price distortions (Diaz-Bonilla and Schamis, 2001). Firms are admittedly concerned with more than just economic growth. Commercial firms may prefer pegged exchange rates if they owe significant amounts of debt to foreign investors, or may prefer floating exchange rates if depreciation of the currency would improve competitiveness. Pegs, however, can provide much of the exchange-rate stability commercial firms desire while providing opportunities for economic stimulation. Public support for monetary policy autonomy in times of recession helps explain why governments rarely employ rigid fixes.

Financial Systems

Before examining why banks would have different preferences for ERRs under different financial systems, it pays to examine different financial systems. The preferences of banks for ERRs depend on the nature of the financial system. Financial systems are here divided into three broad ideal types, depending on whether capital markets or banks link savers and borrowers (Zysman, 1983, pgs. 60-61) or whether the financial system does not provide much intermediation. In a "capital-market system," enterprises acquire most of their financing through organized markets for bonds, stocks, and commercial paper. In a "bank-credit system," enterprises acquire most of their financing through bank loans. In many developing countries, however, financial systems are not sophisticated enough to provide much intermediation between savers and borrowers, so most domestic investment is financed out of the private savings of the investors. For the purposes of this project, I have dubbed this the "private-savings" system.

Those who invest in a firm have a stake in the firm's performance. Consequently, banks and commercial firms have more shared interests in a bank-credit system. Since banks demand information from their debtors, banks are more privy to private information about the health of commercial firms when they are the main source of investment. Such information is more publicly available in a capital market system or relatively unavailable in a private savings system. Laws concerning corporate disclosure may even reinforce these flows of information, as they have done in Germany, Japan, and the U.S. for most of the postwar period. Since banks acquire more information in a bank-credit system, banks also perform more of the risk analysis concerning firm performance and take on far more investment risk in a bank-credit system. In a capital-market system, of course, stock analysts and bond-rating agencies perform much of the risk analysis. In private-savings systems, commercial firms share little information and retain most of the risk.

In addition, the control of corporations also varies among different financial systems. In private-savings systems, individual or family owners normally control a firm without interference from other private agents. In capital-market systems where there are secondary markets for trading claims, investors sell bonds and equities on short notice when corporations pay lower dividends or report unsatisfactory performance. Bond and equity prices become ongoing approval ratings for corporate performance. Thus, investors collectively tend to exercise control over corporations to the extent that they are ready to withdraw their capital and invest it elsewhere (Zysman, 1983, p. 63). In bank-credit systems, by contrast, creditors rarely have that option. Banks often make more long-term loans for the financing of the corporation, since the equity markets of nations with bank-credit systems tend to be more restricted. Faced with the possibility of defaulted loans and no way of unloading such loans, banks can only influence failing corporations by voicing their concerns and advice to managers.

The Preferences of the Banks

Banks' preferences for ERRs are largely indeterminate in a capital-market system or a private-savings system. The most universal preferences of banks are for low inflation, a stable monetary policy, and for fewer state restrictions on their activity (Henning, 1994, p. 26). Low inflation protects the value of monetary assets. Any choice of ERR, however, may be compatible with low inflation. Rigidly fixed rates and pegs are often used as nominal exchange-rate anchors, as an exchange rate fixed to a low inflation currency requires a non-inflationary domestic monetary policy. But fixed exchange rates are not necessary for lower inflation. Floating exchange rates may be used in conjunction with other anti-inflation policies such as money supply targets or inflation targets.

Banks have an interest in stable monetary policy, since an unstable monetary policy forces them to alter interest rates frequently. Central banks often conduct monetary policy by altering the interest rates they charge for loans to commercial banks. To maintain profit margins, banks pass these changes in interest rates through the banking system to customers. Volatility in interest rates makes long-term relationships banks and their loan customers difficult. No particular ERR necessarily has a more stable monetary policy than the others. If a state adopts some form of fixed exchange rate, high capital mobility could expose the state to frequent changes in the foreign demand for domestic currency, which in turn would produce frequent changes in interest rates. A floating exchange rate allows the central bank more discretion to alter interest rates and does nothing to restrain the government from frequently adjusting interest rates if it so chooses.

In a bank-credit system, however, banks have two interests in addition to low inflation and stable monetary policy. First, as mentioned above, the predominance of loans for the financing of commercial firms gives banks an interest in the long-term health of commercial firms. When banks become dependent on good industrial performance for their performance, banks develop an interest in avoiding rigidly fixed exchange rates and the prolonged recessions they may exacerbate. Second, in many middle-income countries, the domestic banks are the main channels of investing external debt (Baily, et. al, 2000, p. 102). A common practice for domestic banks in middle-income countries has been to take out unhedged dollar-denominated loans from foreign banks and then issue domestic-currency loans to commercial firms. Banks that acquire dollar-denominated debt absorb the exchange-rate risk and also acquire an interest in exchange-rate stability. A functioning pegged exchange rate often provides long periods of exchange-rate stability with the occasional flexibility needed in times of severe recession. A peg avoids the increased exchange-rate risk of a float while also avoiding the lack of flexibility in a rigid fix. Banks in a bank-credit system thus have more incentive to favor the maintenance of a peg for as long as possible.

Admittedly, the patterns of corporate finance are in some ways more complex in developing countries than they are Japan, Germany, or the U.S. Significant flows of investment in developing countries come directly from governments. In some developing countries governments have nationalized their banks. In many of these cases, political motives rather than profit motives govern banking decisions concerning the distribution of credit and interest rates. Credit can be distributed in ways that provide less-than optimal returns and interest rates may not reach market equilibrium. In such cases where political considerations primarily govern nationally-owned banks, government ownership often retards financial intermediation, and the country is best described as having a private savings system. The banking system does not develop financial strength and thus does not develop political clout. The banking systems in Mexico and Peru during the 1980s, described in Chapters 5 and 6 respectively, are cases in point. The government retains a lot of autonomy over the banking sector. The political weakness of the banks in countries with nationalized banking sectors, however, is similar to the political weakness of banks in disintermediated economies in which banks are in private hands.

Foreigners also supply a significant amount of capital directly to commercial firms in developing countries. Foreign commercial lenders who lend directly to developing country firms are likely to support fixed exchange rates in order to decrease the risk of non-repayment and increase the risk-adjusted rate of return (Shambaugh, 2004, p. 284). Foreign portfolio investors are also likely to support the reduced risk associated with a fixed exchange rate (Frieden, 1991; Maxfield, 1997, pgs. 42-45) but domestic governments that rely on such portfolio investment are likely to prefer a floating exchange rate. The autonomous monetary policy associated with floating provides the developing country less vulnerability to sudden capital flight from portfolio investors (Shambaugh, 2004, p. 286). Long-term foreign bank lending does not present that concern. The point is that it is not the *source* of the investment (public or private, domestic or foreign) that matters as much as the *form* of the investment (capital-market or bank-credit).

The Power of the Banks

Why would governments respond to the demands of banks when deciding whether or not to maintain a peg? Bankers in a bank-credit system have an advantage in organizing for their interests due to the concentrated nature of banking systems as compared with other banking systems. As bank-credit financing grows in a developing country, the financial system tends to become more concentrated in its structure unless capital markets grow more quickly. In addition to advantages in organization, a bank-based system of finance gives bankers two resources of power: a critical role in the economy and private information on the health of the financial system. When the state does not have a bank credit system, the banks often do not have these advantages, and this gives the government more discretion to abandon a peg in the face of hollowing out pressures or other considerations.

In countries with strong bank-credit systems, the banking sector tends to be concentrated among a few large banking firms. Japan, Germany, and France, the classic examples of bank-credit systems in advanced economies, all have a few large firms dominating their banking industries. As the case studies of Thailand and Mexico illustrate, a small number of banks often dominate strong banking systems in industrializing developing countries. By contrast, the financiers in a capital-market system are many and diverse, including a variety of individual and institutional investors. In private savings systems, the various rich citizens and private firms in an economy rely more on their retained earnings for financing. According to Mancur Olson, (1966, p. 35) a smaller group is more likely to provide a collective good than is a larger group. A few, large bankers can organize more effectively to defend their interests than many, diverse captial-market investors or private firms are. The smaller the number of firms that benefit from a pegged exchange rate, the larger the average share of the benefits is for each individual firm (Olson, 1966, p. 34). A small, concentrated group also has an easier time in bargaining over how to divide the costs of lobbying and in monitoring a member's participation in lobbying (Olson, 1966, p. 45-47). In many developing states, banker's associations organize the banks for collective interests.

Bankers in a bank-credit system often lobby for maintaining an exchange-rate peg to reduce repayment costs for foreign liabilities. In this case, the pegged exchange rate is the collective good and the costs of lobbying are the costs of paying for the collective good. Bankers' associations can voice direct appeals to the government to maintain the peg. Private bankers also have an advantage in lobbying for looser banking regulations and less government oversight. This additional collective good for the bankers has an indirect effect on exchange-rate policy. In a more relaxed regulatory atmosphere, bankers have more discretion over lending practices, but non-performing loans (NPL's) accumulate. As non-performing loans accumulate, the risk of a banking crisis increases. Should the government devalue or float the currency while banks hold significant amounts of unhedged foreign liabilities and non-performing loans, a banking crisis could result, giving the government an another incentive to maintain the peg. Figure 2.1 illustrates these points.

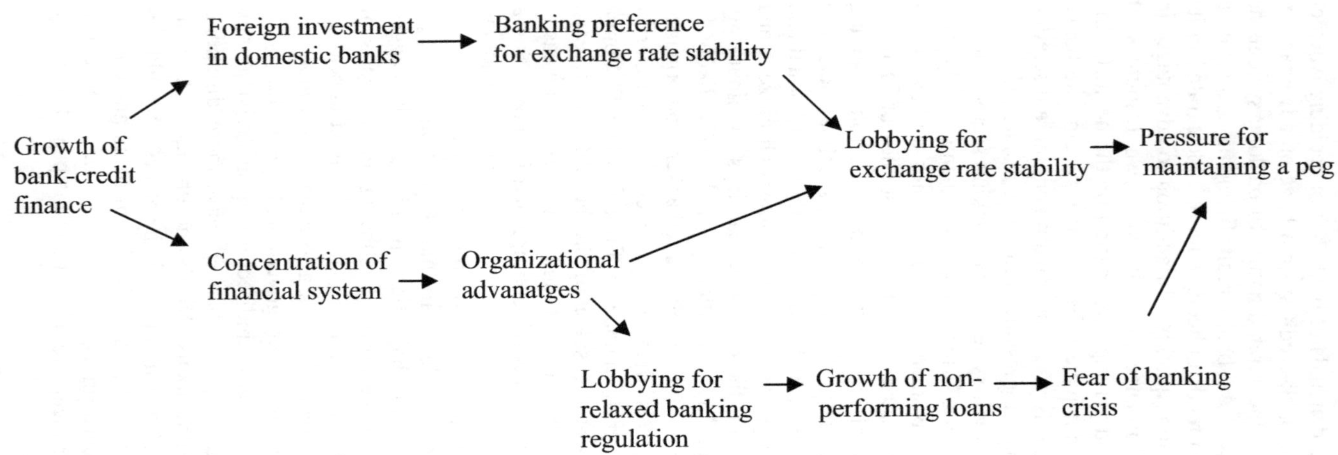

Figure 2.1 Casual pathways of the financial intermediation hypothesis

When a country has a strong bank-based system of finance, governments are more sensitive to bankers for two reasons, the central role of the banking system in the economy and the private information bankers have about the health of the financial system. In the past several years economists have found cross-country evidence that financial intermediation has a significant influence on long-run economic growth (King and Levine, 1993; Levine, 1997). Increasing the costs of foreign liability repayment for banks strains the health of the domestic economy's main channel of capital. The point helps explain why banking crises are so feared in some developing countries. Given that currency crises often trigger banking crises (Kaminsky and Reinhart, 1999) currency crises can thus trigger significant damage to economic growth. Governments would thus have incentive to prevent a currency crisis from crippling the banking system.

Furthermore, bankers in a bank-credit system have special access to information helpful to economic policy-making, as discussed above. This is not just a by-product of financial intermediation, but also a source of power. The effectiveness of lobbying often depends on the strategic use of asymmetric information (See Austen-Smith and Wright, 1992; Wright, 1996; Rich and Weaver, 1998). Even with staff that can provide technical expertise, government officials may not know what the exact consequences of exchange-rate policy may be for the banks, due to the technical nature of monetary and financial policy and banker's private information on the health of their balance sheets. Given that banks have more private and relevant information about the health of the financial sector in a bank-credit system, governments may find the input of the banks indispensable. Consequently, banks have opportunities to structure policy analysis on exchange-rate questions.

When the country does not have a strong bank-credit system of financing, banks borrow less from abroad, have a smaller role in the economy, and have less special information on the health of the financial system. Banks thus have less incentive to maintain a peg and less influence in lobbying for their interests. Key actors in the financial system are also more diverse, and more difficult to organize for direct appeals to the government. Governments have more discretion to abandon an exchange-rate peg, all other things being equal.

Admittedly, the mere pressure of the banks does not necessarily mean that governments will adopt their recommended ERR policies. Pressure from trade unions or agricultural workers may instead encourage a government to attempt a populist economic program of expansionary fiscal and monetary policy to increase consumption and employment. Such a program normally requires capital controls, a floating exchange rate, or at least a relaxation of the peg through successive devaluations in order to provide the necessary monetary stimulation. Alternatively, a government may have the capacity to resist pressure from all societal actors, regardless of their stance on exchange-rate policy. It is conceivable that a government might adopt floating exchange rates to improve the autonomy of monetary policy. Many developing states have turned away from populist economic programs, however, and governments generally do not ignore the banking sector unless the sector is already weak.

The hypotheses

To restate the research question, a number of developing states have employed intermediate ERR options, or pegs, only to drop them in the past several years. Why did it take some states longer to do so than others? This chapter has reviewed seven main hypotheses:

1) The trade hypothesis: states with higher levels of trade exposure are more likely to maintain a peg.
2) The GDP hypothesis: states with larger economies are more likely to abandon a peg.
3) The capital mobility hypothesis: states with more exposure to capital mobility are more likely to abandon a peg (this is a version of the HOT that invokes a rational actor assumption).
4) The election hypothesis: states are more likely to maintain a peg if they have an upcoming election.
5) The transparency hypothesis: states with an authoritarian government are more likely to maintain a peg.
6) The manufacturing hypothesis: states with a larger manufacturing sector are more likely to abandon a peg.
7) The financial intermediation hypothesis: states that rely on bank-credit financing for firms are more likely to maintain a peg.

If states were to simply abandon pegs as their exposure to capital mobility rises then the rise of capital mobility worldwide would explain why a number of states have shifted from pegs to floating over the past few decades. States would simply be seeking to avoid the higher costs of managing pegged exchange rates. But recent currency crises have taught us that a number of states have continued to peg despite the increasing risks and costs. The other six hypotheses provide the most likely explanations of why some states would tempt fate.

The following chapters discuss evidence for and against these hypotheses, with particular emphasis on the financial intermediation hypothesis. Chapter 3 tests the financial intermediation hypothesis while controlling for the other hypotheses in a number of statistical tests. Chapters 4 through 7 examine the cases of Thailand, Mexico, Peru, and Colombia to examine the causal logic of the financial intermediation hypothesis. The case studies also allow the other hypothesized variables to be examined as a way of providing context for the role of financial intermediation.

Strictly speaking, only the financial intermediation hypothesis and the rational actor version of the HOT have been theorized as a choice between pegs and corner solutions. The other hypotheses are theorized as a choice between fixed and floating exchange rates. It is not clear how trade exposure, GDP, elections, government transparency, and the size of the manufacturing sector might influence the choice between pegs and rigidly fixed exchange rates. The inability of these hypotheses to account for a state that might resort to a rigid fix to solve the problems of an unsustainable peg is theoretically problematic. It is not a crippling problem since these hypotheses are not the focus of this book. Also note that when states face difficulties in managing pegs, and their political and economic conditions encourage a fixed exchange rate, states are most likely to maintain their existing pegging regime rather than sacrifice monetary policy autonomy for a rigid fix. Few follow Argentina's example of renouncing a peg and adopting a rigid fix in its place. One could theorize that Argentina, by contrast, adopted a rigid fix in place of a peg in 1991 because it had trouble managing a peg, political coalitions that encouraged some form of fixing, and hyperinflation (Wise, 2000; Diaz-Bonilla and Schamis, 2001). Severe economic problems such as hyperinflation are needed to overcome domestic resistance to rigid fixes.

Notes

[1] The most significant model incorporating economic fundamentals is Ozkan and Sutherland, 1994. On self-fulfilling crises in foreign exchange markets, see Obstfeld, 1994. For a good overview of the causes of speculative attacks, see Eichengreen, Rose and Wyplosz, 2003. A new literature on the "new fundamentals" (Krugman, 1998; Pomerleano, 1998) emphasizes the role of financial bubbles instead of weak macroeconomic performance as the source of investor panic in exchange-rate crises. The related question of how financial bubbles and pegged exchange rates reinforce one another is developed later in this chapter.

[2] See Hefeker, 1996. On the role of hedging instruments in the formation of interest group preferences, see Ruland and Viaene, 1993.

Chapter 3

Statistical Tests

This chapter discusses some statistical tests used to test the hypotheses examined in chapter 2. The tests estimate the influence of political and economic conditions on official ERR policies. Another set of tests, presented in the appendix, estimates the influence of the same variables on the actual ERR behavior of governments. The tests on official ERR policy demonstrate support for the financial intermediation hypothesis and no support for the capital mobility hypothesis. The tests on actual ERR behavior are more problematic, as they provide no support for any of the hypotheses in chapter 2. Those who are concerned about alternative ERR codings and what this second set of tests may mean can consult the appendix. The following section describes the data used in the first set of tests on official ERR policies. The second section discusses the hazard models used in the tests. Following sections discuss how the indicators for the key variables are developed and the results of the tests on official ERR policies. A further discussion of the results, in the light of the evidence of the case studies, is left to chapter 8.

Data and case selection

The data are drawn from middle-income countries and cover quarterly periods from 1987 to 2000. The countries were selected on the basis of income level, population, type of government, and data availability. They were listed as either "upper middle-income" or "lower middle-income" countries according to the World Bank in 1998, reflecting their status in the last year in the time-series. "Low income" countries normally have little exposure to capital mobility and are often dependent on a single developed country for trade. Countries with a population under one million people also exhibit similar economic dependence. Transition economies were also left out of the sample, as communist ideology promoted capital immobility and the use of non-convertible currencies for part of the period under review. The tests thus focus on developing countries that have some exposure to capital mobility and have definite options in choosing an ERR. 44 countries fit these criteria.

The truly limiting factor in case selection was data on capital mobility and ERR. The capital mobility indicator requires data on interest rates for financial assets using a method described below. Only 27 countries out of the 44 had the data available for calculating measures of capital mobility. The period from 1987 to 1998 was chosen because it was the longest series of years for which data on capital mobility was available for these countries. According to the IMF system of coding ERRs (described below) only fifteen states of the full sample of 27 had periods or "spells" in which a government pegged the exchange rate, while the rest employed an alternative to pegging throughout the 1987-1998 period.[1]

Hazard models and the role of time

To test the hypotheses discussed in chapter 2, I present the results of some hazard models. The research question asks under what conditions states maintain or abandon a peg. The most appropriate model for such a research question is a hazard model. Hazard models estimate what effect political and economic variables have on the likelihood that a given country pegged its exchange rate at a specific time (t), given that it has pegged before at time (t-1). In this case, the likelihood that a state will switch from pegging to an alternative is called the "hazard rate." The hazard equation estimates the logarithm of the hazard rate. The tests can then estimate what effect different political and economic variables may have on the likelihood of abandonment of a peg for a given state at a given time.

Note that hazard models only apply to datasets in which all of the cases exist in a given state until they switch to another state. They apply here because all of the cases pegged in 1987 and either switched to floating or maintained a peg. If some of the cases switched from pegging to floating and back to pegging, cross-section, time-series logit models would be more appropriate, as hazard models are not designed to analyze cases that switch back and forth between states.[2] But since the cases in the dataset only switch from pegging to floating, and hazard models are used because they estimate results more efficiently than cross-section, time-series logit.

A number of parametric hazard models are available, depending on how time is to be modeled in the hazard equation. The tests presented here employ a Weibull model, in which the log of the hazard rate increases or decreases linearly with the log of time. In equation 1 below, this is represented by the variable "c log (t)." The advantage of the Weibull model is that it accounts for how the hazard rate can increase or decrease over time even when controlling for other factors. It is possible that the longer the state pegs the more credibility the peg has in the eyes of investors, reducing the likelihood of speculative attacks that force a state to abandon a peg. This would imply that the hazard rate decreases over time, all other things being equal. A Weibull model can estimate this decrease in the hazard rate, if there is any, even if the decrease is a linear or a non-linear function.

The hazard models take the general form of:

1) $$\log h(ERR) = \alpha + b_1(CM) + b_2(FLIA) + b_3(INFL) + b_4(CA) + b_5(TRADE) + b_6(FI) + b_7(MANU) + b_8(DEMO) + b_9(ELECT) + c \log(t)$$

where α is a constant, and $b_{1...9}$ and c are coefficients. CM is the capital mobility indicator. FLIA represents foreign liabilities of a state as percentage of M2. INFL is the logarithm of inflation. CA represents the surplus or deficit in the current account as a percentage of GDP. TRADE, is the indicator for trade exposure. FI represents one of the indicators for financial intermediation. MANU represents the percentage of GDP devoted to manufactured goods. DEMO is an indicator of how democratic a state is. ELECT indicates if the state has had, is about to have, or is having an election during that quarter.

Exchange-rate regimes

This chapter treats the dependent variable as a dichotomous variable: either a state pegs its exchange rate for most of a given year or it does not. The IMF and various scholars have developed different methods of measuring and classifying ERRs. The IMF developed the most standard method of classification, which classifies states according to their official ERR policy. Many economists have criticized this method noting that what states claim to do with exchange rates and what policies they actually follow can be quite different (Benassy-Quere and Coeure, 2000; Glick, et. al., 1995; Poirson, 2001; Reinhart, 2000). Economists have developed alternative methods of measuring ERR differences, which classify ERRs based on actual exchange-rate behavior.[3] Reinhart and Rogoff's (2003) method provides the most complete and up-to-date data on ERRs derived from actual market exchange rates. The details of this coding method and the tests performed on dependent variables based on this system are provided in the appendix.

Most research on ERRs up until recently has used the IMF's classification system. The IMF settled on a three-fold classification of ERRs in 1983: pegged currencies, currencies with limited flexibility, and more flexible arrangements. "Pegged" exchange rates in this system represented all forms of fixed exchange rates, including monetary union and currency boards (although most states had some form of intermediate regime instead of a rigid fix). The IMF disaggregated pegging states into different categories according to whether they pegged to a single currency or to a basket of currencies, and those pegged to a single currency according the currency to which the state pegged. States with "limited flexibility" were special cases of adjustable pegs that fell into two categories. One group of states floated their currency within a wide band against the U.S. dollar, although they had officially declared a policy of pegging to the SDR or a group of currencies. The other group of states participated in the European Monetary System (EMS) in which member states pegged their currencies to the Deutsche Mark and negotiated occasional adjustments of the pegs amongst themselves. The "more flexible" ERRs were listed under three categories, "adjusted according to a set of indicators," "managed floating," and "independently floating." Those "adjusted according to a set of indicators," were essentially forms of crawling pegs. "Managed" and "independent" floating refer to two forms of floating that I defined in chapter 1.

The IMF coding procedure provides quarterly cross-section time-series data. Periodic issues of *International Financial Statistics* classify each member country's ERR choice for the end of March, June, September, or December in that year. The classification of the ERR at the end of the quarter is the basis for coding the ERR of that quarter. To separate pegging states from floating states, I count all countries listed as managed or independently floating as floating. States in all of the other categories are coded as pegging unless I found a record of a rigidly fixed exchange rate for those states in that year. I consulted works that examine the use of monetary union and currency boards in recent decades (Cohen, 1998; Ghosh, et. al, 1998) to identify cases of rigidly fixed rates. States that pegged in a given quarter, in the sense defined here, were coded as a value of zero. States that chose corner solutions in a given quarter, such as a float or a rigidly fixed exchange rate, were coded as a value of one. Of the fifteen states that pegged according to the IMF data, twelve abandoned their pegs for a floating exchange rate, and three retained a peg until the end of the observation period. None abandoned a peg for a rigid fix.[4]

The main criticism of this IMF classification system is that actual exchange-rate behavior may not conform to official claims. Some states that promise exchange-rate stability with a peg may in fact adjust their pegs several times. Some states that claim to be floating their currency may in fact tightly manage their exchange-rate movements. In 1999, the IMF revised its classification system to account for this and other problems. Their classification system now has two dimensions. One dimension of the classification system classifies states according to a revised spectrum of declared ERR policies: monetary unions, currency boards, adjustable pegs, adjustable bands, crawling pegs, crawling bands, managed floating, and independent floating. Under the new system, classifications of pegged exchange rates now include those states whose floating exchange rates are so strictly managed that they are de facto pegs. The other dimension classifies states according to their monetary policy strategies, noting whether a state fights inflation through exchange-rate anchors, money-supply targets, inflation targets, or through a IMF-supported or other monetary program. Unfortunately, the IMF has not yet applied this new classification system retroactively to data from years prior to 1999. Thus, cross-section, time-series data on ERRs using this new classification system is unavailable.

Capital mobility

Researchers have developed three methods of measuring the degree to which capital is able to cross borders. One method is to develop an index of the controls states impose on international capital movements (Haggard and Maxfield, 1996; Quinn, 1997). This approach does have the advantage of generating a wide body of cross-section, time-series data.[5] Capital controls, however, are only one barrier to capital movements. Others include brokerage fees, the costs of acquiring information about foreign investments, and asymmetries in tax systems among different countries, and so indexes of capital controls do not capture all of the barriers to capital mobility. A second method of measuring capital mobility is to measure the degree of correlation among the savings and investment rates of countries (Feldstein and Horioka, 1980). Unfortunately, this method offers a measure of capital mobility for a group of countries rather than for individual countries at any particular time. Moreover, since the measures are in the form of regression coefficients, using them as variables in another statistical analysis presents methodological questions and difficulties.

This book adopts a third approach, the comparison of nominal interest rates across countries. In a world of perfect capital mobility, financial arbitrage will encourage the buying and selling of financial assets until interest rates in different countries reach an equilibrium, or parity, level. The amount that nominal interest rates deviate from their parity level over time is a rough approximation of how mobile capital is across specific states. Interest rate parity comparisons are also capable of generating cross-section, time-series data.

How does one determine when interest rates would be at parity? Several parity conditions may apply. Ideally, one would compare interest rates for assets denominated in the same currency and with similar maturity dates (known as "onshore-offshore" differentials). Parity is achieved when these interest rates are equal. Unfortunately, while some developing countries like Mexico issue some financial assets in U.S. dollars, not enough developing countries do so to generate a large sample of data. One must make comparisons between assets with similar maturity dates denominated in different currencies, which involves accounting for expectations of exchange-rate movements.

How does one determine what the exchange rate is expected to be at the time of a financial asset's maturity? In countries with forward and futures markets, the prices for foreign-exchange cover should in principle provide good indications of what the exchange rate is expected to be. Unfortunately, few developing countries also have forward and futures market for foreign exchange, and those that do have often not had them for long. To develop the largest possible sample of countries, my capital mobility measurements rely on the admittedly weaker assumption that spot exchange rates at the time of asset maturity are in fact good proxies for exchange-rate expectations. In other words, I assume that financial agents have rational expectations of what the exchange rate will be. The parity condition is thus:

2) $$(1 + i_d) = (1 + i_f)\, s_{t+1} / s_t$$

where i_d is the domestic interest rate, i_f is the foreign, or U.S. interest rate for a similar security, s_t is the current exchange rate or "spot rate" at the time the security is sold, and s_{t+1} is the spot rate at the time the security matures. The achievement of parity among interest rates under equation 2 is called "uncovered interest rate parity" (UIP).

Deviations from UIP result from either changes in real exchange rates or differences in real interest rates among states. In developed states, changes in real exchange rates explain much of the deviations in UIP. Since developing states have larger inflation differentials, greater financial risks, and greater use of capital controls, however, deviations from UIP tend to reflect real interest rate differentials (Tanner, 1998). Deviations from UIP can thus make a rough approximation of the barriers made by financial risk and capital controls to capital mobility in specific developing states.

To measure deviations from UIP for a given country and year, I collected data on the domestic interest rate (i_d), the equivalent US interest rate (i_f), the spot exchange rate between the domestic currency and the dollar for that month (s_t) and the spot exchange rate three months in advance (s_{t+1}). These data are in the form of monthly observations. The domestic interest rate is either the 90-day deposit rate or the 90-day treasury security rate. The equivalent deposit or Treasury rate for the U.S., listed in the IMF's *International Financial Statistics*, is used as the basis of comparison.[6] The spot exchange rate is expressed in terms of domestic currency units per dollar averaged over the monthly period. For each monthly observation, the U.S. interest rate is adjusted for the expected change in the exchange rate, by multiplying i_f by (s_{t+1}/ s_t). I then take the absolute value of the difference between the domestic interest rate and the adjusted foreign rate ($|i_d - i_f(s_{t+1}/ s_t)|$). This represents the degree to which the domestic interest rate deviates from the foreign interest rate under UIP, what I shall call the "UIP deviation." I then calculate the averages of the both the adjusted U.S. interest rate and the UIP deviation for the same five-year period, beginning with January observations. I divide the average UIP deviation by the average adjusted U.S. interest rate to yield a ratio that, multiplied by a hundred, is the percentage of deviation from UIP for the five-year period. This ratio is a cross-national measure. In algebraic terms, the measure of capital mobility is:

$$3) \qquad CM = avg(|i_d - i_f(s_{t+1}/ s_t)|) \,/\, avg\,(i_f(s_{t+1}/ s_t))$$

where "CM" is capital mobility and "avg" represents the average value. The capital mobility ratio for a five-year period represents the measure for the last quarter of the period. For example, the capital mobility ratio for the period from the fourth quarter of 1992 to the fourth quarter of 1996 represents the measure for fourth quarter of 1996. Moving five-year averages yield measures for a consecutive series of years. Data from 1983 to 1996 are thus required to make the calculations for measures from 1987 to 1996. Only 27 emerging-market countries that fit the case selection criteria listed above had the necessary data for all these years. A value of zero deviation indicates perfect capital mobility. The larger the percentage deviation, the less capital mobility there is. Therefore if states are more likely to abandon pegging as capital mobility increases, then a low capital mobility indicator should increase the hazard rate and a high capital mobility indicator should decrease the hazard rate.

Using the condition of UIP as a baseline for interest rate comparisons faces three potential problems. First, in many developing countries, exchange-rate expectations may suffer from a "peso problem" in which investors anticipate the possibility of a devaluation, which colors investors' decisions even if no devaluation occurs. The second and more serious problem is that the assumption of rational expectations in predicting exchange-rate changes introduces some random, nonsystematic error into the indicator's measurement of capital mobility. Financial agents can identify patterns in exchange-rate movements under a floating exchange rate, while pegged exchange rates are prone to unexpected revaluations and devaluations. The validity of the rational-expectations assumption thus varies according the dependent variable. The third difficulty with using the UIP condition as a baseline for comparisons of interest rates is that many states in developing countries regulate domestic interest rates, a practice commonly called "financial repression." But financial repression is normally, although not necessarily, maintained in conjunction with capital controls to prevent arbitrage. Evidence from developing countries demonstrates that if a state engages in financial repression, it often employs capital controls as well (Williamson and Mahar, 1998).

The indicator for capital mobility is not perfect. The measure is, however, valid under most circumstances, and it yields continuous measures of cross-section time-series data that captures the effects of a number of barriers to capital mobility, while other methods commonly used in political economy literature do not do so. Nevertheless, the difficulties listed above provide enough reason to interpret the results of tests using this indicator with some caution.

Financial intermediation

The economics literature has developed a number of indicators for financial intermediation, including the ratio of broad money to GDP and the ratio of bank credit to GDP.[7] Shambaugh (2004) follows in this tradition, measuring private sector reliance on bank debt as the private nonguaranteed debt burden of the private sector as a share of GDP. This research uses two narrower indicators of financial intermediation, the ratio of broad money to the monetary base and the ratio of credit to the private sector to the monetary base.[8] These narrower indicators focus relatively more attention on the measurable activities of banks on monetary creation and monetary variables. Measures that use GDP as a denominator, while standard measures, are often measures of all financial intermediation in an economy (bank-based or capital-market based) or do not measure the direct consequences of bank operations.

The ratio of broad money to the monetary base is more commonly called the "money multiplier." It captures the degree to which banks create deposits and use these deposits as a basis for extending credit to the economy. As banks extend credit to clients, the money cycles through the economy, and is deposited again in banks and lent again as credit. The monetary base thus expands to become the total money supply. The ratio of broad money to the monetary base thus measures the degree of bank activity in the economy. Note that the multiplication of money is a feature unique to banks, as only they perform loan functions.

The ratio of credit to the private sector over the monetary base is a good measure of the extent of bank-based investment in an economy. For the purposes of this book I call it the "credit ratio." It differs from the money multiplier in two ways.[9] First, the money multiplier does not capture the uses of finance in the banking system. Second, the money multiplier measures purely domestic financial intermediation. The credit ratio captures financial intermediation from international sources as the capital for private sector credit derived from deposits in domestic banks by either domestic or international residents. Both indicators, however, capture the degree to which banks are involved in financing. For both indicators, the higher the ratio, the greater the use of bank-credit in an economy.

The monetary base is the sum of the total amount of currency in circulation plus bank reserves of currency. The broad money supply (M2) is the sum of the narrow money supply (M1) plus the total amount of savings deposits. *International Financial Statistics* has a separate listing for domestic credit to the private sector in each country.[10] In algebraic terms:

4) money multiplier = M2/MB = M2/(C + D) = (M1 + S)/(C + D)
5) credit ratio = PSC/MB = PSC/(C + D)

where MB is the monetary base, C is currency in circulation, D is bank reserves of currency, S is the volume of savings deposits, and PSC is domestic credit to the private sector. If the financial-intermediation hypothesis is correct, an increase in these indicators should make the abandonment of pegged exchange rates less likely.

The indicators present three possible problems. First, the indicators do not specify the degree to which foreign banks are involved in financing emerging-market firms. Second, reserve requirements partly determine the values of the indicators. Reserve requirements determine the amount of deposits banks must keep on reserve. The higher the reserve requirements, the higher the monetary base and the lower the financial-intermediation measure. The financial-intermediation measures, then, are partly a reflection of the state's banking policies. Third, the money multiplier indicates not only the degree to which the banking sector processes loans but also influences the efficacy of monetary policy in a country. Assuming that the money multiplier is stable, the higher the money multiplier, the more effective is an increase in the monetary base in inflating the economy and the more effective a decrease is in deflating the economy. The credit ratio, however, does not reflect the efficacy of monetary policy as well as the money multiplier does. Its use in statistical tests serves as a check on the results of the money multiplier indicator.

The theory behind the financial intermediation hypothesis argues that strong banks in middle-income states often borrow loans in foreign currency from abroad. This liability dollarization gives the banks in middle-income states an interest in maintaining a pegged exchange rate. If that is true, perhaps it is the percentage of liabilities in foreign currency that accounts for the maintenance of the pegged exchange rate or the interaction of financial intermediation and foreign liabilities that matters. To control for this, the hazard models include an indicator for foreign liabilities. The indicator is the ratio of foreign liabilities divided by the broad money supply multiplied by one hundred.

Economic variables

The statistical tests control for the level of trade exposure (or "trade openness") as OCA theory argues that states with higher levels of trade exposure are more likely to peg. Trade exposure is calculated as the sum of exports and imports in a given year divided by that year's GDP, multiplied by one hundred to put the ratio in percentage terms. The indicator is lagged one year. The tests do not control for GDP, another major variable cited in OCA theory, as GDP was collinear with several of the other control variables.

Inflation rates constitute another control variable. The hazard tests control for inflation rates by including the logarithm for the percentage change in a country's consumer price index over the past four quarters. Logarithms are used so that countries that experienced hyperinflation (such as Brazil) do not bias the results of the tests.[11] The higher the level of inflation, the more likely a state should be to abandon a pegged exchange rate.

The hazard equations also control for variation in the current account of a state's balance of payments. Since a current account deficit represents an outflow of foreign currency for developing states, a state is more likely to devalue or abandon a peg during a current account deficit. The indicator for the current account is the current account as a percentage of GDP, lagged by one year.

Other tests, not presented here, control for other economic variables, such as GDP per capita, the growth in domestic credit, the level of foreign exchange reserves (measured as reserves over M2) and the degree of overvaluation in the real exchange rate (measured as the deviation of the real exchange rate from a calculated trend in the rate). Unfortunately, these variables were collinear with each other and with some of control variables reported here. When separate tests were run using one of these variables and omitting other collinear variables, both of the indicators for financial intermediation were significant at the 0.05 level when controlling for domestic credit, foreign exchange reserves, or overvaluation of the real exchange rate. The financial intermediation indicators are not significant when controlling for GDP per capita, although in these tests no variables achieve significance.

Political variables

As mentioned in chapter 2, some research indicates that tradables producers may actually favor a floating exchange rate if a pegged exchange rate causes an appreciation of the real exchange rate and a loss of competitiveness. In these tests, the share of GDP produced by manufacturing is used as a proxy for the political strength of the tradables sector.[12] These tests use the same indicator, drawing on annual data from the World Bank's *World Development Indicators*.

Broz (2002) argues that the higher the level of democracy and transparency in decision-making, the more likely a state is to use an independent central bank rather than a fixed exchange rate to fight inflation. In his tests, he uses the POLITY indicator (here called DEMO) drawn from the POLITY IV database as a measure of the level of democratization in a state.[13] The POLITY IV database has two separate indicators assigning each state a score for democracy and a score of autocracy in a given year. These democracy and autocracy scores range from 0 to 10. DEMO is the score that results from taking a state's democracy score and subtracting the autocracy score. Values for DEMO thus range from -10 to 10, with 10 being the most democratic. According to Broz, a higher DEMO score should yield a higher likelihood of abandoning a peg.

The election hypothesis posits that devaluations and abandonment of pegs are less likely in the run up to elections and more likely after an election has been held. In these tests the quarter during an election and the previous quarter are coded with a 1, while the quarter after an election is coded with a –1. All other quarters are coded with a 0. Positive scores for elections should be correlated with a lower likelihood of abandoning a peg. This is consistent with the coding in the studies mentioned in chapter 2 testing the election hypothesis.[14]

Results of tests on official exchange-rate regimes

Table 3.1 provides summary statistics of the tests using the IMF's classification of ERRs. The variables show no real surprises in their means and standard deviations, although the mean score of 94.75 for trade exposure among the cases signifies how much these developing states rely on trade. The mean score for capital mobility is 22.21, meaning that the three-month securities had an 22.21% average deviation from UIP over a five-year period, but unfortunately a few quarters of extremely high interest rates during a hyperinflationary period in Brazil skews the mean. The deviation from UIP varies from 1.05% (signifying how high capital mobility can be in some developing countries) to 2886.32% (the extreme case in one Brazilian quarter). Without Brazil, the average deviation is just above five percent. The mean score for the money multiplier is 5.55 and the mean score for the credit ratio is 4.45. Scores below these means represent low degrees of bank-based financing and scores above these means represent high degrees of bank-based financing.

Table 3.2 displays the correlation matrix for the variables in the tests, which is important for identifying possible sources of collinearity. For the most part, the variables do not exhibit much correlation with each other, except for some notable exceptions. The money multiplier and the credit ratio have a 0.656 correlation, as they should. The foreign liabilities indicator has a 0.487 correlation with the credit ratio, but only a 0.044 correlation with the money multiplier. The

Table 3.1 Descriptive statistics for the tests using the IMF system

	Mean	St. Dev.	Minimum	Maximum
Money Multiplier	5.55	2.23	1.79	11.45
Credit Ratio	4.45	2.62	0.24	12.11
Capital Mobility	22.21	165.91	1.05	2886.31
Foreign Liabilities	12.49	13.01	0.14	84.71
Inflation	2.15	1.17	-1.34	8.37
Current Account	-0.33	7.31	-12.55	40.84
Trade Exposure	94.75	41.66	15.12	171.93
Manufacturing	19.53	9.08	4.31	37.42
Democracy	3.90	7.09	-10.00	10.00
Elections	0.0425	0.3620	-1.00	1.00

Table 3.2 Correlation matrix for the tests using the IMF system

	Cap. Mob.	For. Liab.	Inflat.	CA/ GDP	Trade Exp.	Mon. Mult.
Cap. Mob.	1.000					
For. Liab.	0.219	1.000				
Inflation	0.598	0.343	1.000			
CA/GDP	-0.007	-0.261	-0.022	1.000		
Trade Exp.	-0.261	-0.429	-0.338	0.234	1.000	
Mon. Mult.	-0.024	0.044	-0.192	0.068	-0.001	1.000
Cred. Rat.	0.208	0.487	0.028	-0.363	-0.278	0.656
Manufact.	0.134	0.061	0.035	-0.258	0.382	-0.275
Democracy	0.086	-0.105	-0.052	-0.049	-0.283	0.489
Elections	0.157	0.024	0.082	-0.013	-0.067	0.031

	Credit Ratio	Manu- fact.	Demo.	Elect.
Cred. Rat.	1.000			
Manufact.	0.150	1.000		
Democracy	0.325	-0.514	1.000	
Elections	0.057	-0.010	0.032	1.000

capital mobility indicator has a 0.598 correlation with the log of inflation, which may indicate that high inflation explains many cases of strong interest-rate differentials or that the Brazilian case has a strong influence on the capital mobility and inflation indicators.

The results of four hazard tests are shown in Table 3.3. All four tests use the indicators reported above. Each cell of the table has a number without parentheses above and a number in parentheses below. The numbers without parentheses above are the hazard ratios, the magnitude by which one unit of change in the independent variable multiplies the odds of abandoning a peg. Hazard ratios greater than one indicate variables that increase the likelihood of abandoning a peg. Hazard ratios less than one indicate variables that decrease the likelihood of abandoning a peg and the increase the likelihood of maintaining one. The numbers with parentheses below are standard errors for the hazard ratios.[15] Equations I and III employ the money multiplier as the indicator for financial intermediation, while equations II and IV employ the credit ratio. In equations I and II, each indicator is independent of all others. Equations III and IV include interactive product variables that test whether financial intermediation and foreign liabilities interact. In equation III, collinearity problems with the interactive variable seem to prevent chi-squared tests from being performed. In all of the other equations, a chi-squared test of the full equation achieves significance at the 0.05 level.

The capital mobility indicator lacks significance in all of the equations. The hazard ratios for capital mobility are below one, which means that a one per cent increase in deviation from UIP (representing a slight increase in the immobility of capital) would cut the hazard rate or likelihood of abandoning a peg, as expected. Lack of significance here could have many meanings. Either these tests provide no evidence for the hollowing-out thesis, no evidence for the hypothesis that government officials anticipate the risks associated with higher capital mobility or the indicator is simply not valid. Chapter 8 discusses these possibilities in more detail, in the light of evidence from the case studies.

Both the money multiplier and the credit ratio are significant at the 0.05 level in equations I and II. Moreover, the hazard ratios are less than 1, indicating that as financial intermediation rises, the likelihood that a state will abandon a peg drops. According to equations I and II, a state has a likelihood of abandoning a peg about 0.6 times (or three-fifths) that of a state with one-unit less of one of the indicators. Some might argue that the significance of the money multiplier might reflect the fact that monetary policy is stronger in a state with a higher money multiplier, as the effects of interest changes are more pronounced in the banking system. But the significance of the credit ratio makes this interpretation unlikely and more likely that it reflects the strength of the banking sector as a mediator of capital in the economy.

Table 3.3 Results of tests using the IMF system

Variable	I	II	III	IV
Capital Mobility	0.916 (0.068)	0.964 (0.035)	0.921 (0.062)	0.966 (0.036)
Foreign Liabilities/M2	1.018 (0.034)	1.039 (0.053)	0.977 (0.062)	1.020 (0.061)
Inflation (log)	1.384 (0.576)	1.262 (0.553)	1.473 (0.693)	1.282 (0.586)
Current Account/GDP	0.913 (0.133)	0.894 (0.121)	0.918 (0.131)	0.894 (0.118)
Trade Exposure	0.985 (0.011)	0.977** (0.010)	0.988 (0.013)	0.978** (0.010)
Money Multiplier	0.575** (0.125)	-	0.517* (0.175)	-
Credit Ratio	-	0.619** (0.137)	-	0.587 (0.196)
Interactive Variable	-	-	1.008 (0.013)	1.003 (0.011)
Manufacturing Sector	1.020 (0.032)	1.080** (0.037)	0.998 (0.051)	1.069* (0.041)
Democracy	1.216 (0.165)	1.199 (0.140)	1.186* (0.121)	1.181* (0.111)
Elections	1.647 (1.167)	1.612 (1.061)	1.632 (1.178)	1.624 (1.076)
Dependence on time (log)	0.685 (0.481)	0.650 (0.430)	0.703 (0.459)	0.667 (0.419)
N	329	329	329	329
chi-squared	88.61	81.45	-	110.21
Prob>chi^2	0.0000	0.0000	-	0.0000

* indicates significance at the 0.10 level
** indicates significance at the 0.05 level
*** indicates significance at the 0.01 level

The foreign liabilities indicator does not achieve significance in equations I and II. More puzzlingly, the hazard ratios in three of the tests are above one implying that an increase in foreign liabilities leads to an increase in the likelihood of abandoning a peg. But since the indicator is not significant and the hazard ratios are close to one, the unusual hazard ratios could be due to chance. A test of a hazard model (not shown here) using the foreign liabilities indicator but none of the financial intermediation variables yields a hazard ratio of 0.949.

Whether or not financial intermediation and foreign liabilities interact to affect exchange-rate policy is admittedly problematic. In equations III and IV, the interaction between foreign liabilities and financial intermediation is also not significant. One could argue that if banks with high volumes of foreign liabilities lobby for a peg, the interactive term should be significant. The lack of significance for the interactive variable in equation IV and the equation's apparent lack of collinearity problems raise this question. Should the financial intermediation hypothesis imply that financial intermediation and foreign liabilities interact? Given the levels of significance reported in equations I and II, it may be that the strength of the banking system matters more to official policy than the mere level of foreign liabilities that it and others hold. While foreign liabilities measure the interest domestic groups may have in maintaining a pegged exchange rate, the financial intermediation indicator is more a measure of the power banks have to get what they want, which seems to be more crucial to the determination of policy. In the test mentioned in the last paragraph where foreign liabilities are included in the equation but financial intermediation is not, the foreign liabilities indicator still did not demonstrate any significance. Furthermore, the chi-squared score for this equation was 8.27. Compared to the chi-squared score of 110.21 in equation IV, where the credit ratio and its interactive variable are included, the presence of the credit ratio seems significant in equation IV.[16]

Of the control variables, trade exposure and the strength of the manufacturing sector are significant if the equations control for the credit ratio. Democracy is significant at the 0.10 level if controlling for interactive terms, but it is not clear that much should be made of this given the lack of significance for the tests with interactive terms. Moreover, the tests inexplicably imply that an upcoming election actually raises the likelihood of abandoning a peg. It is difficult to tell how much of this is due to the use of a different dataset than used by proponents of the election hypothesis.[17] The duration of time has hazard ratios less than one, implying that more durable pegs may generate greater credibility, but the indicators are not significant in any of the tests.

To check the robustness of the results two further sets of tests were performed, with results not reported here. The tests in Table 3.3 use a dataset that includes all states that pegged their exchange rate for some spell between 1987 and 1998. Most of the spells begin with the first quarter of 1987, but two begin their spell of pegging after that time. This raises questions of whether observations about cases that did not peg before a spell of pegging began are biasing results. The tests were re-run without the two cases that began pegging after 1987. In tests without an interaction term, the money multiplier and the credit ratio are significant at the 0.10 level and have similar hazard ratios. Unfortunately, collinearity problems prevent chi-squared tests from determining if the full equations in these tests are significant. The tests are disappointing but not disconfirmation of the financial intermediation hypothesis.

Finally, the tests were run again with all of the cases except the data from the Brazilian case. Since Brazilian hyperinflation created extreme values for interest rates and the capital mobility indicator, the tests were run again without the Brazilian data. The capital mobility indicator remains insignificant, while the financial intermediation indicators retain their original levels of significance. Interactive terms and the inflation indicator also remain insignificant. Trade exposure and the manufacturing sector continue to be significant at the 0.05 level in a non-interactive test controlling for the credit ratio. In short, the results of the tests in table 3.3 are fairly robust in the face of some basic sensitivity checks.

Conclusions

The tests on a dependent variable coding the official ERR policies of states provide evidence for the following conclusions:

- Higher levels of financial intermediation are associated with a higher likelihood of maintaining a pegged exchange rate.
- The strength of the banking sector (represented in the financial intermediation indicators) is probably more relevant to policy than the sheer volume of foreign liabilities.
- Higher trade exposure seems to increase the chances of maintaining a peg while a stronger manufacturing sector increases the chances of abandoning a peg, when controlling for the credit ratio.

The tests use data from middle-income states with different levels of GDP and from different regions of the world. The tests are fairly robust to checks for outliers and censoring. Combined with Shambaugh's (2004) results, they indicate that patterns of financial intermediation do have an effect on the choice of ERR. While Shambaugh's data include more countries and a longer period of observation, the tests here test the financial intermediation hypothesis with more than one form of measurement for financial intermediation and while providing better controls for capital mobility.

The capital mobility indicator yields negative results. As argued above, this could be the result of failings in the indicator, the failure of government officials to anticipate the costs of rising capital mobility, or the failure of the HOT. To the extent that government officials do fail to anticipate the higher costs of capital mobility, the financial intermediation hypothesis can help explain why states persist in pegging as the costs of maintaining a peg climb. Government officials appear to be concerned with what effects a devaluation or floatation would have on the banking sector, and its political allies that also hold external debt. If the banking sector is strong, it increases the likelihood that states will pay the costs of maintaining a peg, even if these costs are increasing. In Asia and Latin America, this pressure contributed to exchange-rate crises once the costs of pegging became unbearable. The cases of Thailand and Mexico in following chapters demonstrate how this applied dynamic to specific, recent cases.

Notes

[1] The countries used in these statistical tests include: Algeria, Belize, Botswana, Brazil, Chile, Ecuador, Egypt, El Salvador, Guatemala, Jamaica, Malaysia, Mauritius, Papua New Guinea, Swaziland, and Thailand.

[2] Since Shambaugh (2004) uses a different method of estimating capital mobility, he is able to employ a dataset incorporating more countries and a longer time period. Shambaugh's dataset thus includes states that do switch from pegging to floating and back again, and so he uses cross-section, time-series logit methods in his tests.

[3] Levi Yeyati and Sturzenegger (2003) the main alternative to Reinhart and Rogoff, use cluster analysis on nominal exchange rates, volatility in nominal exchange rates, and foreign exchange reserves to classify states as fixes, crawling pegs, dirty floats, and flexible ERRs for individual years in the 1990s. Unfortunately, their method yields a number of inconclusive data points and ignores the role of interest rate movements in exchange-rate management. The Reinhart and Rogoff method described here provides a more complete dataset over a longer period of time.

[4] Ecuador and El Salvador both adopted the U.S. dollar as its domestic currency in 2000, which would code them as rigid fixes. But the data end at 1998, so the rigid fixes do not show up in the data.

[5] Shambaugh (2004) uses dummy variables that record whether a state did or did not have controls on the capital and current accounts.

[6] All of the raw data for these calculations come from data series in the IMF's *International Financial Statistics*, various years. Interest rates for treasury securities come from data series 60L. Interest rates for 90-day deposits come from data series 60C. Exchange rates come from data series RF.

[7] King and Levine, 1993.

[8] See Rother, 1999 for more discussion of these indicators.

[9] Rother, 1999, p.9.

[10] The raw data for these indicators also come from *International Financial Statistics*, various years. Currency in circulation comes from data series 14A. Bank reserves of currency come from data series 20. The narrow money supply is given in data series 34. Volumes of savings deposits are given in data series 35. Domestic credit to the private sector is given in data series 22C.

[11] Data for consumer price indexes were drawn from *International Financial Statistics*, series 64.

[12] Frieden, Ghezzi and Stein, 2001; Blomberg, Frieden and Stein, 2002.

[13] Broz, 2002. Data on the Polity IV database can be found at http://www.cidcm.umd.edu/inscr/polity/.
[14] Frieden, Ghezzi, and Stein, 2001; Blomberg, Frieden, and Stein, 2002.
[15] The results reported here use the Huber/White estimation method for standard errors.
[16] A Wald test is not available when using Huber/White standard errors. Significance levels for individual variables are not valid when one of the indicators is used to compute an interactive variable, so a comparison of equations with and without the indicator and its interactive term are more appropriate.
[17] The appendix reports results on tests that provide more support for the election hypothesis.

Chapter 4

Thailand

The case of Thailand illustrates the main features of the financial intermediation hypothesis fairly well. Thailand has a strong banking sector and pegged its exchange rate for longer than most middle-income countries. This chapter will argue that not only did the peg strengthen the banking sector, but that the banking sector and the fear of a banking crisis helped maintain the peg. The next section of this chapter summarizes the history of exchange-rate policy in Thailand in the 1980s and 1990s. The third section examines the economic context of growth, trade, foreign investment, and inflation in Thailand during this period and their influence on exchange-rate policy. Thailand has had a small, open economy with relatively low inflation during the past few decades. Pegged exchange rates have been beneficial for such an economy, protecting export and import prices from volatility in the exchange rate. Later sections trace out the elements of the financial intermediation hypothesis and evaluate how well other hypotheses apply to ERR policy in Thailand. These sections address the three basic points behind the financial intermediation theory: 1) how the financial system is structured (section four) 2) what the banks and other interest groups wanted for ERR policy (sections five and six) and 3) what affected the policy-making procedure for ERR policy (section seven). As the story of government policy unfolds, the Thai government deliberately maintains a peg even as the risks of doing so become more apparent. One key reason for doing so involves the financial sector. Fearing the effects of a floatation or devaluation on banks with foreign liabilities and non-performing loans, the central bank of Thailand fought a long, hard battle to protect the pegged exchange rate. When it lost the battle in July 1997, the fears of the government were realized: heavier external debts burdened both banks and commercial firms.

Exchange-rate policy in Thailand

Thailand had some form of pegged exchange rate up until the financial crisis of 1997, which is a longer period of time than most middle-income countries (IMF, various years). In the sample used in chapter 3's statistical tests, Thailand pegs for ten and a half years after January 1987, which is longer than eleven states in the sample and shorter than three others.[1] Thailand first established a basket peg in 1978. Thai officials fixed the value of the baht against a basket of foreign currencies including the U.S. dollar, the Japanese yen, and other trading partners.

While ostensibly calculated according to a trade-weighted formula, economists generally reckoned that the U.S. dollar had a weight far greater than 50% in the basket, making the basket peg a de facto peg to the dollar.

Although Thailand managed to maintain its official pegged rate for most of the period from 1978 to 1997, this period before the Asian financial crisis saw two devaluations. In May of 1981, the Thai government devalued the baht by 1.083% and by a further 8.7% in July 1981, as a response to worldwide recession, which provoked a loss of exports and persistent current account deficits. The government also abolished the basket peg that July and introduced a simple dollar peg. This helped until 1983, when the value of the dollar skyrocketed in global currency markets, making Thailand and other states pegged to the dollar lose competitiveness in world markets. In November 1984, Thailand devalued the baht yet again by 14.9%, and reintroduced the basket peg.

From 1984 to 1997, Thailand maintained a basket peg with little alteration in exchange-rate value. After 1987, the exchange rate normally fluctuated between values of 25 to 26 baht to the dollar. Once again, the dollar accounted for the majority of weighting in the basket, and some economic tests implied that the dollar's weighting grew over time during this period (Warr and Nidhiprabha, 1996, pp. 215-217). During this period, Thailand received large influxes of foreign investment, which enabled it to finance larger current account deficits. While the foreign investment stimulated economic growth, it caught the managers of interest rates in a dilemma. Attempting to restrain inflation with higher interest rates would ironically encourage further investment and borrowing from abroad, which in turn would increase the domestic money supply and domestic inflation. Given the mobile capital and pegged exchange rate, the Thai central bank found it difficult to move interest rates away from prevailing world levels. As debts piled up in a shaky banking system, the current account deficit became persistent and unsustainable. After defending the peg for as long as it could, the Thai finance ministry let the baht float on July 2, 1997. The government declared, however, that it reserved the right to intervene in currency markets on occasion. The baht fell from 24.5 baht to the dollar to 28 baht to the dollar that day, a 14.2% depreciation. This action encouraged other investors to question what other East Asian currencies might be overvalued and exposing other East Asian currencies to similar overwhelming speculative pressures, which of course was the Asian financial crisis. After stabilizing its currency, Thailand has maintained a managed float.

Economic conditions in Thailand

What conditions led up to the crisis? Much has already been written about the crisis and its aftereffects, and this chapter will focus on what was behind Thailand's persistence in pegging its exchange rate, a key cause of the crisis. The following sections examine how well the different hypotheses presented in chapter 2 explain Thailand's persistence in pegging. This section examines the role of five economic conditions: industrialization, GDP growth, trade exposure, foreign investment and inflation.

Industrialization

The most striking aspect of the Thai economy is the rapid, consistent growth it has experienced over the past few decades, a product of industrialization. In the period from 1965 to 1980, real GDP grew at an average rate of 7.2% (Warr and Nidhiprabha, 1996, p. 42). At no time from the beginnings of its industrialization around 1965 to the Asian financial crisis of 1997 did Thailand experience negative growth, although many developing countries did. Industrialization serves as the backdrop for all of the economic conditions relevant to exchange-rate policy.

The government of Thailand has been pushing for the industrialization of the economy since the 1950s. Thailand distinguished itself by adhering to a capitalist economic model at a time when neighbors such as Myanmar and Vietnam were employing socialist economies. Beginning in the 1960s, it tried to stimulate industrialization through import-substitution, as many developing countries were doing at the time. But with industrialization proceeding slowly, Thailand switched to a strategy of export-led growth in the 1970s. The public sector received significant amounts of foreign investment that financed infrastructure and other public works projects (Narongchai, et. al., 1993, p. 31), which helped the economy to grow. The combination of the 1979 oil shock and two devaluations in the early 1980s, however, forced painful adjustments on the private sector, leading to the slowdown of growth from 1981 to 1987. Even in 1985, however, Thailand's manufacturing sector was 21.92% of its GDP, which was higher than the average of 19.53% for the sample of countries in chapter 3. By 1997, the manufacturing sector was 28.75% of GDP.

Export-led growth led to three transformations of the Thai economy: the influx of foreign investment directed at the private sector, the growth of the manufacturing sector, and the development of consumerism. By the late 1980s and 1990s, investors in Japan and the Newly Industrializing Countries (NIC's) were looking for new investment opportunities outside their own countries, as their domestic labor costs had risen. Cheap, productive labor in Thailand and the relatively low value of the baht made Thailand attractive to investment. Thailand's private sector received an influx of foreign investment, sparking an economic boom. Investors provided the capital for new factories. From 1985 onward, industry accounted for a bigger share of GDP than did agriculture (Falkus, 1995, p. 13). The industrializing boom created an urban middle class, which predictably sought a higher standard of living. Foreign borrowing and consumer spending, however, continued even after the boom slowed down in the middle of the 1990s. After a few years, the current account deficits appeared unsustainable.

GDP Growth and Trade Exposure

Industrialization has transformed Thailand's GDP and trade exposure. Thailand's rapid growth, however, has not altered Thailand's status as a small economy. In 1975, around the end of the Bretton Woods par value system, Thailand's nominal GDP was just over 303 billion baht (see table 4.1). From 1987 to 1992, the Thai economy took off, hitting an average growth rate over ten percent. By 1995, Thailand GDP was at almost 4,099 billion baht of GDP, an increase by a factor of 13.5 over 1975. Nevertheless, GDP per capita was roughly 69,000 baht in 1995, almost $2,740 at contemporary exchange rates. According to the World Bank this made Thailand qualify as a "lower-middle income" country. Despite being a "fifth tiger," Thailand still lags behind compared to the size of other Asian states. In 1995, Thailand's GDP was $168 billion, small compared to the GDP of the more populous Indonesia ($202 billion) or the more industrialized South Korea ($489 billion).[2]

Thailand's exposure to foreign trade also grew over the 1990s (see Table 4.1). During much of the 1980s, trade exposure was equivalent to half of Thailand's GDP. But beginning in 1987, when foreign investment began to pour into private sector, trade exposure began to rise. By 1997, trade exposure was equivalent to 93% of its GDP. Because Thailand is a small, open economy, pegging has provided benefits for the aggregate economy.

Three features about the destination of Thai exports put the role of a dollar peg in perspective (Warr and Nidhiprahba, 1996, p. 53). First, a large fraction of Thai exports go to developing countries, which normally use the dollar in international trade. For lower middle-income countries, exports to developing countries account for an average of 27% of total exports. Exports to developing countries in the 1990s accounted for 38% of Thai exports. Second, much of Thai exports to developing countries are to neighboring East Asian countries. Most East Asian countries use the dollar in international transactions. However, of exports to industrialized countries, 26% went to Japan, a third point that undercuts the need for a dollar peg.

As OCA theory predicts, Thailand's relatively small and open economy benefited from a pegged exchange rate. The pegged exchange rate isolated the small economy from foreign monetary shocks and gave it price stability in its major export markets. The economic benefits, however, were not the primary reasons key interest groups pressured the government to maintain the peg in the 1990s.

Foreign Investment

As capital mobility increased, Thailand had more opportunities for foreign investment. The peg had the added benefit of helping to encourage foreign investment by giving foreign investors a sense of reduced exchange-rate risk. As

Table 4.1 Economic data on Thailand

Year	Real GDP (billions of baht)	Real GDP Growth	Inflation (CPI)	Exchange Rate (baht /US $)	Trade Exposure
1985	1,191.3	4.6	2.4	27.16	49.2
1986	1,257.2	5.2	1.9	26.30	49.2
1987	1,376.8	9.5	2.5	25.74	57.2
1988	1,559.8	13.3	3.8	25.29	67.4
1989	1,750.0	12.2	5.4	25.70	72.4
1990	1,945.4	11.2	5.9	25.59	75.8
1991	2,111.9	8.6	5.7	25.52	78.5
1992	2,282.6	8.1	4.1	25.40	78.0
1993	2,473.9	8.4	3.3	25.32	79.1
1994	2,695.4	9.0	5.0	25.15	81.8
1995	2,946.3	9.3	5.8	24.92	89.6
1996	3,119.6	5.9	5.9	25.34	82.8
1997	3,074.5	-1.4	5.6	31.37	93.4
1998	2,743.4	-10.6	8.1	41.37	92.9
1999	2,859.2	4.2	0.3	37.84	97.7
Year	Money Multiplier	Credit Ratio	Capital Mobility	TED /GDP	TED/ Exports
1987	7.194	5.469	4.3	39.60	172.41
1988	7.281	6.063	3.9	34.21	133.70
1989	7.898	6.840	3.1	31.55	114.57
1990	8.090	7.453	2.8	34.34	127.95
1991	8.738	8.092	3.5	38.59	133.92
1992	8.785	8.484	3.8	39.12	135.40
1993	8.886	8.991	4.6	41.33	142.35
1994	8.796	10.272	5.2	44.91	145.19
1995	8.237	10.175	5.3	59.91	180.97
1996	7.927	9.973	4.7	59.58	198.72
1997	8.074	10.658	n.a.	72.33	192.77
1998	10.264	11.421	n.a.	93.94	198.68
1999	8.155	8.148	n.a.	78.38	168.31

TED = total external debt
n.a. = not available
Trade exposure, money multiplier, credit ratio, and capital mobility indicators are those used in chapter 3. Figures for growth, inflation, trade exposure, capital mobility, and total foreign debt in percentages.

Sources: Bank of Thailand and International Monetary Fund.

was mentioned above, Thailand began to receive massive inflows of foreign investment in 1987. The capital account measures the net amount of investment across borders, whether in the form of direct investment, portfolio investment, or loans. In 1985 the capital account of Thailand recorded net inflows of $1.5 billion. By 1991, the inflows had grown to over $11 billion, and remained around ten billion dollars for the next few years. By 1995, the capital inflow was almost $21 billion. The vast majority of this investment capital went to private rather than public investment. After the financial crisis in 1997, foreign investors shied away from investing in Thailand, and the capital account exhibited net outflows for the next few years. For most of the period up until the financial crisis, however, billions of dollars were flowing into the Thai economy, and Thais needed to earn dollars to pay back loans and pay dividends and interest to foreign investors. This gave many private firms in the economy an interest in avoiding a devaluation, which would have made earning dollars far more difficult.

Table 4.2 shows the structure of foreign investment and the relative sizes of each form of investment from 1970 to 1990. The table shows not only the growth of foreign investment over time but a telling shift from investment in public enterprises to private enterprises. For most of the period from 1970 to 1986, capital inflows did not average more than four percent of GDP but after 1987 capital inflows began to average six percent of GDP. From 1975 to 1986, most of the foreign investment was in the form of long-term loans, and much of these inflows went to the public sector or state-owned enterprises. After 1987 the public sector and state-owned enterprises were now repaying their previous loans and not taking in new ones. The private sector now took the predominant share of long-term loans. Direct investment, portfolio investment, and short-term loans all increased as a share of total inflows. The ratios of debt to GDP and debt to exports in Table 4.1 demonstrate that foreign investment kept growing well after 1990. Consequently, Thailand exposed itself to more short-term private investment that depended on the confidence of foreign investors.

Foreign investment was still a small but significant fraction of all investment in Thailand. Until 1997, foreign sources of investment also accounted for at least a fifth of all investment in Thailand. Gross fixed investment is the total amount of capital domestic private firms spend on investment in a given year, and Table 4.3 summarizes some statistics on gross fixed investment and total investment. Figures for the capital account and the portion of the capital account devoted to private investment represent allow one to calculate how much of gross fixed and total investment came from foreign sources. From 1991 to 1996, the capital inflow was equivalent to 21 to 32% of gross fixed investment. Foreign private investment accounts for 20 to 31% of gross fixed investment. Domestic savings thus powered most of Thailand's economic boom in this period, but foreign sources of capital made up a significant portion of investment. When foreign capital poured out of Thailand after the 1997 crisis (represented by the negative percentages), Thailand experienced the first negative growth in its economy for decades. Foreign investment, then, could produce significant changes in total flows of investment capital and alter the business cycle. The significant

Table 4.2 International capital flows into Thailand

As a Percentage of GDP

	DFI	PFI	NFL	NFL (pr)	NFL (se)	NFL (gv)	NFS	CaAc
1970-74	0.81	0.11	0.78	0.43	0.18	0.17	0.20	1.90
1975-79	0.39	0.08	2.29	0.43	1.13	0.72	0.79	3.56
1980-82	0.65	0.08	5.08	1.69	2.39	0.99	0.74	6.54
1983-86	0.74	0.16	2.57	0.46	1.18	0.93	0.51	3.98
1987-90	1.88	1.10	0.33	1.09	-0.46	-0.29	2.67	6.01

Percentage of Capital Account

	DFI	PFI	NFL	NFL (pr)	NFL (se)	NFL (gv)	NFS	CaAc
1970-74	42.7	5.8	41.1	22.8	9.3	8.9	10.4	100.0
1975-79	11.1	2.3	64.4	12.2	31.9	20.3	2.2	100.0
1980-82	9.9	1.2	77.6	25.9	36.5	15.1	11.3	100.0
1983-86	18.5	4.0	64.7	11.7	29.6	23.4	12.8	100.0
1987-90	31.3	18.3	5.5	18.1	-7.7	-4.9	44.5	100.0

Key:
DFI = Direct Foreign Investment
PFI = Portfolio Foreign Investment
NFL = Net Inflow of Long-Term Loans
NFL(pr) = Net Inflow of Long-Term Loans to Private Sector
NFL(se) = Net Inflow of Long-Term Loans to State Enterprises
NFL(gv)= Net Inflow of Long-Term Loans to Government
NFS = Net Inflow of Short-Term Loans
CaAc = Capital Account

Source: Narongchai Akrasanee, et. al., *International Capital Flows and Economic Adjustment in Thailand* (Bangkok: Thailand Development Research Institute, 1993), p. 35.

Table 4.3 Foreign investment as a percentage of investment in Thailand

Year	FI/TI	FI/GFI	FPI/TI	FPI/GFI
1991	26.8	27.6	24.4	25.1
1992	21.3	21.7	21.0	21.3
1993	21.0	21.2	20.6	20.8
1994	20.9	21.1	20.7	20.8
1995	31.1	31.8	29.5	30.2
1996	25.7	26.2	24.0	24.4
1997	-10.3	-10.2	-17.7	-17.7
1998	-43.9	-40.2	-68.6	-62.7
1999	-32.3	-32.1	-56.2	-55.8

Key:
FI = foreign investment
FPI = foreign private investment
TI = total investment
GFI = gross fixed investment

Figures in percentages

Source: author's calculations based on Bank of Thailand data.

role that domestic savings played in investment, however, also meant that Thai commercial firms depended heavily on domestic financial intermediation, which Thai banks dominated.

Inflation

Low inflation also made the peg easier to maintain and improve the investment climate, helping to stimulate long-term growth. From 1982 to 1998, the annual rate of inflation, as measured by the consumer price index, did not go above six percent. The last spikes in prices hit during the oil shocks of 1973-1974 and 1977-1982. Cautious fiscal and monetary policies were largely responsible for this consistently low inflation. Over the period from 1970 to 1988, the government did not run a deficit higher than nine percent of GDP (Warr and Nidhiprabha, 1996, p. 139). Indeed, after 1988, the government began to run budget surpluses. Revenue from indirect taxes, such as import duties, business taxes, and sales taxes, rise and fall with the performance of the economy, while expenditures are often subject to a rigid, bureaucratic process (Warr and Nidhiprabha, 1996, p. 166). Thus, Peter Warr and Bhanupong Nidhiprabha argue that automatic stabilizers in the budget, rather than discretionary policy, had stabilizing effects on the business cycle. They also argue that discretionary monetary policy had stabilizing effects (Warr and Nidhiprabha, 1996, pp. 197-203). But given that Thailand adhered to a pegged exchange rate, the rise of capital mobility after the mid-1980s caused monetary policy to lose autonomy in Thailand over time. Nevertheless, consistently low inflation helps to explain why there was little demand to abolish the Bank of Thailand and replace it with a currency board or monetary union.

Traditional economic considerations seem to help explain the pegged exchange rate in Thailand. Thailand's small, open economy benefited from a pegged exchange rate as it industrialized and developed new export markets. Restrained fiscal and monetary policies produced relatively low inflation, which made it easier to maintain a peg with a low-inflation dollar. The peg also encouraged foreign investors to assume that Thailand presented little exchange-rate risk. But the influx of private investment, and short-term investment in particular, posed the growing possibility of an exchange-rate crisis. A loss of confidence in the peg or the economy could provoke investors to pull their mobile capital out quickly. Why then maintain a peg as the risks of crisis grew? The benefits of the peg to a small, open economy are not enough of an explanation, as these benefits did not automatically translate into political support from government or private groups. Politicians could have easily ignored the long-term benefits of price stability if it meant abandoning a peg to avoid a short-term crash. An analysis of the more political hypotheses indicates that the most likely explanation for pegging in Thailand came from the financial and commercial sectors, rather than the economic characteristics of the country.

The rest of this chapter argues that the interests and influence of the financial system was probably the most crucial factor for explaining the persistence of pegging, even if it is not the only one. Ideally, the influence of bank lobbying should be demonstrated through direct process-tracing in a case study. But in developing countries, evidence of lobbying efforts is rarely documented in sources open to the public. This chapter therefore, will trace the process more indirectly, by evaluating evidence for different elements of the financial intermediation argument. Four elements establish the argument. First, banks represented the primary source of financing in the Thai economy and a key interest group. Second, despite what a devalued exchange rate could do for competitiveness, many commercial firms had reasons for maintaining the peg. This meant that banks were not alone in lobbying for a peg, and could rely for support among some of their main customers. Third, banks had significant foreign liabilities that gave them an interest in maintaining a peg. Fourth, the government's behavior during a currency crisis reflected a determination to peg in spite of an environment of high capital mobility. The government's behavior indicates that it was trying to prevent a banking crisis from erupting. The next sections present evidence for these propositions.

The financial system

Thailand, like most countries, has a variety of financial institutions. They include commercial banks, specialized development banks, finance and securities companies, insurance companies, savings cooperatives, and mortgage institutions. Commercial banks dominate the Thai financial scene. In 1987, at the beginning of the period studied in chapter 3, commercial banks accounted for 69% of the total assets of financial institutions, 73% of the total savings mobilized, and 76% of the total credit extended (Warr, 1993, p. 226). Even after the influx of foreign investment from 1987 to 1993, domestic commercial banks held a commanding position in Thai finance. Just prior to the Asian financial crisis, commercial banks accounted for three-quarters of all deposits placed with financial institutions (Warr and Nidhiprabha, 1996, p. 39; Warr, 1993, p. 23). In 1999, commercial banks commanded 75% of the total assets in Thai financial institutions and, more critically, lent 79% of the total credit extended (Bank of Thailand, 2001).

In addition to banks, finance companies are the second largest share of the Thai loan market. Finance companies in Thailand differ from banks in three ways: finance companies raise funds through promissory notes instead of deposits, face more restrictions on opening branches, and focus more on financing personal consumption and real estate ventures (Paiboon, et. al., 1995, pp. 37-38). The total assets of finance companies are equivalent to one quarter of the assets of commercial banks. Between the banks and the finance companies, Thailand's money multiplier is higher than most other middle-income states. As shown in Table 4.1, the money multiplier for Thailand is between eight and nine during most of the 1990s, while the mean for the countries in the statistical tests was 5.55. The credit ratio falls between eight and just over ten in that same period, while the mean is 4.45.

Besides commercial banks and finance companies, Thailand has a variety of smaller financial institutions. These include credit foncier companies, which loan money for property development, insurance companies, government development banks, and cooperatives, which mobilize the savings of members of various occupations and supply credits for members. In 1999, these institutions had 1.5 trillion baht in assets (Bank of Thailand, 2001). Commercial bank and finance companies, however, had almost 7.7 trillion baht in assets that same year. The smaller financial institutions, then, are not serious rivals to the banks.

Banks vs. Capital Markets

The Stock Exchange of Thailand (SET) grew significantly in the 1990s, but still lags behind those of other countries. In 1990, the SET's total market capitalization (the total value of all stocks issued by companies listed on the exchange) was almost $24 billion, equivalent to 28% of Thailand's GDP (International Finance Corporation, 1999, p. 321). By 1995 market capitalization peaked at almost $142 billion, equivalent to 84% of its GDP. The market, however, tumbled after the Asian financial crisis. After 1997, the capitalization of SET amounted to $23.5 million, 15% of GDP. By the end of 1998, Thailand had the 36th largest stock exchange in the world (International Finance Corporation, 1999, p. 24). This, however, was behind other middle-income countries that had also weathered the Asian financial crisis. The Philippines had the 35th largest stock exchange, Malaysia had the 23rd largest, and South Korea the 20th largest. The SET was 31st in terms of values of shared traded, while Malaysia was 29th and Korea was 17th. In short, by international standards, Thailand's capital markets are small. Thailand's continuing reliance on bank-credit has probably restrained the growth of its equity markets.

One can see further evidence of bank dominance over capital markets in comparisons of debt. Commercial banking accounts for more of the financing of corporate liabilities than capital markets do. In 1997, the year of the financial crisis, commercial banking accounted for $25.7 million of long-term debt, equivalent to 17% of Thailand's GDP.[3] Bonds accounted for $14.1 million of long-term debt, equivalent to 9% of Thailand's GDP (World Bank, 1999, pp. 532-535). Nor was 1997 an atypical year. Throughout the 1990s, commercial bank loans accounted for more long-term debt than bonds did, although the bond market in Thailand saw significant growth during this period.

This pattern of bank-based financing is also evident in the balance sheets of individual corporations. Bata Shoe of Thailand, an exporter, recorded 638 million baht in bank loans and overdrafts in 1997, which constituted 80% of its liabilities (Bata Shoe, 1997, p. 24). Admittedly, many other corporations involved in international trade have taken greater advantage of capital markets. In 1996, loans from banks and other financial institutions amounted to 2.8 billion baht for the Precious Shipping Company, almost 42% of its total liabilities. Debentures and bonds, though, amounted to 3.6 billion baht, or almost 54% of its total liabilities (Precious Shipping, 1996, p. 23). Nonetheless, it is evident that Thai corporations generally rely on bank credit to a greater degree than in countries with stronger capital markets. This reliance on bank credit stems from the period after the recessions of the 1970s, when sources of foreign investment dried up and businesses had to look to banks for credit, as capital markets were only just developing (Suehiro, 1989, p. 265). It also reflects extent to which Thai corporations tried to emulate Japanese models rather than British or American models.

The Concentration of the Banking Sector

Thailand's banking sector has a fairly concentrated structure. In the 1990s Thailand had 13 domestic banks and 21 banks incorporated abroad. Thai law has long favored existing domestic banks (Warr and Nidhiprabha, 1996, p. 39; Warr, 1993, pp. 230 & 236). Since 1962, Thai law has restricted entry of any new banks into the banking business. Foreign banks are limited to wholesale banking activities and cannot open new branches. Foreign banks must also pay a withholding tax on dividends transferred abroad. And since they can only be incorporated as subsidiaries of foreign companies, they are not eligible for the lower corporate tax rate offered to domestic banks. Most foreign banking activity is restricted and conducted offshore, which explains why foreign banks accounted for only five percent of all bank assets in 1990 (Warr and Nidhiprabha, 1996, p. 39).

While financial activity was concentrated in the banking sector, much of the banking was concentrated in the hands of a few major bankers. Much of this concentration in the banking industry began in the 1960s, when the banking industry was one of the fastest growing sectors of the economy. Between 1962 and 1972, the total deposits in Thailand grew by an average annual growth rate of 20.6% (Suehiro, 1989, pp. 246-247). During this period, four wealthy, influential Chinese-immigrant families became the major shareholders of four of the top banks in Thailand: Bangkok Bank, Thai Farmers Bank, Bangkok Metropolitan Bank, and Bank of Ayudyha (Suehiro, 1989, pp. 251-260). Also during this period, most major banks saw their deposits grow faster than did those of smaller banks (Suehiro, 1989, pp. 246-247). One economist argued that with new banks barred from entry, the larger banks could improve market shares due to their advantages of size and efficiency (Supoj, 1976). Family participation in the ownership of banks later gave way to investment company ownership as families sought partnerships with investment companies and banks developed into diversified conglomerates (Suehiro, 1989, 249-250).

The four banks most successful in developing modern conglomerate operations became the market leaders by 1980: Bangkok Bank, Thai Farmers Bank, Krung Thai Bank, and Siam Commercial Bank (Warr, 1993, pp.233-235). The domination of these four banks has persisted during the 1980s and 1990s. By the late 1980s, the total assets of the top four banks accounted for 66% of the assets in the banking industry. Bangkok Bank alone accounted for almost 30% of the banking industry's assets. Top four banks also accounted for almost 68% of the total deposits and 66% of the credit banks extended. After the financial liberalization of the 1990s, large domestic banks continued to grow faster than medium-sized and small domestic banks (Leightner and Lovell, 1998).

Laws designed to reduce the concentration of ownership and activity in the banking sector have not worked (Warr, 1993, p. 237; Hewison, 1989, pp. 191-192). Back in the 1970s, the government tried to encourage the creation of new finance companies to provide more competition for the banks. This initiative failed because most of the banks ended up becoming major shareholders in many of the finance companies. The government also encouraged capital divestiture by making it illegal for a shareholder to own more than five per cent of a bank's shares, but the government did not apply this law to existing shareholders, only new investors. One observer argued that these laws were not honest attempts to reform the banking sector, but simply the state's attempt to modernize the smaller banks and make them operate more like the larger banks (Hewison, 1989, p. 191).

The Thai Bankers' Association (TBA) is the trade association for the banking industry, the forum through which the bankers organize for their interests. All domestic banks are members of the association. It has a small staff. Only in 1977 did the TBA have a permanent staff, and as late as 1987 it had only seven paid staff members (Anek, 1992, pp. 49-50). Its size belies its importance. Through the TBA, bankers collectively set standard rates for service charges and loans (Warr and Nidhiprabha, 1996, p. 40). These collective decisions influence the cost and allocation of credit in Thailand, in addition to the interest rate ceilings and the central bank lending rate. The TBA has traditionally been active in the formation of economic policy in Thailand. The government sent the original 1962 legislation, limiting role of foreign banks and restricting entry in the banking sector, to the TBA for advice before it was enacted (Anek, 1992, p. 50). According to the association, the TBA was represented on 81 government committees or subcommittees by 1990 (Anek, 1992, p. 50).

The banking sector has all of the ingredients of an effective lobbying group. Assets, deposits, and credit activity are concentrated in the hands of a few. Domestic law and bank operations organize the industry as a cartel. The TBA also serves as a forum for Thai banks to share information with one another about general economic conditions and monitor the activities of banks. Moreover, the TBA has numerous avenues for contact with the government. Given these advantages, what did the banks and the commercial firms in which they invested want concerning exchange-rate policy?

The preferences of commercial firms

Before examining the interests Thai banks had in exchange-rate policy, it pays to examine those interests in the context of what interests commercial firms had in exchange-rate policy. Empirical evidence for how domestic groups view their preferences in exchange-rate policy, however, is difficult to gather. When governments alter exchange-rate policy, government officials commonly talk about how they expect the policy change to affect aggregate variables in the economy, but not specific sectors. Business and financial firms rarely make public statements designed to address questions of exchange-rate policy specifically. To the extent that firms do comment on economic conditions or policy, they normally address the more familiar problems of inflation, employment, and competitiveness. Moreover, while exchange-rate movements are often reported in the financial sections of newspapers, journalists rarely report on popular reactions to exchange-rate movements. Only when an exchange-rate crisis erupts or the government announces a sudden shift in exchange-rate policy do journalists normally report the reactions of various business and financial firms. Thus most evidence only shows up after the fact. For Thailand, the major periods of transition were the devaluations of 1981 and 1984, and the Asian financial crisis of 1997.

Theory allows us to identify a number of factors that can condition what interests commercial firms have in the exchange rate. Exporting firms may be interested in a floating exchange rate if it improves competitiveness (the manufacturing hypothesis), but commercial firms of all sorts could prefer a peg if they are concerned with macroeconomic price stability (the trade hypothesis of OCA theory), the price of imported inputs, or the cost of servicing foreign liabilities (the financial intermediation hypothesis). Hence, it is difficult to formulate generalizations about what all commercial firms wanted. But evidence in how firms reacted to the devaluations of 1981, 1984, and 1997 indicate that the cost of imported inputs and servicing foreign liabilities appeared to grow in importance for many firms over time.

Commercial Firms after the Devaluations of the 1980s

The devaluations of 1981 and 1984 led to predictable reactions among commercial firms. Exporters expected to gain from more competitive prices abroad while importers bemoaned higher prices for their products. Producers of goods that compete with imports also expected to gain, since the prices of foreign competitors were increasing. Price inelasticities complicated the picture, since they determined how market demand reacts to price changes. Some critics of the devaluation argued that while the government claimed the devaluation would improve agricultural exports, manufacturers would benefit from devaluation more, since agricultural prices are relatively more inelastic in demand (Paisal, 1984, p. 113). All this is evidence for the manufacturing hypothesis. But with the 1981 devaluation, businesses were also worried about increases in the price of imported oil, already high due to previous oil shocks (Paisal, 1981, p. 49).

External debt complicated this situation further. Devaluation made it more difficult for holders of dollar-denominated debt to earn the money to repay the loans. In 1981, the private sector owed \$2 billion dollars in external debt, while the public sector owed \$4.5 billion (Paisal, 1981, p. 49). In 1984, the private sector owed approximately \$4.8 billion dollars, while the public sector owed \$7.2

billion. Thus, some companies found devaluation painful regardless of whether they produced tradable or non-tradable goods.

Along with low inflation, the effects of the devaluations help explain why few commercial firms had an interest in any form of rigidly fixed ERR. The Thai economy adjusted quickly after each devaluation. After the shock to import prices and oil prices following the devaluation in 1981, the economy grew 7.1% in 1983 and imports grew by 20.1%. After the devaluation in 1984, the economy grew over nine percent in 1987 and imports grew by 39.0% (Warr and Nidhiprabha, 1996, p. 43), while inflation remained at 6% or less from 1982 to 1997. Thus, a rigidly fixed exchange rate would have made little difference to the price level compared to the conditions Thais already had with a peg and a conservative central bank. A rigidly fixed exchange rate, however, would have made adjustment to current account imbalances more difficult as compared with a peg.

Commercial Firms and the Asian Financial Crisis

The growth of trade exposure from 1984 to 1997 complicated the interests of commercial firms. As was noted above, trade exposure grew considerably during the 1990s, from 49.2% in 1985 to 82.8% in 1996. According to Frieden and Stein (2001, p. 5), only levels of trade exposure over 100% tend to show a tendency to fix exchange rates, but the Thai economy was also now highly integrated into the world economy. Thailand had more reason to be concerned with export competitiveness, since as mentioned above by 1997 the percentage of GDP devoted to manufacturing was 28.75%, higher than most countries tested in the previous chapter.[4] But due to low inflation, the real exchange rate had only been appreciating by 0.33% to 4.11% per year since 1986,[5] making the peg a small threat to export competitiveness. Thus many manufacturers were caught in a dilemma. Depreciating or devalued exchange rates could on the one hand improve competitiveness, but on the other hand they could also increase the prices of imported inputs. Increased input costs would send ripple effects through the Thai economy as producers of non-tradables depended on workers in exporting firms for a consumer base and depended on imports of oil, steel and other basic products for inputs in production.

Such a double-edged sword became evident when the government dropped the pegged exchange rate in 1997 and the baht fell against the dollar by almost 15%. Most of the business reaction concerned the short-term effects of the depreciation in the baht rather than the long-term effects of the floating exchange rate. Rice exports were poised to pick up after a poor showing earlier in the year (*Bangkok Post*, "Floating," 4 July 1997, p. B3). But exporters whose production depended on imported materials, such as automobiles and textiles expected higher export volumes and higher input costs to offset one another (*Bangkok Post*, "Private," 3 July 1997, p. B12; "Automotive" and "Exporters," 4 July 1997, pp. B3 & B12). An importer of scientific and medical equipment, the Beck Thai Company, lost up to 100 million baht, since the price of its goods rose 15% (*Bangkok Post*, "Private," 3 July 1997, p. B12).

Prices of raw materials and other inputs shot up for the whole economy. Even by conservative estimates, the Thai energy sector was expected to pay $700 million dollars more for petroleum and natural gas in 1997 after the depreciation, since these commodities are priced in dollars (*Bangkok Post*, "Retail," 3 July 1997, p. B12). This was expected to lead to an increase in the domestic price of oil by up to 0.5 baht/liter. Other basic inputs, such as steel and ocean freight rates rose 15% (*Bangkok Post*, 5 July 1997, p. 1; *Bangkok Post*, "Private," 3 July 1997, p. B12). The government ordered a price freeze on seventy types of consumer items, but that lasted only for as long as the current inventories of those items did (Tasker, 1997, p. 88).

The other pressing question was what effect the floatation would have on external debt in Thailand. The depreciation of the baht made the debt more difficult to pay, and the floating exchange rate made it difficult to know how expensive the long-term debt would be. External debt, which was almost entirely denominated in dollars, amounted to $91.9 billion dollars in 1996 and $85.2 billion in 1997 (Bank of Thailand, 2001). $46.9 million of the debt in 1997 was long-term, but $38.3 billion was short-term debt, with a maturity of three years or less. If the value of the baht had remained at 15% below its original value during the peg, that would have added the baht equivalent of $240 million to the repayment of Thailand's debts (*Bangkok Post*, 3 July 1997, p. 2).

The crisis was so difficult because much of the Thai economy was leveraged. According to one analyst at Goldman Sachs, the ratio of total loans to GDP was 140% at the time of the crisis, while it was only 45% for Mexico at the time of its peso crisis in 1994 (Charoen, 8/97, p. 24). Major non-tradable businesses, such as telecoms and property, were heavily affected (*Bangkok Post*, "Private," 3 July 1997, p. B12). Siam Cement, Thailand's biggest industrial conglomerate, had $4 billion in dollar-denominated debt, none of it hedged. The company estimated that at an exchange rate of 29 baht to the dollar it would lose 7.5 billion baht in extra debt costs (Barnes, 1997, p. 26). Nevertheless, president of Siam Cement declared that his company could service its debt due to a strong positive cash flow. Many others were not so fortunate. A study at Paribas Asia Securities found that the depreciation in the value of the baht effectively wiped out most of the profits in Thai companies that year (Barnes, 1997, p. 26).

While large corporations hedged their overseas loans as a matter of policy, many small companies and exporters accepted currency risk to save 1-2% on their loan expenses (*Bangkok Post*, "Tax," 3 July 1997, p. B12). Jasmine International arranged a fourteen-year sale of bonds worth $180 million to American investors with the help of CS First Boston to finance a subsidiary, Jasmine Submarine Telecommunications. The company's banker at CS First Boston declared in an interview that fourteen years was probably the "longest currency hedge ever extended on behalf of a Thai company" (Charoen, October 1997, p. 21). Most Thai companies could not afford such an arrangement. Phatra Thanakit, a Bangkok stock brokerage firm, found that while nine out of ten corporations it surveyed had external debt (Charoen, August 1997, p. 24), only half of those surveyed had hedged their debt. By 1997, the government had not devalued in thirteen years and the risk of a change in the exchange rate seemed to be low. But as long as producers of goods and services took on unhedged debt, they had an interest in the government maintaining the pegged exchange rate.

The preferences of the banks

What interests did Thai banks have in exchange-rate policy? Many of the banks' customers were commercial firms hit hard by the depreciation and floating currency. Thai banks had mediated a lot of external debt by borrowing from banks in developed countries and loaning the funds to local companies. During the boom years of the 1990s, banks dispersed several loans, more and more of which turned out to be loans that would not be repaid. When the crisis came, it dumped more non-performing loans on Thai banks.

Domestic commercial banks and finance companies raised an increasing share of their funds from overseas sources up until the 1997 financial crisis (Paiboon et. al., 1995, p. 38). The establishment of Bangkok International Banking Facilities (BIBF's) in 1993 formalized offshore banking in Thailand. BIBF licenses allow financial institutions to finance businesses with foreign currency. All domestic banks and 33 foreign banks had BIBF licenses. After the government licensed domestic banks to borrow and lend in foreign currency through the BIBF's and lifted a number of capital controls, Thai banks had unique access to a large pool of foreign capital. By 1994, BIBF credits accounted for 457 billion baht or 13.4% of total domestic bank credit in Thailand, demonstrating that a significant portion of the foreign investment into Thailand was flowing through banks.

Thai interest rates were set a little higher than world interest rates. Thus domestic banks could exploit a 2-5% interest differential and the booming economy appealed to foreign investors who thought they found low-risk returns. Foreign capital thus financed a gap in Thailand between local demand for investment capital and the supply of domestic savings. Thai firms used the foreign loan capital for investment projects, hoping that returns on investment would be enough to repay the loans and still have profit left over to pour into the stock market. Thai financial institutions often provided short-term bridge loans to Thai businesses which the businesses were to repay when they were listed on the stock market (Nukul Commission, 1998, para. 22). Most Thais and foreign investors assumed the foreign loans were safe because the exchange rate had remained stable since the mid-1980s. Unfortunately, many lenders had relaxed loan requirements and the funds often ended up in unproductive real estate and business ventures.

In many cases, banks had mediated much of the funds that allowed external debt to pile up. Of the $85 billion that the private sector owed, non-bank debt amounted to $46 billion, or 54% of the debt (Bank of Thailand, 2001). Debt intermediated through BIBF sources amounted to $30 billion or roughly 35% of the debt. Banks owed $9 billion themselves, or almost 11% of the debt. Combining BIBF credit with bank debt, banks accounted for 46% of the private sector debt endangered by the Asian financial crisis. Thai banks, however, did not have adequate capital behind these international operations. Instead of strengthening banking regulations, the central bank permitted banks and finance companies to have capital adequacy ratios below the requirements of the Bank of International Settlements, the organization that crafts international banking regulations (Nukul Commission, 1998, para. 4).

Banks had also lent significant sums to sectors that were hurt in a variety of ways by the devaluation. Table 4.4 provides the breakdown of how banks distributed bills, loans, and overdrafts among different sectors of the economy at the end of June 1997. Banks extended the most credit, 1.4 trillion baht, to manufacturing businesses, accounting for 27.6% of the credit at that time. Wholesale and retail interests received the second largest share of credit, 18.6%. Thus a significant portion (46.2%) of bank credit went to sectors with sensitivity to the price of imported inputs. Personal consumption, which suffered from loss of purchasing power with a devaluation, received the third largest share of bank credit, 12.7%. Real estate, which was developing the properties of an asset price bubble, received the fourth largest share of bank credit, 8.3%. The export sector, for which a devaluation meant increased competitiveness, only accounted for 201 billion baht, or 3.9% of bank credit.

Once the government dropped the peg, banking officials initially praised the move as a long overdue corrective and a way to let the baht reflect economic fundamentals (*Bangkok Post*, "Private," 3 July 1997, p. B12). But in the aftermath of the switch to floating exchange rates, the government raised interest rates to make the baht more attractive on currency markets (*Bangkok Post*, "Pain," 3 July 1997, p. 1). This tightening of monetary policy contributed to a liquidity crunch. Meanwhile, non-performing loans (NPL's) piled up as companies found it harder to pay their dollar-denominated debt. One American investment bank estimated that the amount of NPL's in Thailand was equivalent to 20% of GDP at the end of 1996 and threatened to increase to 35%. During the Mexican peso crisis, by contrast, NPL's were equivalent to 18% of GDP (Charoen, August 1997, p. 24). Considering the strain the floating exchange rate put on the financial system, bankers undoubtedly had incentive for the peg to continue for as long as possible prior to the crisis, despite their pronouncements immediately after it.

Public statements from the chairperson of the Thai Bankers' Association and president of Siam Commercial Bank at the time, Olarn Chaipravat, confirm this view (*Bangkok Post*, 2 July 1997, p. 1). Just prior to the switch to a floating exchange rate, Olarn argued against a devaluation, arguing that it would not boost exports as much as conventional wisdom said it would. He also warned that it would raise production costs for many industries, raise interest rates, and increase the external debt burden. Olarn wanted the government to alter the weighting of currencies in the basket peg to allow the currency to appreciate up to two percent. This would allow the Bank of Thailand to lower interest rates and stimulate the economy, Olarn claimed. While Olarn was not necessarily speaking in his official capacity as TBA chairperson, the public statements were a clear call from a major banker opposing a fall in the baht's value or an abandonment of the peg.

Table 4.4 Bills, loans and overdrafts of commercial banks, classified by economic sector as of June 1997

Sector	Amounts	Percentage of total
Agriculture	157,713.7	3.1
Mining	33,633.0	0.7
Manufacturing	1,402402.0	27.6
Construction	249,463.4	4.9
Real Estate Business	421,867.1	8.3
Imports	152,724.7	3.0
Exports	201,048.5	3.9
Wholesale and Retail Trade	948,657.5	18.6
Public Utilities	149,295.1	2.9
Banking and other Financial Business	332,607.5	6.5
Services	396,336.6	7.8
Personal Consumption	644,117.4	12.7
Total	5,089,866.5	100.0

Amount figures in the second column in millions of baht.

Source: Bank of Thailand.

Government Policy

The last question is what effect, if any, did the preferences of banks and commercial firms have on exchange-rate policy, and if so, how did banks and commercial firms exert that influence? To put these questions in their context, consider again the hollowing-out thesis and the threat that capital mobility posed to the exchange-rate peg. As can be seen in Table 4.1, capital mobility in Thailand was quite high in the years leading up to the Asian financial crisis. Interest rates deviated from uncovered interest parity by 3% to 6% of the parity value in the decade before 1997. Contrast this with the Philippines, where interest rates deviated from uncovered interest parity by 4% to 9% before the Asian financial crisis.[6]

Other economists have reached similar conclusions about capital mobility in Thailand using other tests of interest parity. Warr and Nidhiprabha (1996, p. 175) estimated how much the variation in differential between Thai and U.S. interest rates affected the forward exchange-rate premium over time, correcting for first-order autocorrelation. This analysis tested how much Thai interest rates deviated from covered interest parity. The regression coefficient for the differential of interest rates is less than one, indicating that capital mobility is not perfect, but it is close at 0.88.[7] Evidence shows that capital has been mobile enough on world markets to keep Thai interest rates close to covered and uncovered interest parity.

The effects of strong capital mobility also made themselves evident in Thai financial markets. After the peso crisis in Mexico, Thai and other investors began to sell baht for dollars for fear of devaluation in Thailand (*Bangkok Post Economic Review*, 30 June 1995, p. 8; *Bangkok Post Economic Review*, 30 June 1995, p. 13). The 1994 peso crisis made investors around the world nervous about the possibility of devaluation and abandoned pegs in a number of developing-country markets. The Thai central bank raised the bank rate from 9.5% to 10.5%. It also injected funds through the loan and repurchase markets to improve liquidity. A baht-dollar window was also opened to satisfy the demand for exchanging currency, but purchases of dollars were subject to a charge. Though confidence returned and the peg remained, the episode demonstrated how vulnerable Thailand was to changes in short-term capital flows. Capital flows also increasingly presented the central bank with a dilemma. If the central bank lowered interest rates, it could ignite inflation. Raising interest rates in an environment of high capital mobility and an exchange-rate peg, however, would lead to capital inflows, which could also ignite inflation (*Bangkok Post Economic Review*, 30 June 1995, p. 13). Foreign investment also had the capacity to affect the stock market after the government liberalized capital market regulations. Foreign capital flowed into the stock market and foreigners accounted for thirty percent of the total trading volume by 1995 (*Bangkok Post Economic Review*, 30 June 1995, p. 9).

In 1994 and 1995, the IMF warned the Thai government that the basket peg was probably not compatible with financial openness and suggested that a more flexible exchange-rate system would help stabilize inflation and economic growth (Nukul Commission, 1998, para. 46). The Bank of Thailand ignored these warnings. While the central bank had examined the financial crises in Mexico and other states, the central bank leadership tended to think that the situations of other states were significantly different from Thailand's and that Thailand's current economic troubles were temporary (Nukul Commission, 1998, para. 60, 61 & 89).

Thailand's defenses against a crisis, however, only worsened. By 1996, the Bank of Thailand had only barely enough foreign exchange reserves to cover one year of foreign short-term loans (Nukul Commission, 1998, para. 41). Moreover, Moody's downgraded the ratings of Thailand's short-term foreign debt on September 3, 1996 (Nukul Commission, 1998, para. 132). More trouble from international financial markets came during the first half of 1997. Speculators attacked the baht in February and May of that year, calculating that Thailand's persistent current account deficit and weak export outlook made the baht a likely candidate for a devaluation.[8] The attack in mid-May came from financial centers all across the world: Singapore, Hong Kong, Tokyo, London, and New York. Speculators sold billions of baht short, making contracts to sell baht they did not have, in expectation of borrowing it later at cheaper exchange rates. The Bank of Thailand responded with a coordinated battle plan. The central bank bought up the baht on world markets, with the assistance of other monetary authorities in Southeast Asia, such as Hong Kong, Singapore, and Malaysia who also bought up baht. The Bank of Thailand also ordered domestic commercial banks not to lend baht on interbank markets. Speculators suddenly found that baht was scarce on the interbank market, which made it difficult for them to borrow the baht needed to satisfy their contracts. The scarcity of the baht on the interbank market raised its value in currency markets and the peg was temporarily defended. Many speculators lost money betting against the baht. Since Thailand's fundamental economic problems were unlikely to go away, however, the episode was evidence that the baht was vulnerable to another speculative attack.

Thus Thailand was exposed to a high degree of capital mobility but persisted in maintaining its peg in spite of the risk of speculative attack. If Thailand had been a rational, unitary state calculating how much of a threat capital mobility was to its exchange-rate management, it would have had good reason to abandon the peg for an alternative ERR, yet it did not. This is even more of an anomaly for the assumption of rational expectations in the capital mobility hypothesis when one considers that Thai officials were aware of other examples of exchange-rate crises, such as the case of Mexico. The Bank of Thailand began to investigate various designs for a floating exchange rate in the last half of 1996 (Nukul Commission, 1998, para. 48-50; *Bangkok Post Economic Review*, 2 July 1996, p. 35). A month before the 1997 crisis, an assistant governor of the Bank of Thailand also declared at the time that the Bank would allow for a more flexible exchange rate, but did not commit himself to a date (Sender, 1997(a), p. 52). If the Thai government was facing pressure on the peg, why did it wait until a crisis erupted to switch to a floating exchange rate?

Elections and Transparency

The persistence in pegging is not simply the result of elections, although elections explain some of the persistence in pegging once the pressures of capital mobility intensified. Much of Thailand's modern politics has been an oscillation between military juntas and democratic governments. From 1979 to 1988, Thailand had a hybrid system of military officials running parliamentary governments. After the retirement of General Prem in 1988, Thailand experimented with a more democratic government that elected the corrupt Chatchai administration. A military coup removed this administration in 1991, and civilian rioting pushed the military to allow elections again in 1992. An unstable party system led to the formation of a three short-lived governing coalitions: the Chuan administration (formed in 1992), the Banharn administration (1995) and Chavalit administration (1996). 1997 was not scheduled to have an election, and thus the government's insistence on maintaining the peg that year did not spring from the government's fear of what a pre-emptive devaluation or floatation could do to its immediate electoral chances. But given that a devaluation or floatation could cause any of these unstable coalitions to collapse, government officials were unwilling to alter the peg even while financial troubles accumulated during the 1990s (Haggard, 2000, pgs. 51-55; MacIntyre, 2003, pgs. 58-69).

The form of government seems to have less to do with the explanation. Broz (2002) argues that usually democratic governments only have the transparency necessary to make central banks credibly independent. But while Thailand alternated between dictatorship and democracy, an independent central bank has consistently managed to evolve. According to Alex Cukierman and Steven Webb, the best indicator of central bank independence in developing countries is the turnover in central bank governors (1992) or the degree to which central bank governors change after a change in government (1995). Thailand has done well on these measures, changing central bank governors almost every five or six years from 1971 until the crisis in 1997 regardless of turnover in the government and changes of regime. Sylvia Maxfield (1997, pp. 78-86) argues that during periods when Thailand needed the trust of global investors for external financing, the central bank could use the need to establish credibility for the monetary policy as a tool to make even military governments back down from demands on the central bank. Moreover, despite the relative independence of its central bank Thailand also maintained a pegged exchange rate during most of the 1980s and 1990s. Central bank independence and pegging were not treated as rival alternatives as Broz claims they are.

The Role of the Banks

Instead of government institutions, many observers in the business press blamed the pressure of domestic interests for prolonging Thailand's exchange-rate troubles. The day after the floating exchange rate was established, the *Bangkok Post* ran an editorial claiming that the decision took "courage" because "vested political and business interests" opposed any drop in the baht's value due to the country's heavy debt burden (*Bangkok Post*, "Bold Move," 3 July 1997, p. 1). Another writer at *Asian Business*, Brian Mertens, noted that when the Thai government accepted IMF conditions for financial discipline and reform in exchange for financial assistance, it provided the government with political cover against business interests. Though many "powerful domestic interests" requested that the government bailout failing companies in the wake of the crisis, with the IMF agreement the government was in a position to refuse them (Mertens, 1997, p. 22). The implication, of course, was that the government felt obliged to accommodate their requests prior to the crisis.

Internal central bank memoranda revealed that the leaders of the Bank of Thailand were indeed worried about private sector finances during the speculative attacks of 1996 and 1997. Central bank officials worried that financial firms were too fragile to accept any alteration in the exchange-rate regime would exacerbate private sector debt problems (Nukul Commission, 1998, para. 198 & 223). Officials at the central bank thought that Thailand's declining export performance at the time was temporary and also worried that an alteration of the exchange-rate regime would provoke the very financial panic they were trying to prevent. These concerns seem to have animated much of the central bank's foot-dragging over exchange-rate policy.

Moreover, the Thai government did have a record of crafting policy for the benefit of the banks and finance companies. When the government first began to consider financial deregulation, large banks were initially opposed to the possibility of new competition (Doner and Unger, 1993, pp. 119-120). Deregulation went ahead when it relaxed controls on banks' ability to manage portfolios, underwrite debt instruments, sell mutual funds and open branches, operations in which large banks had the advantage (Haggard, 2000, p. 34). The BIBF licensing agreements, described above, allowed domestic banks to engage in offshore banking while limiting foreign competition in banking in Thailand.

The Bank of Thailand also bailed out the ailing Bangkok Bank of Commerce (BBC) (*Bangkok Post Economic Review*, 2 July 1996, p. 33; Sender, 1997(b), p. 53), demonstrating how enforcement of regulations could serve individual banks more than the national economy. Even as early as 1991, a bank examination revealed that the BBC had non-performing loans equivalent to 26.73% of its total assets, while the industry average was 7.41% (Nukul Commission, 1998, para. 283). Rakesh Saxena, the BBC's de facto director, had appropriated bank funds for himself and extended loans to business and political friends with little collateral, running up $3 billion in bad debts in the end. The bank went broke in 1995. The governor of the Bank of Thailand, Vijit Supinit, bailed out the bank. After a run on the BBC began, the Bank of Thailand bought a 32% stake in the company with 16 billion baht. It took another infusion of central bank cash to encourage a private firm to buy the BBC. Vijit refrained from requiring the BBC to write down its capital losses, which would have punished the bank's old management before providing the bank with new capital (Nukul Commission, 1998, para. 296 & 313). After the scandal, Vijit resigned as governor for failing to exercise market discipline on the banking sector. As one reporter discussing bank reform put it "... the greatest problem in Thailand is not that certain banks are too big to fail, but that they're too *political* to fail (emphasis in original)" (Sender, 1997(a), p. 53). In late May 1997, the Finance Ministry and the Bank of Thailand tried to redeem some credibility by suspending sixteen financial companies that were failing (*Bangkok Post*, 1 July 1997, 1; Vatikiotis, 1997, p. 70). But by then the scandal had seriously damaged the government's reputation.

Governmental neglect in monitoring the financial sector also led to the eventual suspension of several finance companies. The finance companies were the first to develop noticeable problems with bad debt in 1996. The Financial Institutions Development Fund (FIDF) extended a total of fifty billion baht to fourteen finance companies that year (Nukul Commission, 1998, para. 343). A later Ministry of Finance report claimed that eighteen finance companies and three banks suffered from difficulties from bad debt (Nukul Commission, 1998, para. 368). The second largest party of the governing coalition, Chart Pattana, prevented the government from taking action to restructure many of the ailing financial institutions, as it had controlling interest in some of them (Haggard, 2000, p. 53). Given the ties some parties had with some financial institutions, bad debts were allowed to fester for some time. The bailouts and protection of several banks and finance companies created a moral hazard in which bad debts were allowed to accumulate, which in turn scared the government into thinking it could provoke a financial crisis if it was not careful. In the end, of course, conditions were unsustainable and the financial crisis erupted anyway.

Summary

Thailand maintained a pegged exchange rate for longer than other middle-income countries. Capital mobility was high for most of the 1990s, as foreign investment flowed into Thailand and the Bank of Thailand had to fend off more attacks on the pegged exchange rate. Yet Thai officials maintained the peg. Why? Thailand was a relatively small, open economy, and economic theory predicts that such countries are more likely to peg. The peg did contribute to low inflation and stable exchange-rate expectations. These conditions alone do not explain why the government fought to maintain the peg for as long as it did, however. Manufacturing firms were growing in Thailand, but were not facing a serious appreciation in the real exchange rate. Instead, many sectors of the economy had serious concerns about the price of imported inputs. This, combined with the repayment of foreign-denominated debt, gave some manufacturers an interest in maintaining a peg.

Additionally, all of the key ingredients were in place for the financial intermediation hypothesis to work. First, given the low inflation and strong growth of the Thai economy, commercial firms and other sectors of the economy had little reason to support a rigid fix. Second, due to their external debts and a growing problem with non-performing loans, banks had an interest in maintaining the peg.

The leader of the banker's association also provided evidence of this when he publicized his opposition to devaluation and floatation before the crisis erupted. Third, banks had power to influence economic policy as banks largely financed Thailand's economy and operated like a cartel. Central bankers worried that abandoning the peg would provoke a banking crisis. The government even relied on the banks for some assistance in implementing policy, as the banks' refusal to sell baht to international investors helped to defend the peg earlier that year. Political parties relied on some credit institutions for political support. These political parties, in turn, were critical in maintaining support for unstable government coalitions. Given these facts, it is reasonable to conclude that the government defended the peg for as long as it did in part to protect the banking sector from facing crisis. The pressure of the banks to avoid a banking crisis seems to be one of the critical political explanations for the government's frequent attempts to defend its peg in the first half of 1997.

Notes

[1] In the appendix, the statistical tests use a different coding system for ERRs, a different sample of states, and the data run from 1987 to 2000. Thailand has a "de facto" pre-announced peg for ten and a half years even under this alternative coding system, which means that it pegged for longer than seven other states in the sample, less than six other states, and as long as one other state.
[2] Based on author's calculations using IMF data drawn from *International Financial Statistics*, various years.
[3] These long-term debt figures include all publicly guaranteed debt and non-guaranteed debt.
[4] The data are drawn from the World Bank's *World Development Indicators*, various years.
[5] Based on author's calculations using IMF data drawn from *International Financial Statistics*, various years.
[6] The deviation of Thai interest rates from UIP is mostly below the mean of 5% for most of the countries used in the statistical tests in chapter 3.
[7] Warr and Nidhiprabha also test whether or not interest rates reflect real interest rate parity with a similar regression equation that estimates the effect of the forward exchange rate and the differential of inflation between Thailand and the U.S. on the differential of interest rates (Warr and Nidhiprabha, 1996, p. 177). The regression coefficient is 0.13, significantly different from one and much closer to zero. Real interest rate parity does not even hold under the assumption of perfect foresight in forecasting exchange rates (Warr and Nidhiprabha, 1996, p. 178). Real interest rate parity, however, only occurs under more stringent assumptions than covered or uncovered interest rate parity does.
[8] For accounts of this episode, see Charoen, July 1997, pp. 28-29; *Bangkok Post*, 16 May 1997, pp. B1 & B12; Nukul Commission, 1998, para. 168-185.

Chapter 5

Mexico

The case of Thailand demonstrated how a bank-credit system helped to prolong a pegged exchange rate. The case of Mexico, by contrast, appears to be a case that falsifies the financial-intermediation hypothesis, at least at first blush. In the early 1990s, Mexico privatized its banking system after almost a decade of government control. Financial intermediation through banking increased, and Mexico developed a banking system much more active than in most other developing countries in a short time. According to the IMF, Mexico also maintained a managed float until December 1994, after which it had an independent float. On the surface it looks as if Mexico's bank-credit financial system failed to yield the pegging predicted by the financial intermediation hypothesis. But on closer examination, Mexico's managed float involved more governmental management than floating. Mexico actually maintained a crawling band from 1991 to the peso crisis in 1994. A crawling band is a peg according to the definitions used in this book, while Mexico's crawling band was technically loose enough to satisfy the IMF's definition of managed floating. By 1994, however, the exchange rate exhibited little flexibility, and this chapter investigates the causes behind the rigidity of the exchange rate that contributed to the peso crisis later that year.

This chapter will argue that the way that a bank-credit financial system contributed to the peso crash of 1994 was roughly similar to the way that Thai banking contributed to the Thai financial crisis in 1997, despite many differences and mitigating factors. Privatization and liberalization of the banking sector in the early 1990s led to the growth of banking in Mexico. Growing bank-credit intermediation led to the re-establishment of financial-industrial groups (groupos) as well as strong links between banks and brokerages. Banking also had a concentrated, cartelized structure. Banks and large commercial firms had an interest in perpetuating the crawling-band regime, as it reduced the burden of external debt. The middle class and labor, in addition, also benefited from the increased purchasing power that resulted from the crawling-band policy. A combination of electoral pressures, pressure from domestic banks and commercial firms, and foreign investors pushed the government to maintain a pegged exchange rate for longer than was prudent, and an exchange-rate crisis was the result. Instead of falsifying the financial-intermediation hypothesis, the Mexican case actually demonstrates its validity in a Latin American context.

This chapter has a similar structure to the previous chapter. The second section analyzes the history of exchange-rate policy in Mexico since the end of the Bretton Woods regime. Exchange-rate policy in Mexico has a long history of state intervention in various forms, from simple pegs to dual exchange-rate systems to crawling bands. According to the IMF, Mexico engaged in managed floating during this period, but this chapter makes the case that the crawling-band policy qualifies as a form of a peg. The following sections analyze the applicability of the financial intermediation hypothesis to the Mexican case, especially when set against competing hypotheses. The third section analyses some of the economic conditions surrounding the crawling-band policy, such as the growth of Mexico's trade exposure and the growth of foreign investment in Mexico. The fourth, fifth, and sixth sections establish the elements of the financial intermediation hypothesis, arguing that the banking system was active and concentrated, had an interest in exchange rate stability, and had an influence on government policy. The fourth section describes how the privatization of banks under the Salinas administration deliberately promoted a concentrated and protected banking industry. The fifth section analyzes the preferences different interest groups had in exchange-rate policy. As in Thailand, both banks and major industrial firms were amassing dollar-denominated debt in the early 1990s, giving them an interest in keeping the peso fixed at its overvalued rate. The middle and working classes also had reason to favor the crawling band, because the strong peso made imports cheaper and increased purchasing power. The last section analyzes the government's motives and actions. Numerous conditions and factors have been cited as contributing to the peso crisis. A complex web of conditions thus explains the government's decisions. The crawling band probably contributed to persistent current account deficits. The government was loath to devalue because of pressures from the electorate, banks, large commercial firms, and foreign investors. Raising interest rates would have shaken a fragile banking system. In the end, the government hoped to maintain the confidence of foreign investors to finance the deficit. When this was no longer feasible, a sudden devaluation contributed to a financial panic, and the government was finally forced to float the exchange rate.

Exchange rate policy in Mexico

Between 1971 and 1991, Mexico had an unfortunately predictable pattern in its exchange rate crises.[1] The government would pursue deficit spending and loose monetary policies and borrow from abroad to cover the spending. This would stimulate imports and worsen the current account. As foreign and domestic agents worried about the Mexican ability to repay its debts, the borrowing would become unsustainable. A crisis would result, forcing Mexico to devalue. After the crisis, the government would pursue expansionary policies again, often to help the economy recover from its troubles.

During this time, the government would alter exchange rate policies to help manage various balance of payments crises. Mexico initially tried to maintain its adjustable peg with the U.S. dollar after the U.S. goes off the gold standard in 1971. After a balance of payments crisis in 1976, the peso lost 40% of its value (Lustig, 1998, p.19) and the new government encouraged a managed float. With the infamous debt-crisis of 1982, the government nationalized the banks, forbade dollar-denominated bank accounts, resorted to tight exchange controls to prevent capital flight, and established a dual exchange rate system (see IMF, *EAER*, 1983). In this system, the government established a controlled exchange rate for transactions of exports and imports and non-factor payments and another free, open-market exchange rate applied to all other transactions (IMF, *EAER*, various years). The government, however, also established the rate of depreciation in the free foreign exchange market (Lustig, 1998, p.234). Mexico maintained its dual exchange-rate system from 1982 to 1991 (IMF, various years). In practice, the government kept the free and controlled exchange rates close to each other and let both exchange rates depreciate quickly in order to boost exports, which would in turn generate foreign exchange for Mexico (Kessler, 1999, p.64). As inflation grew during the 1980s, the government did not have the foreign exchange reserves to defend a tight peg. Thus the government lets the exchange rate go into a "free fall" until 1988 (Reinhart and Rogoff, 2003b). The depreciation of the currency from 1982 to 1988 exacerbated the country's inflation, but it also allowed Mexico to build up foreign exchange reserves that it could use to pay off debt and defend later exchange rate targets.

The government's attention would later turn to inflation as the balance of payments improved. In December 1987, the government began sincere efforts to reduce inflation by negotiating an Economic Solidarity Pact (pacto) with business and labor leaders. The pacto mandated tight macroeconomic policies, wage freezes, and structural reforms including trade liberalization and privatization (Lustig, 1998, p.51; Gould, 1996, p.25). In tightening macroeconomic policies, the government abandoned the highly managed float and established a de facto crawling peg in the controlled exchange rate market (Reinhart and Rogoff, 2003b). The government mandated a preannounced, fixed rate of devaluation in the peso that was to be less than the rate of inflation (IMF, *EAER*, various years). In real terms, the exchange rate began to appreciate.

The Salinas administration, which lasted from 1988 to 1994, maintained a de facto peg for its entire term. On November 11, 1991, the dual exchange-rate system was abolished and replaced with a unified system (IMF, *EAER*, 1992, p. 319). With the new unified system the government widened the band within which the exchange rate could float from 35 pesos to 60 pesos. The buying and selling rates for the government, which constitute the upper and lower limits of the band, would depreciate at a slower rate of 2.4% per year, where they had depreciated at a rate of 5% before (IMF, *EAER*, 1992, p.319).[2] This rate of depreciation was slower than the rate of inflation, and thus the real exchange rate appreciated. The details will be explored in more depth below, but the appreciation of the peso encouraged persistent current-account deficits financed though foreign private investment. When foreign investors began to panic, the current-account deficit became unsustainable, and the government had to let the value of the peso fall. The exchange-rate crisis hit in December 1994, a few weeks after Salinas left office and after Ernesto Zedillo began his term. Since the crisis of 1994, Mexico has had a managed float for its exchange rate.

The case of Mexico is an example of how coding methods for ERRs can sometimes be misleading. Accurate descriptions of ERRs are crucial for the analysis of the case studies. Mexico, as will be argued below, has had a strong system of bank-credit financing for a developing country. According to the financial-intermediation hypothesis, Mexico should have pegged for most of this period. But according to the IMF's original classification system, found in various issues of *International Financial Statistics*, Mexico had a managed float from 1982 to 1994 and must be an anomaly. Since this is the classification used in the statistical tests in chapter 3, Mexico is coded as a state with no history of pegging in recent times and so it is left out of the statistical sample.[3] Since significant amounts of foreign exchange were traded on the outside the controlled market from 1982 to 1991 or within a changing band from 1991 to 1994, these exchange rate systems are presumably managed floats.

If one examines how the ERR worked in practice, however, the anomaly mostly disappears. Many economists have described the crawling band as a nominal exchange-rate anchor in an inflation-reduction program (See Lustig, 1998, p.155; Dornbusch and Werner, 1994; Sachs, et. al, 1996; and Pastor, 1998, pp.123-124). During much of 1994, the exchange rate did not float within the band but remained at the ceiling of the band (Banco de Mexico, 1995, p.38). According to the definition of pegging in this book, a pegged exchange rate includes any exchange-rate regime with a commitment that the government can revoke at its discretion. The crawling band for a unified exchange rate from 1991 to 1994 committed the government to maintaining a range in which the exchange rate could float, a commitment that was contingent on the government's stock of foreign-exchange reserves. Hence, Mexico maintained a form of pegging while capital mobility grew.

Economic conditions in Mexico

Economic Size and Trade Exposure

According to the GDP hypothesis, a large economy is more likely to float its exchange rate and a small economy is more likely to fix. As of 1999, Mexico had a nominal GDP of 4.6 trillion pesos, equivalent to $484 billion at current exchange rates (IMF, *IFS*, various years). According to PPP exchange rates, Mexico ranked as the twelfth largest economy in the world that year (World Bank, *WDI*, 2001). By these standards, Mexico's economy is large enough to float, and the crawling pegs and bands employed during the Salinas administration are an anomaly for the GDP hypothesis. But perhaps this characterization is unfair, since the GDP hypothesis essentially argues that developed states float and developing states fix. Given that Mexico is a developing country so geographically close to the U.S., one might expect Mexico to peg. But this argument does not explain why Mexico had a managed float (or free fall) from 1982 to 1988, nor the facts of why the government fought to maintain its crawling band in 1994 (discussed below).

Moreover, Mexico has historically had less trade exposure with its neighbors than one might think. Mexico employed an import-substitution strategy until the mid-1980s. Trade liberalization later proceeded gradually (Loser and Kalter, 1992, pp.28-30; Pastor and Wise, 1994, pp.460-461; see also Lustig, 1998, pp.117-120). Beginning in 1983, the tariff structure was simplified and the government removed import permits for certain industries. The government phased out official import prices. After negotiations with the U.S., the Mexican government agreed to reduce export subsidies. The government shifted protection from quantitative restrictions to tariffs and then progressively lowered tariffs. Mexico lowered many tariffs in order to become a member of GATT in 1986. The government cut tariffs further as part of the Economic Solidarity Pact of 1987 and also removed all remaining official import prices. In 1994, NAFTA created a free trade and investment zone encompassing Canada, the U. S., and Mexico. In a single decade, Mexico went from being one of the world's most closed economies to one of the most open of all developing economies.

Figures for trade exposure demonstrate that trade liberalization has had an effect (see Table 5.1). The total of exports and imports as a share of GDP rose from 25.9% in 1985, when Mexico had only just begun its trade liberalization, to 62.8% in 1999, five years after NAFTA took effect. According to the trade hypothesis, the higher the level of trade exposure the more likely a country will peg or use a rigid fix. In this case, OCA theory does not predict the behavior of Mexico very well, even though it predicts the ERRs of many states in a number of statistical tests. From 1985 to 1988, trade exposure hovered between the relatively low levels of 25% and 39%, but Mexico had a dual exchange-rate regime that was effectively a managed float. From 1988 to 1994, while Mexico pursues exchange rate stabilization with crawling pegs and bands, trade exposure remained between 35 and 39%, which was more consistent with the theory. In the years while Mexico floats after the peso crisis, however, trade exposure was at its highest at levels near 60% most of the time. Thus while OCA theory is often a good place to start to explain ERRs, Mexico's policy was the result of variables other than GDP and trade exposure.

Foreign Investment and Capital Mobility

Inflows and outflows of foreign investment seem to matter more to exchange-rate policy in Mexico. During the first part of Mexico's post-Bretton Woods history, from 1973 to 1989, laws on foreign investment were quite restrictive (see Loser and Kalter, 1992, pp.27-28; Lustig, 1998, pp.125-29). In 1973, the Law to Promote Mexican Investment and Regulate Foreign Investment mandated that several key industries, such as oil, raw materials, electricity and transportation were to remain the exclusive domain of the Mexican government and Mexican nationals. Foreigners could own partial shares in all other industries. Different industries were allowed different ceilings for foreign ownership, the maximum percentage for any industry being 49%. Hence, Mexicans legally had controlling interest in all industries. In practice, foreigners could circumvent the restrictions

Table 5.1 Economic data on Mexico

Year	Real GDP (billions of pesos)	Real GDP Growth (%)	Inflation (CPI) (%)	Ex. Rate (peso/ US $)	Trade Exposure (%)
1985	1044	2.53	57.75	0.26	25.89
1986	1011	-3.16	86.23	0.61	30.93
1987	1029	1.78	131.83	1.38	32.91
1988	1042	1.26	114.16	2.27	38.47
1989	1086	4.22	20.01	2.46	38.06
1990	1141	5.06	26.65	2.81	38.31
1991	1189	4.21	22.66	3.02	35.64
1992	1232	3.62	15.51	3.09	35.51
1993	1256	1.95	9.75	3.12	34.42
1994	1312	4.46	6.97	3.38	38.39
1995	1231	-6.17	35.00	6.42	58.07
1996	1294	5.12	34.38	7.60	62.69
1997	1381	6.72	20.61	7.92	60.47
1998	1448	4.85	15.92	9.14	41.25
1999	1501	3.66	16.60	9.56	62.80

Peso values measured in the new pesos Mexico introduced in 1993.

Sources: International Monetary Fund and World Bank.

by holding assets in a trust with a Mexican bank as the trustee, or using Mexicans as fronts for de facto foreign ownership (Lustig, 1998, pp.127-128). Nevertheless, the government nationalized many key industries and did what it could to discourage foreign investors.

In 1985, the government began to open the country to some limited foreign direct investment by allowing foreign firms to build maquiladora (in-bond industries) of which foreigners could own 100%. This led to the proliferation of American-owned factories along the Mexican-American border. In 1989, the government significantly amended the foreign investment law. The government further streamlined the investment process, opening up 73% of Mexican industry to 100% foreign ownership and removing barriers to foreign participation in the stock market laws (Loser and Kalter, 1992, p.30). Foreigners were now allowed to own up to 30% of Mexican stock brokerages, financial groups, and banks (Lustig, 1998, p.129).

Statistics demonstrate that foreign investment has significantly increased since these changes. As shown in Table 5.2, the indicator for capital mobility has increased during the 1990s. The capital mobility indicator, as was described in Chapter 3, measures the percentage deviation of interest rates from their estimated uncovered interest parity level for a five-year period. In the period from 1985 to 1989 (signified by the figure for 1989), the period immediately before the reform of foreign investment, interest rates averaged a 41.4% deviation from uncovered interest parity. In the period from 1990 to 1994 (signified by the figure for 1994), after the reform of foreign investment law and before the peso crash, the average deviation fell to a low of 14.8%. Deregulation of interest rates allowed more flexibility in interest rates and more openness to international financial markets meant more arbitrage among interest rates. Capital mobility in Mexico does not appear to be as strong as it was in Thailand during this period, which had capital mobility figures under 6%. Nevertheless, Mexico became more exposed to international capital flows in the early 1990s than in its previous history. According to the hollowing-out thesis, this growing exposure to international financial markets put Mexico's crawling band at greater risk of exchange-rate crisis. Given that foreign private investment financed persistent current-account deficits during the 1990s, it is no surprise that a loss of confidence ultimately erupted and an exchange-rate crisis resulted. The question is why the government did not try to prevent the crisis earlier, which it might have done by floating the exchange rate or establishing a more rigid fix.

Figures comparing levels of foreign investment with total Mexican investment also demonstrate that the change in the law encouraged the growth of foreign investment. In Table 5.3, figures for foreign investment come from the capital account and figures for gross fixed investment and total investment come from Mexico's national accounts. From 1988 to 1990, foreign investment accounts for less that 10% of gross fixed investment or total investment. From 1991 to 1994, however, foreign investment jumped to a minimum of 20% of investment in

Table 5.2 More economic data on Mexico

Year	Money Multi-plier	Credit Ratio	Capital Mobility	Total External debt/ GDP (%)	Total External debt/ Exports (%)
1985	2.076	0.810	n.a.	n.a.	n.a.
1986	2.455	0.895	n.a.	n.a.	n.a.
1987	3.473	1.264	0.365	n.a.	n.a.
1988	1.904	1.631	0.408	n.a.	n.a.
1989	3.710	2.977	0.414	n.a.	n.a.
1990	5.115	3.617	0.413	41.1	191.4
1991	5.965	4.480	0.365	37.3	198.4
1992	6.431	6.270	0.266	31.7	183.0
1993	6.856	7.302	0.175	33.6	195.1
1994	6.623	8.092	0.148	34.4	179.4
1995	3.057	2.653	0.168	61.1	172.5
1996	2.199	1.295	0.190	50.0	137.1
1997	6.135	4.077	n.a.	38.4	114.2

Sources: International Monetary Fund and World Bank.

Table 5.3 Foreign investment as a share of investment in Mexico

	Foreign investment as a share of gross fixed investment (%)	Foreign investment as a share of total investment (%)
1988	5.43	4.68
1989	5.05	4.54
1990	8.68	7.91
1991	24.49	22.52
1992	29.02	26.10
1993	44.50	39.34
1994	25.58	22.22
1995	-0.67	-0.64
1996	82.26	72.03
1997	55.98	47.46
1998	36.14	30.90
1999	74.15	66.05

Source: Calculations based on Banco de Mexico data. See http://www.banxico.org.mx.

Mexico. In 1993 it reached a height of 44.5% of gross fixed investment and almost 40% of total investment. Since foreign investment had become a motor for growth in the early 1990s, Mexico had an incentive against devaluing or floating the peso in order to keep the confidence of foreign investors. Foreign private debt and the promise of further foreign investment also gave domestic banks and major commercial firms in Mexico a preference for maintaining the crawling band, detailed below. After the peso crash, however, foreign investors pulled their money out of Mexico. Investment capital leaving Mexico outweighed the investment capital entering it, making the net outflow equivalent to 0.64% of total investment. But foreign investment returned to Mexico after 1995, often at dollar levels similar to those before the peso crash. Because the peso had depreciated, foreign investment accounted for a greater share of total investment.

Tables 5.4 and 5.5 provide data on the form that foreign investment has taken in Mexico, by measuring different forms of foreign investment as a share of capital-account liabilities and as a share of GDP, paralleling Table 4.2 in the previous chapter. Some notable patterns stand out. In the aftermath of the 1982 debt crisis, foreign direct investment and foreign loans flowed into Mexico, while portfolio investment flowed out. During most of the period where Mexico used a crawling band, from 1991 to 1993, the situation was reversed, and foreign portfolio investment became the predominant form of foreign investment. As in the Thai case, a lot of short-term capital powered the foreign investment boom. After the peso crash, direct investment was the most consistently dominant form of foreign investment, while portfolio investment remained strong.

The financial system

Was a system of bank-credit financial intermediation responsible for the governments' defense of a crawling band in the early 1990s? To answer that question and put it in its context, it helps to examine the nature of the Mexican financial system, the preferences different interest groups had for the exchange rate, and the role of different political conditions. The Mexican financial system, I will argue, is mostly based on bank credit, but it differs from the Thai financial system in three ways. First, banks went through a period of nationalization. Second, equity and securities markets are relatively more prominent. Third, a combination of development and commercial banks dominate the Mexican banking sector. Some scholars argue that capital markets are the basis of contemporary Mexican finance (Minushkin, 2002). Nevertheless, banks and bank-credit financing definitely grew, and grew considerably, in the early 1990s. The banking sector has been concentrated in a few firms shielded from foreign competition, making it easy to organize when bankers need to articulate their interests. Mexican banks also have strong links to industry. This section begins with a brief history of

Table 5.4 Forms of foreign investment as a share of the capital account

Year	Foreign direct investment as a share of the capital account (%)	Foreign portfolio investment as a share of the capital account (%)	Net foreign loans as a share of the capital account (%)
1980	16.56	0.46	82.98
1981	9.97	3.23	86.80
1982	17.56	5.97	76.46
1983	54.45	-12.89	58.44
1984	48.03	-13.57	65.53
1985	187.11	-56.20	-30.91
1986	94.18	-20.34	26.16
1987	73.00	-27.82	54.82
1988	487.29	169.16	-556.46
1989	73.07	8.08	18.85
1990	15.49	19.83	64.68
1991	18.67	50.00	31.33
1992	21.05	86.46	-7.51
1993	12.16	80.14	7.69
1994	54.17	40.40	5.43
1995	41.85	-42.68	100.83
1996	88.23	128.89	-117.13
1997	141.81	55.68	-97.49
1998	67.37	-3.36	35.99
1999	64.96	59.79	-24.75
2000	131.51	28.20	-59.71

Source: Calculations based on Banco de Mexico data. See http://www.banxico.org.mx.

Table 5.5 Forms of foreign investment as a share of GDP

Year	Foreign direct investment as a share of GDP (%)	Foreign portfolio investment as a share of GDP (%)	Net foreign loans as a share of GDP (%)
1988	1.57	0.55	-1.80
1989	1.42	0.16	0.37
1990	1.00	1.28	4.18
1991	1.51	4.06	2.54
1992	1.21	4.96	-0.43
1993	1.09	7.17	0.69
1994	2.61	1.94	0.26
1995	3.33	-3.39	8.02
1996	2.76	4.04	-3.67
1997	3.20	1.26	-2.20
1998	2.76	-0.14	1.47
1999	2.48	2.29	-0.95

Source: Calculations based on Banco de Mexico data. See http://www.banxico.org.mx.

the Mexican financial system. This history puts into context an examination of intermediation sources, concentration in the banking sector, and links between banks and industry.

The Development of the Mexican Financial System

Up until the nationalization of the banking system in 1982, banks have dominated the Mexican financial system (see Rodriguez, 1988; Minushkin, 2002 pp.917-918; Maxfield, 1991, pp.435-436; Kessler, 1999). Many banks had close ties to major industrial firms, forming financial-industry conglomerates called "groupos." In some cases, banks had crossholdings of shares with industrial firms, while in others the banks were legally and administratively integrated with industrial firms. The stock market was little more than a private club of small businesspeople. Given that a few wealthy families often owned controlling shares in large Mexican corporations, and that government regulations prevented many stock brokages from incorporating as independent, limit-liability firms, brokers traded relatively few shares in this period. Banks thus provided most of the financing. The government actively promoted the banking system and controlled many key banking functions with directed credit and several regulations on banking activity. With a robust banking sector, the government could finance public debt and direct credit to favored domestic industries in its import-substitution programs.

Bankers, however, could exercise some leverage over the government by threatening to withhold funds. During the administrations of Luis Echeverria (1970-1976) and Jose Lopez Portillo (1976-1982), the government reformed the laws on securities markets to allow brokerages more independence from banks in trading stocks and to allow the growth of a Mexican bond market. Peso-denominated bonds, "cetes," allowed the government a new channel of financing public debt. Meanwhile, inflation spiraled upward and current account deficits grew during the Lopez Portillo administration. During most of this administration investors felt confident about the Mexican economy because Mexico had become an oil exporter just at the time when oil prices had skyrocketed. But when oil prices tumbled in 1982 and worldwide recession hurt Mexico's oil export opportunities, many investors lost confidence in the economy, causing significant capital flight. The government experienced its now infamous debt crisis, and Lopez Portillo blamed the bankers for draining the country of funds in its time of need (Lopez Portillo, 1988). In retaliation, Lopez Portillo ordered the nationalization of the banks in 1982 (Gruben and Welch, 1996, p.64; Kessler, 1999, pp.33-35). With the banks firmly under government ownership and regulation, people saved less of their capital and banks and the newly liberated capital markets saw growth in investment.

With the Salinas administration (1988-1994), Mexico turned toward an export-led neo-liberal development strategy. The new neo-liberal strategy of the government was partly an attempt by the ruling party, the PRI, to respond to the growing popular appeal of the National Action Party (PAN), a conservative, pro-business opposition party (Kessler, 1999, pp. 84-85). After the 1988 election, the

PRI also needed the support of the PAN to get the 2/3 majority in the legislature needed to amend the constitution, which was necessary for economic reform (Starr, 1999a). As part of this new strategy, the government deregulated the banks beginning in 1988 and sold off eighteen banks from 1991 to 1992. Two other commercial banks had never been nationalized, so the total number of private commercial banks in Mexico rose to twenty (Gruben and Welch, 1996, p.66). Many of firms that bought the banks were domestic brokerage firms (now flush with capital) or domestic industries (Garrido, 1994, p.171). The banking industry grew as a channel of finance once again. New groupos were established, this time with new elites in charge drawn from brokerage and industrial firms. A banking crisis in 1995 precipitated by the peso crisis in 1994 crippled the newly privatized banking sector for a time, and Mexican banks spent years afterward recovering from the crisis.

Bank Credit vs. Capital Markets

Given all of the developments in the Mexican financial system, did Mexico end up with a financial system based on bank credit or capital markets after the privatization of the banks? Direct comparisons of bank credit and capital markets are difficult to make, since such comparisons are like comparing apples to oranges. Direct comparisons of aggregate figures in banking and capital markets can be misleading. One can, however, find a few clues by looking at changes in the composition of M4 (the broadest measure of the money supply) over time in Table 5.6. Banking instruments here include savings deposits (M2 minus M1) and longer-term deposits, while non-bank financial instruments include bonds, commercial paper, and promissory notes. The growth of capital markets during the 1980s is reflected in the observation that at the end of 1977 and 1978, non-bank financial instruments were less than one percent, while by the end of 1988 they have grown to 27.66% of M4. Meanwhile after the banks are nationalized, bank instruments as a share of M4 decline from 64.29% at the end of 1982 to 46.42% at the end of 1991, the last year of public ownership. Mexico makes a clear shift to more reliance on capital markets in the 1980s. After the privatization of the banks in 1991, the relative shares of M4 do not change much, but since the government liberalized both banks and capital markets by this time, the numbers may not have changed since investors had new investment opportunities in both bank-credit and capital markets. After the banking crisis in 1995, Mexicans seem to have saved less in banks and invested more in capital markets.

So are capital markets the basis of Mexican finance now? Susan Minushkin (2002) argues that Mexico's brokers dominate the financial system, not the bankers. When one looks at patterns of ownership, this is true, as the old elite of bankers lost their dominant position with nationalization and a new elite of brokers ended up purchasing many of the banks after privatization. But when looking at the assets of financial firms and measures of how financial capital flows through the financial system, it is accurate to say that Mexico has a mixed financial

Table 5.6 Financial instruments as a share of M4

Year	Banking instruments as a share of M4	Non-bank financial instruments as a share of M4
1977	59.46	0.34
1978	60.19	0.68
1979	59.51	2.60
1980	61.09	3.73
1981	64.38	4.02
1982	64.29	8.01
1983	64.76	9.27
1984	65.29	9.77
1985	62.36	10.48
1986	61.50	13.62
1987	58.46	18.68
1988	50.37	27.66
1989	49.09	31.61
1990	48.58	31.54
1991	46.42	24.03
1992	49.07	22.52
1993	46.08	25.85
1994	50.75	24.13
1995	61.18	14.53
1996	58.93	14.32
1997	52.26	19.13
1998	51.34	18.78
1999	45.44	21.84
2000	35.87	28.78

All figures in percentages. Figures represent shares of M4 at the end of a given year.

Source: Calculations based on Banco de Mexico data. See http://www.banxico.org.mx

system with both capital markets and banks that are relatively strong for a developing country.

Banking regained a significant presence in Mexican finance after privatization. At the end of 2000, commercial banks held 27.4% of the total assets of all Mexican financial intermediaries, and development banks held 41.2% of assets (Banco de Mexico, 2001). Development banks are publicly owned banks that focus on providing lending to enterprises that the government has targeted for development. But combined, the commercial banks and development banks accounted for 68.6% of the total assets among financial intermediaries at the end of 2000. The other intermediaries included (in order of asset holdings) investment firms, the Economic Promotion Fund, insurance companies, brokerage firms, and savings and loan associations. But the investment firms, the Economic Promotion Fund, and the insurance companies each accounted for only 7-12% of the assets among financial intermediaries.

Mexico also has relatively strong capital markets for a developing country. As of the end of 1998, the market capitalization of the Mexican Stock Exchange was $91.7 billion, equivalent to 23.3% of GDP. $33.8 billion of shares were traded that year (IFC, 1999, p.257). Mexico's stock market ranks 25th in the world according to market capitalization, and 28th in the world according to the value of shares traded (IFC, 1999, p.24). Of all the Latin American countries, only Brazil, with a market capitalization ranked 18th in the world, had a larger stock market.

Securitized debt also rivals bank credit as a form of financing. By 1990, the broadest measure of total public debt was equivalent to 50.4% of GDP (Banco de Mexico, 1991, p.124). Securities have become the favored instrument for foreign investment. By 1990, securities in the hands of foreign private investors accounted for $40.1 billion of long-term public debt, while foreign commercial bank loans accounted for $6.6 billion of long-term public debt (World Bank, 1998, p.377). Securities overtook bank loans as the predominant debt instrument for private investment in the early 1990s. By 1993, the stock of private non-guaranteed debt in the form of securities was $9 billion, more than the $6 billion foreign commercial banks held (World Bank, 1998, p.377). After the peso crisis in 1994, the securities market fell abruptly, and foreign bank loans took a commanding lead in debt issues again in the wake of domestic bank restructuring. But the largest stock of private non-guaranteed debt would remain in securities.

Nevertheless, it is fair to argue that with deregulation and privatization, Mexico went from being a state with little bank-credit intermediation to relatively high levels of bank-credit intermediation for a developing country. Hence the banking sector increased its role in the economy, became linked with non-bank firms, and its preferences for exchange rate policy had more weight with policy-makers. Prior to the neo-liberal reforms, government regulation discouraged a lot of banking activity. Even before nationalization, the government put ceilings on interest rates and heavy reserve requirements on banks (see Kessler, 1999, pp.36-38; Morris, et. al., 1990: pp.37-48). The combination of inflation and interest rate ceilings led to negative real deposit rates during the 1980s, discouraging saving activity (Morris, et. al., 1990, p.38). Since domestic savings were low and government borrowing (whether through bank loans or securities) was high, private borrowing was crowded out. In 1986, 60% of net bank credit went to the government (Gruben and Welch, 1996, p.65). The government, in effect, used a captive banking system to finance its spending and kept interest rates low to lower government costs.

The figures for financial intermediation in Table 5.2 bear this out. The money multiplier measures the ratio at which the monetary base of a country expands to become a broader money supply through bank credit intermediation. Between 1985 to 1989, the money multiplier hovers between 1.9 and 3.7, compared to 7.2 to 7.9 in Thailand from 1987 to 1989. During the same 1985-1989 period, the credit ratio, which measures the ratio bank claims on the private sector over the monetary base, climbs from 0.8 to almost 3.0, whereas it grows in Thailand from 5.5 in 1987 to 6.8 in 1989. Mexican figures are also below the averages of 5.55 for the money multiplier and 4.45 for the credit ratio in sample of countries in Chapter 3. In 1989, bank lending as percentage of GDP was 20%, lower than what it would be than at any time during the 1990s (Mohar, et. al., 1998, see Table 5.7).

Privatization and deregulation in the early 1990s led to an expansion of banking activity and private lending. The government removed controls on interest rates for deposits and lending. It dropped reserve requirements to 30%, an amount judged necessary to maintain liquidity. The government also abolished its selective credit mechanisms, which directed credit to private firms in order to serve to political objectives (Gruben and Welch, 1996, p.65; Lustig, 1998, p.108). With the banks deregulated, the government could put the banks up for sale. Brokerages and large industrial firms bought the banks at high prices, generating over $12 billion for the government in a period of thirteen months. The average ratio of price-to-book-value for the banks was 3.5, strikingly high considering that banks in the U.S. and Europe typically sell for around 2.2 times their book value (Kessler, 1999, p.93; Minushkin, 2002, p.936).

With deregulation, privatization, and lower reserve requirements, intermediation through the banking system noticeably increased. As shown in Table 5.2, the money multiplier rose from 3.7 in 1989, the year deregulation began, to almost 6.9 in 1993. The credit ratio rose from 3.0 in 1989 to a height of 8.1 in 1994. According to Banco de Mexico data, bank lending grew to 43.3% in 1994 (Mohar, et. al, 1998, p.93). In the early 1990s, therefore, the intermediation of finances through Mexican banks came close to rivaling the degree of financial intermediation in Thai banks.

Concentration and Competition in the Banking Sector

The privatized banking sector in Mexico had a concentrated structure in the early 1990s. Prior to privatization, Mexico had 64 nationalized banks. The government consolidated them into eighteen larger banks for sale. Two banks had never been nationalized. Of the resulting twenty domestic commercial banks in operation,

Table 5.7 Bank lending as a share of GDP, by sector

Sector	1988	1989	1990	1991	1992
Agriculture and Husbandry	3.5	3.6	3.4	3.2	3.4
Industry	7.1	7.4	7.7	8.4	8.9
Services	1.5	2.2	2.5	2.6	4.6
Commerce	2.1	3.7	4.3	5.2	5.5
Housing	1.5	1.6	1.7	1.6	4.6
Consumption	1.3	1.5	2.5	3.7	3.6
Total	16.9	20.0	22.1	24.7	30.7

Sector	1993	1994	1995	1996	1997
Agriculture and Husbandry	3.5	4.0	3.3	2.8	2.1
Industry	9.6	12.4	12.0	9.7	7.6
Services	5.3	7.8	9.3	8.5	7.8
Commerce	6.9	8.7	7.7	5.0	3.8
Housing	6.1	7.4	9.0	8.3	6.7
Consumption	3.3	3.1	2.0	1.2	0.8
Total	34.7	43.3	43.2	35.4	28.8

Sector figures may not equal totals due to rounding. Data on bank lending to public and financial sectors are not included. Figures for 1997 are through September 1997 only.

Source: Comision Nacional Bancaria y de Valores (CNBV), based on Banco de Mexico data. Cited in Mohar, et. al, 1998: 93.

three were market leaders: Banacomer, Banamex, and Serfin. The three accounted for about 60% of all Mexican bank assets (Gruben and Welch, 1996, p.66). They also accounted for over 70% of total bank deposits (Kessler, 1999, p.92). The largest banks were thus in a position to organize for their collective interests and speak for the banking industry in the early 1990s.

The government actually fostered this concentration of the banking sector not only through consolidation but also through regulations on competition (Kessler, 1999, pp.91-94). While the banks had more freedom to decide interest rates and the allocation of capital, regulations still restricted free entry into the banking sector. Until 1994, the minimum amount of capitalization needed to establish a new bank was 0.5% of the capital and reserves of the entire banking system. In 1993, that meant the minimum capital needed to establish a new bank was $30 million, a figure too high for many possible entrants. Regulations discouraged not only new domestic entrants, but foreign entrants as well. To prevent foreign banks from dominating Mexican banking, foreign banks as a whole could only purchase or start up bank subsidiaries that totaled up to 8% of Mexican banking capital (Gruben and Welch, 1996, p.68). Before 1994, Citibank was the only foreign bank chartered to take deposits and issue loans (Gruben and Welch, 1996, p.67).

The NAFTA treaty established a free trade and investment area throughout North America, meaning that Mexican banks would face competition in banking services from large U.S. and Canadian banks beginning in 1994. Mexican bankers and their new owners, however, argued strenuously and publicly during the negotiations that Mexican finance was an infant industry that needed protection from more developed competitors in order to grow.[4] In order to curry favor with those taking ownership of the new banks, Mexico's government bargained for and received concessions that would restrict foreign ownership of Mexican banks. The resulting treaty stipulated that Canadian and U.S. banks could not set up branches in Mexico, only national subsidiaries. Since new bank subsidiaries faced a minimum capitalization requirement, many foreign banks were effectively barred from entry into small-scale retail banking along the U.S.-Mexican border (Vega Canovas, 1995, p.220). Nor could foreign banks get controlling interest in existing Mexican banks until 1998, and even then, the total market share for foreign banks could not rise above 8% (Kessler, 1999, p.94; Minushkin, 2002, p.938). As was mentioned above, foreigners were allowed only a 30% share in brokerage firms, financial groups, and banks (Lustig, 1998, p.129).

The protection of the banking system encouraged inefficiency in banking operations (Gruben and Welch, 1996, p.66). At the end of 1991, the ratio of non-interest expense to total assets, a common measure of bank efficiency, was 5.3% in Mexico whereas it was 3.6% in the more efficient U.S. banking sector. The lack of competition was apparent in consumer service as well. In 1991, Mexico had one bank branch for every eighteen thousand people, whereas the U.S. had one bank branch for every four thousand people.

After NAFTA went into force, foreign firms broke into Mexican banking and finance despite some treaty limitations. In October 1994, the government announced that it would issue licenses for foreigners to establish eighteen commercial banks, sixteen securities firms, and twelve insurance companies (Gruben and Welch, 1996, p.69). The 1994 peso crisis also caused such extensive bank failures that the Zedillo administration felt it had little choice but to open up Mexican banking to foreign competition if only to recapitalize the banking system. With a new banking law in 1995, the government raised the maximum amount of banking capital that a starting foreign bank could hold from 8% to 15%. Foreign banks could now acquire any domestic bank that had up to 6% of the Mexican banking market, allowing foreigners to own any but the three largest Mexican banks (Gruben and Welch, 1996, pp.71-72). European, Canadian and U.S. banks acquired controlling interest in some of Mexico's smaller banks, and HSBC, a bank with operations in London and Hong Kong, managed to acquire a quarter of the equity of Serfin, Mexico's third largest bank (Kessler, 1999, pp.125-126).

Links between Finance and Industry

As mentioned above, the privatization of the banking sector also saw new linkages between banking and non-bank finance and the return of the groupos, the financial-industrial groups (see Garrido, 1994, pp.170-174). New regulations from 1990 encouraged Mexican banks to be like the "universal banks" found in Germany (Aspe, 1993, p.89). Firms could engage in commercial banking, investment banking, and brokerage activity simultaneously. Mexican banks could also invest in domestic or foreign firms, or in a broad range of financial instruments, including derivatives and currency trading. This, of course, allowed brokerage houses to purchase banks once the government put them up for sale.

During the nationalization of the banks, brokerages and investment firms grew in relatively free capital markets and accumulated a 31.61% of M4 by 1989 (see Table 5.6). Non-bank financial firms were thus well positioned to acquire privatized banks. Eight of the banks that brokerages and investment firms purchased, however, were smaller regional banks (Garrido, 1994, p. 171). Of the three largest banks, only Banamex went to a non-bank financial firm, Accival. Two industrial conglomerates, Visa and Vitro, purchased the other two leading banks. Smaller regional banks not acquired by brokerages or investment firms became the property of firms specializing in manufacturing, agrobusiness, or transportation.

While most corporations were not formally allied to banks, many Mexican firms relied on domestic bank loans for financing, even though after 1989 they could increasingly securitize their debt in international capital markets. On the whole, smaller and medium-sized firms tended to rely on bank loans more than did large firms, since larger firms had more access to international capital markets (Mohar, 1998, pp.94-95). But some large firms also predominately relied on bank loans. For example, Femsa, the major bottler and distributor for Coca-Cola in Mexico, had 7.2 billion pesos in long-term bank loans in 1996, which made up 65% of its total liabilities that year (Fomento Economico Mexicano, 1997, p.57). Alfa, a conglomerate producing petrochemicals, steel, automobile parts, synthetic fibers, and food products, had 11 billion pesos in bank loans from different sources in 1996, which accounted for 56% of its total liabilities. Only 20% of their long-term liabilities, however, came from domestic banks (Alfa, 1997, pp.45 & 58). In 1994, the ratio of bank loans to GDP averaged 52% for the sectors that produced goods and services. The ratio of bank loans to net capital stocks averaged 215% for fifty-five sectors for which information was available (Mohar, 1998: p.94).

Banks in turn relied on producers of goods and services for a significant portion of their business. Loans to agricultural, industrial, service, and commercial sectors of the economy made up 76% of all bank lending in 1994 (see Mohar, 1998, p.93). Performing commercial loans accounted for 40.1% of Bancomer's total gross loans in 1997, and 31.9% of its total assets (Bancomer, 1998, p.68).

Compared to their relative powerlessness while nationalized, Mexican banks acquired more political influence after privatization. Deregulation increased the turnover of money in the banking system, as measured by the money multiplier, and the degree to which banks lent to the private sector, as measured by the credit ratio. Banks lent to a number of small and medium-sized firms. Thus, events or policies that threatened the health of the banking system would have strong repercussions throughout the economy. Most banking activity was concentrated in the hands of three or four large banks, allowing the banking sector a greater ease of coordinating their lobbying efforts. Pronouncements of the Mexican Bankers's Association could easily reflect the preferences of its largest members. Moreover, many of the owners of the banks were the brokers or large industrial firms that the government tried to please with a turn to neo-liberal development strategies and the NAFTA negotiations.

The preferences of private interest groups

What preferences did private interest groups have for ERR policy during Mexico's period of growing capital mobility in the 1990s? In the Mexican case, the preferences of a number of groups were relevant, including not just commercial firms and banks but also the middle class and labor. Many commercial firms and banks both favored a crawling band in order to guard against fluctuations in the value of their external debt. The middle class and labor enjoyed greater purchasing power due to an appreciating real exchange rate. Analysis of their preferences indicates that many groups had reason to favor the crawling band and little reason to support either some form of rigidly fixed exchange rate or a floating exchange rate. While banks and commercial firms were not the only interest groups in favor of maintaining the status quo in economic policy in the early 1990s, they represented important voices in the policy debate, especially after the election of 1994. Greater exposure to international capital markets made the crawling-band policy more vulnerable to an exchange-rate crisis, which eventually came to pass. But even while volatile flows in the international financial system endangered the crawling-band policy, most domestic interest groups benefited from it.

Rigidly Fixed Exchange Rates

None of the firms or social classes listed above exhibited support for any form of rigid fix. Why? If Mexico did adopt a rigidly fixed exchange rate, it would either adopt the U.S. dollar as its national currency or establish a currency board in which the value of peso is fixed to the dollar. In either case, a rigidly fixed exchange rate would remove a vital symbol of Mexican sovereignty. Given its history and its proximity to the U.S., Mexico has reason to be more sensitive about American domination than most countries. Much of the reason why Mexico had a closed economy for so long was to protect itself from U.S. domination. More importantly, however, by the early 1990s Mexico had significantly reduced inflation, and high inflation is normally what generates support for a rigid fix. In 1990, inflation was 22.6%, down from 114.2% in 1988. In 1994 inflation had fallen further to 7.0%. The pacto of 1987 had apparently succeeded in reducing inflation, meaning that representatives of business, labor, and agriculture associations had participated in restraining wages and prices. The crawling band also contributed to lower inflation by letting the real exchange rate appreciate, making imports cheaper. With the crawling band operating as a nominal exchange rate anchor, few groups perceived any need for a rigidly fixed exchange rate. And since the economy managed to grow consistently between two and six percent per year, the combination of the pact and the crawling band was preferable to a rigidly fixed exchange rate, which could have contributed to a prolonged slowdown as it did more recently in Argentina. The more complicated question is why so many groups had little incentive to adopt a floating exchange rate.

The Interests of Commercial Firms

The exchange-rate crisis in 1994 led to a 40% fall in the value of the peso in the period of a week (Kootnikoff, 1995, p.28). As is normally the case among producers, Mexican firms dependent on imports and foreign firms exporting to Mexico felt the worst of it. Cifra, a mass-market retailer, had a joint venture with Wal-Mart in running Club Aurrera-Sam's Club, a discount retail and grocery chain. Roughly half of the chain's goods were imported, and sales of imported goods fell 60% across Mexico after the depreciation (Adams, 1995, p.45). Wal-Mart soon announced that it would halt the planned expansion of 25 new stores in Mexico (Chaffin, 1995, p.48). U.S. exporters along the U.S. Mexican border also took a direct hit. One machinery-parts dealer in McAllen, Texas, lost $5000 on Mexican contracts, noting that Mexican law required billing to be in pesos. The dealer claimed that a local marketing business had lost 30% of its business after the depreciation, as Mexican firms suspended marginal projects (Kootnikoff, 1995, p.28).

Mexican exporters, ironically, did not lobby for a devaluation or depreciation prior to the exchange-rate crisis, even though a decline in the exchange rate would have improved their competitiveness. According to the manufacturing hypothesis (Frieden and Stein, 2001), manufacturers should generally prefer floating so that depreciation can improve their competitiveness. Some export-oriented sectors, such as chemicals and mining, were expected to benefit after the peso crisis, since the overvalued peso had hurt their export potential (Adams, 1995, p.48). But while the National Council of Foreign Commerce acknowledged that the exchange rate was overvalued and was hurting the competitiveness of Mexican exports, it ruled out devaluation as a strategy to improve exports (*El Norte*, April 3, 1993, quoted in Kessler, 1999, p.112). For many commercial firms, whether they were exporters or not, the experience of high inflation during the late 1980s was so painful businesspeople feared that any devaluation would ignite another round of inflation. Given that intra-industry and intra-firm trade between Mexico and the U.S. had risen significantly in the 1980s (Pastor and Wise, 1994, p. 464), many Mexican producers also saw the prices of imported capital goods, intermediate goods and other inputs rise, increasing their production costs.

The reactions of foreign firms operating maquiladora industries, who by definition participated in intra-firm trade, depended on the destination of their sales. For those firms that used maquiladora factories to assemble products for export to developed countries, the fall of the peso was beneficial. Mexican labor was now cheaper for foreign firms with a depreciated peso. Firms such as Johnson Controls, Packard Electric, and Briggs and Stratton were some of the beneficiaries (Chaffin, 1995, p.49). Firms that used maquiladoras to assemble products for Mexican production were hurt. Goper Sistemas imported parts for Hewlett-Packard, Toshiba, and IBM computers, assembled them, and sold computer systems to Mexican companies. The company announced that it expected its sales to fall as Mexican companies cut back on buying equipment (Kootnikoff, 1995, p.28). The long-term consequences of the exchange-rate crisis were difficult for U.S. companies to forecast due to the floating exchange rate. When asked shortly after the crisis what the expectations they had for Mexican business and operations in the long-term, officials from Hewlett-Packard, Gillette, and Ford Motor Company all replied that it was too early to tell (Bamrud, 1995, p.29).

Even producers of non-tradable goods and services suffered as the effects of the depreciation rippled through the tradables sector into the non-tradables sector. As the exchange-rate crisis led to government bailouts for banks and to lower government revenues, government cut back on infrastructure projects, hurting construction firms such as Grupo Tribasa and Empresas ICA. Analysts predicted that Grupo Tribasa's revenues for 1995 might drop by 43% (Adams, 1995, p.46). Televisa, which controlled 85% of the advertising market, also got hurt in the resulting recession, as advertising budgets were some of the first cuts that Mexican businesses made (Adams, 1995, pp.45-46).

A more pressing problem for firms in both the tradables and non-tradables sectors was the effect of the depreciation on private sector external debt. During the 1980s, frequent devaluations increased the burden of external debt in Mexico. The appreciation of the real exchange rate under crawling band allowed commercial firms to reduce the peso value of the dollar-denominated debt burden

(Stein Velasco, 1988, p.15). Private sector external debt had grown considerably as Mexico opened up to international financial markets. Dollar-denominated debt doubled between 1988 and 1991 for the 59 largest corporate groups, accounting for over half of their total liabilities in 1991 (Garrido, 1994, p.164). Total external debt for both public and private creditors in 1994 was $142.6 billion (Banco de Mexico, 1995, p.91). According to World Bank estimates, total external debt was equivalent to 34.4% of GDP, and equivalent to 179.4% of total exports (World Bank, 1998, p.376, see Table 5.2). By the end of 1994, the private sector's total external debt was $53.3 billion (Banco de Mexico, 1995, p.92). Private sector debt was approximately equivalent to 13.1% of GDP and 68.3% of total exports of goods and services.[5] Of this private sector debt, $28 billion belonged to non-bank firms.

The growth of dollar-denominated debt gave commercial firms in many sectors an incentive to avoid a devalued or depreciated exchange rate or the fluctuations associated with a floating exchange rate. According to a study by the newspaper *El Financiero*, 87% of the 120 companies on the Mexican stock market had liabilities in foreign currency (*El Financiero*, 21 December 1994, p.6). Grupo Tribasa, which was mentioned above as suffering from government cutbacks on construction, was one of those companies that used foreign securities to finance much of its projects. After the peso crisis, it announced that it would cut its workforce by thirty to forty percent (Adams, 1995, p.46). One corporation, Ceramic, had a leverage index in foreign currency of 95%, making it a prime casualty of the peso crisis. Other corporations such as Apascy and Cemex, had leverage indexes in foreign currency higher than 80% (*El Financiero*, 21 December 1994, p.6).

The Preferences of Banks

Data provided above sketched the argument that many firms in Mexico borrowed from the banks, while larger firms also had access to foreign securities markets. Data also show that domestic banks had issued a significant portion of their loans to firm involved in industrial and commercial activities. Table 5.7 provides a breakdown of how bank lending was distributed among different sectors of the economy. As of 1994, the industrial sector took the biggest portion of loans from Mexican banks, followed by the sector devoted to trade and commerce. Given the discussion above, it is likely that banks had invested capital in some exporters who stood to benefit from the floatation. Other firms, however, would have been dependent on imported inputs or the domestic market, and the floatation put their businesses at risk. Such economic disturbance was not good for banks whose financial positions were already shaky.

More conclusive evidence, however, relates to the problems banks had with external debt and with firms that held external debt. Mexican banks held $25.3 billion dollars of external debt at the end of 1994, 47.5% of all the external debt held by the private sector (Banco de Mexico, 1995, p.92). Banamex alone held a quarter of the banks' external debt, and Bancomer held about another 15%, while the next largest banks, Serfin, Comermex, and Internacional y Mexicano, accounted for a combined portion of 36% of the debt (*El Financiero*, 21 December 1994, p.6). A handful of banks, then, held the bulk of the private sector foreign-currency debt. As in Thailand, domestic banks acquired much of this foreign-currency debt so that they could borrow cheaply abroad and loan money at higher interest rates to Mexican firms in a protected credit market (Kessler, 2000, p.50).

Meanwhile, the assets of the banks were becoming questionable. While the banks were accumulating dollar-denominated liabilities, they also accumulated non-performing loans (NPL's) after privatization. After years of nationalization and state-directed lending, many bank officials did not have the experience and expertise to assess properly the risks of private loans in a deregulated environment (Lustig, 1998, p.165). Furthermore, competition to expand market share in the loan market was intense (Mohar, 1998, pp.96-97), encouraging some risky lending decisions. Banking regulations and supervision did not require as much self-disclosure from banks as would be required in developed countries, meaning that many risky loan decisions were often not discovered until it was too late (Lustig, 1998, p.165). Consequently, bankers made a number of poor credit decisions during the credit boom of the 1990s. NPL's began to pile up as early as 1993 (*Los Angeles Times*, 8 September 1993, p.D4).

Just how many NPL's the banks had came to light with the banking crisis of 1995. A banking crisis erupted in Mexico when, to stifle inflation after the depreciation of the peso, the Banco de Mexico boosted interest rates. Mortgage rates set at 22% in November 1994 shot up to 74% in March 1995. The interbank loan rate also rose to a high of 114% in March (Gruben and Welch, 1996, p.71). The higher interest rates prompted a number of Mexican firms and households to default on their loans. Mexico unfortunately became a good example of Kaminsky and Reinhart's (1999) finding that banking sector problems tend to precede exchange rate crises and exchange rate crises deepen banking crises. According to Mexico's generous accounting standards, nine percent of outstanding loans were past due (Starr, 1999b, p.222), but the problem was probably much worse by then. After the banking crisis hit, one analysis estimated that by the beginning of 1996 up to 35% of all Mexican bank loans could have been considered non-performing according to U.S. accounting standards (Smith, 1996, p.80). As a result, the Mexican and U.S. governments cobbled together a bailout package to absorb the non-performing loans and recapitalize the Mexican banking system. Between their swollen foreign currency liabilities and the growth of non-performing loans, Mexican banks had ample reason to avoid a weaker peso or a floating exchange rate prior to the peso crisis.

The Preferences of the Middle Class and Labor

Banks and commercial firms, however, were not the only groups with an interest in maintaining the crawling band. The middle and working classes had an interest in avoiding inflation and the crawling band helped restrain inflation. While the middle class was not organized and the labor unions were not independent of the

PRI, both the middle and working classes were influential because both groups had voting power relevant to the outcome of the 1994 presidential election. Both the middle and working classes benefited from the purchasing power that came from an appreciating real exchange rate (Kessler, 1999, pp.114-115). In the years following the 1982 debt crisis, Mexico experienced slow economic growth and real wages had not climbed back to pre-crisis levels. The anti-inflation pacto of 1987 encouraged disinflation, decelerating the decline in real wages (Lustig, 1998, p.51). The appreciating real exchange rate also made foreign imports cheaper and allowed Mexicans, particularly those with some means, to engage in a consumption boom. Between December 1989 and June 1993, credit for consumption increased by 260% in real terms (Lustig, 1998, p.166). The consumption of foreign imports was also apparent in a current account deficit that varied between 5.1% and 7.4% from 1991 to 1994, despite consistent export growth. Labor leaders supported the use of the crawling band to fight inflation and would not have supported a devaluation or depreciation (Kessler, 1999, p.115). As a result, any proposal for adjustment in exchange-rate policy risked popular resentment.

The consumption boom was beneficial for the government because it improved public support for neo-liberal policies such as the pacto and NAFTA, and thus the government had incentive to maintain an overvalued exchange rate. Both opposition parties also hesitated to criticize the government's exchange-rate policy. Cuauhtemoc Cardenas, the 1994 presidential candidate for the left-wing PRD, stated that while a devaluation might be likely in the near future, he did not necessarily advocate one (*El Economista*, 14 April 1994, p.48, cited in Kessler, 1999, p.114). The PAN, the free-market opposition party that had been gathering business and middle-class support, also refrained from making exchange-rate policy an issue in the 1994 campaign.

Government policy

The Mexican government faced pressure to adjust the exchange rate almost a year before the crisis erupted. As noted above, capital inflows increased and interested converged toward U.S. levels in the early 1990s, indicating that capital mobility increased as Mexico became more open to international financial markets. Various economists (Dornbusch and Werner, 1994; Ros, 1994) warned that the peso had become overvalued. Mexican inflation had not yet fallen to U.S. levels and Mexico now had persistent current account deficits. For the time being, capital inflows financed the current account deficits, but should investor confidence have collapsed, the exchange rate and the balance of payments would have been in serious trouble. Observers figured that a small, early devaluation would ameliorate the imbalances (Dornbusch and Werner, 1994; Ros, 1994, Sachs, et. al., 1996). Up until the end of 1994, however, the government repeatedly chose to defend the crawling band and the current exchange rate in the face of continuing pressures.

In February 1994, interest rates in the U.S. began to rise in response to inflationary pressures in the U.S. (Banco de Mexico, 1995, p.39). The demand for pesos fell and the demand for dollars rose as investors sold off peso-denominated bonds (cetes), purchased more dollar-denominated investments, and companies scrambled to buy more dollars to pay the costs of dollar-denominated debt. Instead of devaluing, the government defended its exchange rate commitment, initially allowed interest rates on cetes to rise, and financed the capital outflows with its dollar reserves. With this shock to currency markets, the exchange rate traded near the ceiling of the crawling band in February 1994, and would remain there for most of the year (Banco de Mexico, 1995, p.38). The assassination of the PRI's original presidential candidate, Luis Donaldo Colosio in March, the resignation of two major government officials, and renewed fighting in Chiapas in December shocked international finanical markets and contributed to further losses of foreign-exchange reserves (Springer and Molina, 1995, p.62). International investors, wondering whether Mexico's politics were as stable has many had assumed, began to sell Mexican investments. Mexico began to deplete its stock of international reserves over the year. In February, the Banco de Mexico had nearly $30 billion in net international reserves. By December, it had less than $15 billion (Banco de Mexico, 1995, p.41). The assassination of Colosio alone prompted a loss of ten billion dollars in international reserves in one month.

To reclaim the confidence of foreign investors, the Mexican government significantly increased its sales of dollar-denominated liabilities (tesebonos), thereby promising foreign investors that they would not have to be exposed to exchange rate risk because the government would absorb it. The sum of tesebonos increased from $3.1 billion in March 1994 to $12.6 billion in June, to $19.2 in September and $29.2 in December (Lustig, 1995, p.13). Without the increase in tesebonos, the Mexican government would have been forced to cut spending or increase taxes in an election year (Starr, 1999a). Unfortunately, the government put itself in the awkwardly risky position of having sold more dollar-denominated debt than it had dollar reserves.

The tesebono sales, however, did seem to buy the government some time. By April, turmoil in the currency markets had settled, and Mexico maintained foreign exchange reserves between fifteen and twenty billion dollars until November (Banco de Mexico 1995, p. 41). The resignation of the Secretary of the Interior in the middle of the year caused another fluctuation in currency markets and a temporary dip in reserves. Apart from this episode, confidence remained fairly intact during the summer. The election victory of the incumbent party's candidate for the presidency, Ernesto Zedillo, in August 1994 gave investors reason to believe that the neo-liberal economic program of the PRI would continue. In November, however, Mexico faced another increase in U.S. interest rates (Sachs, et. al., 1996, p.45). Fighting in Chiapas in early December and rumors of a devaluation prompted another run on foreign-exchange reserves. Reserves fell to $11 billion on 16 December 1994 (Lustig, 1995, p.15).

Once reserves could no longer defend the exchange rate, the Zedillo administration raised the sell-off price of the crawling band to 4.0016 pesos to the dollar on 20 December 1994, effectively a 15% devaluation. Foreign investors observed Mexican investors selling pesos for dollars. Foreign investors panicked and sold off Mexican assets in favor of foreign assets (Sachs, et. al, 1996, pp.42-47; Lustig, 1998, pp.167-169). The exchange rate hit the new ceiling of four pesos to the dollar and $5 billion left the country in two days (Lustig, 1995, p. 15). Thus reserves fell to near $6 billion after the devaluation (Banco de Mexico, 1995, p.41; Lustig, 1998, p.169). These capital outflows after the devaluation were so pronounced that the government was forced to let the peso float on 22 December 1994. A government auction of tesobonos on the 27th of December failed to raise the $600 million needed to roll over debt (Sachs, et. al, 1996, p.46). The Banco de Mexico raised interest rates to 55% on 10 January 1995 (Kootnikoff, 1995, p.28). As interest rates skyrocketed, non-performing loans piled up, and bank failures resulted. The PRI's reputation for economic competence was painfully damaged.

If investors had put so much pressure on the exchange rate for almost all of 1994, why did the government insist on defending the exchange rate? Immediately after the peso crisis, many wondered how a government that had so many well-trained technocrats and had pursued so many of the free-market policies favored by the experts could have slid into such a disaster. As time went on, several economists and political economists developed a small cottage industry in researching the crisis and now several explanations have been cited. These explanations range from misdiagnosis of the economy by government officials, to electoral pressures, to mismanagement of the transition, to Salinas's desire to increase his international standing, to pressure from the U.S. If anything, what once seemed like a puzzle now seems like an overdetermined case. Electoral pressures, more than any of the other explanations, have much to do with the government's defense of the crawling band. The external debt that the Mexican government, Mexican banks, and Mexican corporations held, however, is one the most plausible explanations for why the government refused to devalue after the election.

Official Explanations

In defending their decision to defend the crawling band instead of devaluing or floating, Mexican officials argued that a devaluation was unnecessary to correct current account deficits and that a devaluation might ignite inflation after a hard-won battle to reduce it. In regards to the current account deficit, the issue was whether the currency was overvalued, thus increasing imports and hurting export competitiveness for as long as it was overvalued, or whether the current account was temporary, the result of foreign investment, and would correct itself over time. If the currency was overvalued a devaluation or floatation would be necessary. If the current account deficits were temporary, a devaluation or floatation would be unnecessary and merely reduce the government's credibility in making exchange rate commitments. In the early 1990s, government officials argued that the exchange rate was not overvalued and that the current account would correct itself.[6] They argued that lower inflation and the neo-liberal reforms had attracted foreign investment inflows, which encouraged the current account deficits. Over time, foreign investment capital would improve Mexican productivity and Mexican exports. Thus the current account gap would close as the Mexican economy took off. NAFTA would allow even more foreign investment and export opportunities in the future. In the view of some government officials, the devaluation and floatation were unnecessary, and the peso crisis the result of a politically triggered panic among investors (Gil-Diaz and Carstens, 1997).

Critics that pushed the overvaluation interpretation, however, noted that several measures of inflation indicated that the real exchange rate was continuing to appreciate and that the use of the exchange rate to stabilize inflation frequently produces overvaluation in other countries (Dornbusch and Werner, 1994; Edwards, 1997). Furthermore, the critics argued that Mexican productivity figures were suspect (Dornbusch, 1997) and that economic growth in early 1994 not growing as quickly as the trade deficit (Wessel, et. al., *Wall Street Journal*, 6 July 1995, p.A4). In the view of the government's critics, the peso crisis was the inevitable outcome of an unsustainable crawling band.

Whether or not the peso was overvalued and whether the peso crisis was due to mismanaged economic policy or a self-fulfilling panic are difficult questions that have been subject to extensive debate and that debate cannot be settled here. Comments by government officials and official government reports, however, show government officials insisting that the crawling band was not responsible for the current account deficits or the peso crisis. Perhaps by insisting that the exchange rate policy was not at fault, these officials were simply trying to deflect blame for their mistakes. It is plausible, however, that the rigid beliefs of officials, however mistaken, were sincere and help explain why the government persisted in defending the exchange rate. Pedro Aspe, then the foreign minister and the architect of the economic reform program, was reputed to have a dismissive attitude to those that questioned his economic policies (Wessel, et. al., *Wall Street Journal*, 6 July 1995, p.A4). This ideational approach alone, however, would not explain why the reigning ideas in the Finance Ministry and the central bank received political support from President Salinas and the PRI, a party ultimately concerned with maintaining political control and divided within itself over the question of economic reform (see Dresser, 1997, Kessler, 1999, and Starr, 1999b.)

Aside from arguing that a new exchange rate policy was necessary for correcting the current account, government officials also argued that a devaluation or depreciation would have led to increased wage demands from unions and inflation (Banco de Mexico, 1995, p.38). That the government was primarily worried about inflation in 1994, however, is less believable. The PRI had a long history of co-opting the labor movement (see Burgess, 2003). If the ruling party had really wanted to coerce labor organizations into accepting higher import prices without a compensating increase in wages, few doubted the party's ability to do it in most circumstances. Furthermore, the central bank allowed an expansion of domestic credit during 1994. As foreign exchange reserves fell in March and April, the central bank sterilized the outflow by expanding short-term domestic credit and letting interest rates drop (even while U.S. interest rates were rising)

(Banco de Mexico, 1995, pp.46-47). This held the monetary base roughly constant from April to November 1994. Note that instead of accepting the disinflationary consequences of a capital outflow and defending the exchange rate with higher interest rates, the central bank protected the size of the monetary supply. Given that it was an election year, the government wanted to deliver economic growth. The expansion of domestic credit to this end was consistent with other expansionary policies, such as spending far more than half of the government in the first half of the year (Starr, 1999a).

Political Pressures

Since official explanations of Mexico's exchange rate policy do not entirely satisfy, it worth examining what the transparency, electoral, and financial intermediation hypotheses can contribute to the explanation. Three other explanations unique to the Mexican case, however, are worth mentioning here: pressure from the U.S. government, pressure from foreign investors, and Salinas' personal preferences.

Some have argued that as the U.S. Congress debated the ratification of NAFTA in 1993, Salinas became convinced that abandonment of Mexico's exchange rate commitments would be viewed in the U.S. as an underhanded attempt to enhance Mexican competitiveness just as the U.S. lowered its tariff barriers (Naim, 1995). Opponents of NAFTA in the U.S. Congress, such as Representative John LaFalce of New York, even held hearings on the stability of the peso as the NAFTA debate raged.[7] While pressure from the Congress was a contributing factor, it was not likely decisive. It is arguable that the difference to the U.S. trade balance from any devaluation early in 1994 would likely have been negligible, and most of the American debate on NAFTA concerned jobs, labor standards, and environmental issues more than the bilateral trade balance. Moreover by November 1994, as Mexico's foreign exchange reserves were becoming scarce, senior officials in the U.S. Treasury Department such as Lloyd Bentsen and Lawrence Summers, with the backing of the Federal Reserve Bank, had expressed concern to the Mexican Finance Minister about the sustainability of the exchange rate. Bentsen advised a devaluation.[8]

The preferences of U.S. investors were more consistent. In April 1994, after the first big shock to Mexico's reserves that year, the Weston Forum, a consortium of premier investment enterprises such as Fidelity Investment Company, Oppenheimer Management Corporation, Putnam Funds Management, Soros Funds Management, Salomon Brothers, and the Weston Group, met in secret meetings with Guillermo Ortiz, the deputy finance minister for Mexico and Augustin Carstens, the central bank research director (Torres and Vogel, *Wall Street Journal*, 14 June 1994, p.A6). The Weston Forum's message to the Mexican officials was that if Mexico wanted to retain the confidence of the international financial community, it should not devalue. The Mexican government immediately began to sell more tesebonos in order to convince international investors that the government was going to absorb the exchange rate risk (Wessel, et. al., *Wall Street Journal*, 6 July 1995, p.A4). Mexican officials seemed to believe that maintaining the crawling band was necessary for maintaining the foreign investment that had powered Mexican development and financed current account deficits during the Salinas administration.

President Salinas also desired to become director of the World Trade Organization after his term ended in 1994. Some have argued that Salinas was desperate to avoid a devaluation or depreciation of the peso in 1994 so as to avoid leaving office in disgrace, thus hurting his post-presidential career plans (Smith, 1997, p.39). This too was probably a contributing factor for the spring and summer of 1994. But when Mexico faced another loss of reserves in November, Salinas met with president-elect Zedillo on 20 November and decided that a 10% devaluation was their only option. Aspe, the finance minister, called up Salinas and threatened to resign if the peso was devalued. Salinas feared that if Aspe left, the problems with investor confidence would turn into a panic, so the devaluation plan was abandoned for the time being (Wessel, et. al., *Wall Street Journal*, 6 July 1995, p.A1). By the fall then, Salinas was not decisive force in favor of defending the peso.

The Transparency Hypothesis

Did the government hold onto a crawling band because it was not transparent enough to give credible independence to the central bank? On the surface, this explanation has some merit. The PRI dominated Mexican politics as a one-party oligarchy from time of the Mexican revolution. The PRI is widely thought to have stolen the 1988 presidential election from the left-wing Democratic Revolutionary Party (PRD) (Starr, 1999a; Kessler, 1999, p.83). Given the "hyper-presidentialism" (Dresser, 1997) that also characterized Mexican politics at this time, could the government credibly claim that the central bank was independent from political control? Perhaps the crawling band was Mexico's only option for committing to disinflationary policies. This view overlooks two points. First, the pacto demonstrated that Mexico's anti-inflation options were not limited to fixed exchange rates and independent central banks, but included incomes policy. Granted, the pacto was an agreement by which the government would commit to a crawling band in exchange for limitations on wage and price increases from business and labor. But the mere existence of incomes policy as a possible third option demonstrates exceptions to the logic of the transparency hypothesis. Second, Sylvia Maxfield (1997, p.104) argues that as the NAFTA debate heated up in the U.S. Congress in 1993, Salinas pushed a new statute that gave the central bank more legal independence. In doing so, Salinas was signaling the PRI's commitment to policies friendly to foreign investment even after he left office. The new statute enshrined the stability of the peso's purchasing power as the central bank's prime goal, prohibited central bank from extending credit to the government, and altered the terms and conditions for central bank governors. Whether this new statute struck others as credible is difficult to tell. It did however signal that the crawling band and central bank independence were not mutually exclusive options for the Mexican government.

Political Coalitions and the 1994 Election

A more plausible explanation why the government worked to defend the crawling band centers on the PRI's presidential ambitions during the election of 1994. As mentioned above, many people inside and outside of Mexico widely believed that the PRI stole the presidential election of 1988. Prior to 1988, the Mexican population had endured six years of painful economic adjustment in the aftermath of the 1982 debt crisis, and the PRI had lost much of the support it once had. Cuauhtemoc Cardenas, the left-wing National Democratic Front (FDN) candidate, was known to be more popular than Salinas, the PRI candidate, but the government declared that Salinas had narrowly won the election. The PRI then faced a dilemma. Many Mexicans now saw the presidency of Salinas as illegitimate. In the late 1980s, the support of working-class and poor people was gravitating to FDN and other left-wing movements, while middle-class and business support was gravitating to the conservative, pro-market PAN. The PRI could have tried imposing coercive measures to remain in power. International attention to Mexican political practices was growing, however, and wrenching political changes in the former Soviet bloc and South Africa had demonstrated that coercive measures did not always keep long-standing ruling parties in power. In response to this dilemma, the Salinas administration chose to rebuild support for PRI governance (see Kessler, 1999, p.84).

In the days of import-substitution policies, the PRI nurtured a coalition of small, uncompetitive businesses, urban workers, and peasant organizations with protectionist policies. With the traditional coalition behind the PRI eroding after the 1982 debt crisis, however, the PRI settled on a strategy of building a new coalition of support with new strategies. Given that the conservative PAN was now winning gubernatorial contests and the PRI needed the PAN to pass 2/3 majorities to amend the constitution (Starr, 1999a) the PRI first sought to reestablish its relations with large influential business interests and smaller entrepreneurs. The PRI designed neo-liberal policies such as anti-inflation commitments, privatization, and opening the economy to please large commercial firms looking to export, financiers opposed to the bank nationalization, and middle class Mexicans frustrated by high inflation. NAFTA in particular pleased large commercial firms that could exploit economies of scale. Some observers argue that since smaller commercial firms had less information on how NAFTA would affect their fortunes, many small businesses supported NAFTA even in spite of the threat of foreign competition or they simply could not mount effective opposition to it (Pastor and Wise, 1994, pp. 480-482). The new neo-liberal strategies, however, had the political drawback of reducing the tools of directed finance and captured markets that the PRI had traditionally used as patronage to satisfy old allies (Kessler, 1999, p.84).

To offset the costs that neo-liberal adjustment placed on those that were not big business, brokers, or bankers, the PRI pursued two other strategies to garner support. One was to temper the neo-liberal program with policies designed to protect or compensate the disaffected (Pastor and Wise, 1994; Dresser, 1997). For example, the government provided export credits, directed some credit through national development banks to promote small enterprises, and developed a National Solidarity Program (Pronasol) to alleviate poverty. The other strategy was to promote limited democratization reforms to placate citizens who claimed that the Salinas Administration was illegitimate and reduce the appeal of the Chiapas rebels (Starr, 1999a). The PRI began to allow rival parties like the PAN to win gubernatorial elections. Salinas granted more legal autonomy to the Federal Election Institute, the government agency charged with counting votes. The 1994 election would also include foreign observers, and many analysts and foreign observers validated the fairness of the election procedures and the independence of the Federal Election Institute (see Scherlen, 1998).

Given that the PRI set out to win an honest election in 1994, it is reasonable to argue that the PRI crafted economic policy with the objective of winning votes and the support of key interest groups (see Kessler, 1999, pp.110-116). Hence the PRI financed capital outflows with reserves and expanded domestic credit, rather let the money supply contract and cripple economic growth. A devaluation or depreciation would also have increased the debt burden for banks and large commercial firms, at a time when the PRI was trying to woo business interests away from the PAN. A devaluation or depreciation would also have cut the purchasing power of numerous middle- and working-class voters who were buying increasing volumes of imports. Rather than fearing that a devaluation would provoke increased wage demands and inflation, it is more plausible to argue that the government simply hesitated to grieve working-class voters with a loss of purchasing power in an election year.

Dollar-Denominated Debt and Finance

After the election in August 1994 and before Zedillo, the PRI victor, took office in December 1994, the government had another opportunity to devalue or float the peso (Pastor, 1998, p.140). After the elections, the Mexico's foreign exchange reserves had remained fairly steady and interest rates between Mexico and the U.S. were beginning to converge (Sachs, et. al., 1996, p. 41). The PRI, meanwhile, did not have to worry about critics claiming that the government had stolen another election, as Zedillo won with a vote total nearly twice that of his nearest rival in an internationally-certified election (Starr, 1999a). The U.S. Congress had ratified NAFTA many months ago. Why did it continue to defend the exchange rate after the election?

At this point one set of significant, interrelated concerns still remained: the volume of dollar-denominated debt Mexican officials, banks, and commercial firms held, and the confidence of foreign investors. This is where the insights of the financial intermediation hypothesis and an examination of Mexican financial patterns apply best. By the mid-1994, the government had converted much of its public debt from peso-denominated cetes to dollar-indexed tesebonos. By December 1994, foreigners held 87% of the holdings of Mexican public debt in the form of tesebonos (Pastor, 1998, p.125; Lustig, 1995, p.13). Deflation or depreciation would have made servicing public debt far more expensive for the government. Moreover, by September 1994, the total volume of tesebonos was $19.2 billion, more than the total amount of the government's reserves (Lustig, 1995, p.13). Should investors have panicked and sold off their tesebonos, the government would not have had the reserves to cover its debts. Banks and large commercial firms, as noted above, also held significant liabilities denominated in dollars, making a fall in the exchange rate costly for the very groups that the PRI had worked hard to include in a new political coalition. Furthermore, if the government tried to defend the exchange rate with higher interest rates, banks would face a wave of defaults from non-performing loans, which the banking system was too fragile to absorb (see Sachs, et. al., 1996, pp.23-24; Pastor, 1998, p.139; Starr, 1999a). Without the options of capital controls, devaluation, floatation, or higher interest rates, all the government could do to maintain its current account was to try to maintain foreign investor confidence to encourage more capital inflows, and finance any capital outflows with reserves. Thus, the preferences of foreign investors, banks, and large Mexican commercial firms became interrelated.

While direct evidence of bank and business lobbying is difficult to attain, insider accounts of high-level government decision-making on exchange rate policy gave foreign investors, banks, and indebted commercial firms what they wanted for as long as events allowed. In September, the government renegotiated and largely renewed the anti-inflation pacto with business and labor groups.[9] Ortiz, the deputy finance minister, argued then that the time had come for a small one-time devaluation of the peso. Aspe, his superior, rebuffed him and argued that any devaluation would lead to lost investor confidence and a run on the peso. When key officials such as Salinas, Zedillo and current cabinet ministers (including Aspe and the then commerce minister Jaime Serra) discussed post-election economic policy that September, devaluation was barely considered, and Zedillo and Serra made clear their opposition to a devaluation. But in November after the U.S. raised interest rates and renewed fighting in Chiapas caused a run on the peso and billions more in reserve losses, Salinas and Zedillo discussed a roughly 10% devaluation with their economic advisors, as mentioned above. Aspe threatened to resign if they carried out the devaluation. Aspe insisted that his reputation was at stake when he promised foreign investors that Mexico would never devalue. Fearing an investor panic if Aspe resigned, Salinas dropped plans for a devaluation.

The hemorrhaging of reserves, however, continued. In mid-December, after Zedillo took office, it became clear that reserves had fallen so low they were no longer sufficient to defend the peso. Officials from government and peak business associations held a meeting to discuss exchange-rate policy on 19 December 1994. The meeting was to provide the sort of corporatist consensus that had provided the political support for the anti-inflation pacto. Included at the meeting were officials such as Jaime Serra, now Zedillo's finance minister, Miguel Mancera, the governor of the Banco de Mexico, and Jose Madariaga Lomelin, the president of the Mexican Bankers' Association. Sidney Weintraub (2000) conducted several interviews with Mexican decision-makers about the peso crisis and reported what happened at this meeting (pp.103-104). According to Weintraub, The Banco de Mexico's position was that the peso should float and allowed to find a sustainable level. This was also Serra's position, and, according to Serra, Zedillo's inclination as well. But the reaction of the business officials was negative, citing worries about market reactions. Business officials argued that only a minor adjustment was necessary. Discussions wore on until the early hours of the morning. Lomelin argued in favor of raising the exchange-rate band by 15% instead of floating. From the point of view of the banks, if a defense of the exchange rate was not an option, a devaluation was preferable to a float. Both devaluation and floatation would have made dollar-denominated debt more expensive to repay, but a limited devaluation would have been less expensive than the float, which could have depreciated the peso more than 15%. The devaluation would also at least have provided relatively more certainty about the future costs of the debt, while the floatation would not. Government officials announced a 15% devaluation hours later on the 20th of December.

Government officials did not announce any changes in economic policy to support the devaluation, nor did they announce how they would manage a withdrawal of investment from Mexico (Edwards, 1997, p.118). With no Aspe at the helm to calm foreign investors, foreign investors felt betrayed and worried that they were going to be stuck with devalued assets (Lustig, 1995, p.17; Hale, 1997, pp.214-215, Edwards, 1997). The devaluation triggered a financial panic, and the Finance Ministry announced that the peso would henceforth float. The peso plummeted to half its value and Mexico plummeted into economic crisis (Kessler, 1999, p.110).

Conclusions

The combination of capital mobility and an overvalued exchange rate put the crawling-band regime in danger of an exchange-rate crisis in the early 1990s. Eventually the government postponed exchange-rate adjustment for so long that a crisis did erupt and the government was forced to adopt a floating exchange rate. Why?

OCA theory, the manufacturing hypothesis, and the transparency hypothesis do not apply to the Mexican case well. Of all the hypotheses covered in this book, the electoral and financial intermediation hypotheses are the most relevant to Mexico, especially after weaving them with some supplementary explanations. The Mexican peso crisis is an overdetermined case, and the most decisive causes of the crisis are a combination of the PRI's desire to forge a new coalition of support, electoral pressures, the dollar-denominated debts of the government, banks, and large domestic firms, plus the fragility of the banking system, and pressure from foreign investors. Maintenance of the PRI's dominance in Mexican politics came to depend on the support of major businesses, brokers, and banks, and winning broad support in the 1994 election. The middle and working classes opposed devaluation in the interests of maintaining purchasing power, and banks and large domestic commercial firms opposed devaluation largely due to their dollar-denominated debt. The fragility of the banking system made it difficult to raise interest rates. Without the options of devaluation, floatation, or higher interest rates, the PRI depended on foreign investors to finance current account deficits, and foreign investors also indicated their opposition to devaluation. After the election, the preferences of foreign investors, banks, and large commercial firms became paramount. The crawling band was ultimately unsustainable and the government floated the exchange rate only after the band was no longer an option.

The financial intermediation hypothesis is part of the explanation because each of the elements of the hypothesis applies to Mexico. While Mexico has a financial system that incorporates both capital markets and banks, Mexican banks are more active than banks in most developing countries. Mexican banks held dollar-denominated debt, and formed a concentrated group with ties to Mexican political authorities. These elements gave banks interest and influence in lobbying. The pattern of bank lobbying in the peso crisis allows for two interesting points of comparison. One compares the peso crisis of 1994 to previous Mexican financial crises, the other compares it with other financial crises of the time. Celso Garrido (2003) argues that Mexico's repeated financial crises are the result of four structural features of the Mexican financial system. First, Mexico has a long tradition of major financial-industrial groups leading the economy. Second, lax enforcement of financial regulations encourages financial and industrial firms to lend and borrow recklessly. Third, the international financial system supplies and withdraws capital from Mexico in investment cycles of boom and bust. Fourth, the government encourages further reckless investment decisions by bailing out Mexican firms in bust times. Garrido argues that these four conditions apply to four cases of financial crises in 1976, 1982, 1987, and 1994, despite significant changes in bank ownership and the shift from import-substitution to neo-liberalism. Since private, dollar-denominated debt was more prominent in the last of these cycles, the financial intermediation hypothesis helps to explain why exchange rate policy played a crucial in precipitating that crisis more than the others.

The financial intermediation hypothesis also identifies a common pattern between the exchange rate crises Mexico and Thailand experienced in the 1990s. Mexico and Thailand have some significant differences in history and culture, and more notably in the size and structure of their economies. Nevertheless, a common underlying process unfolded in both states. Mexico's economy also has a more developed capital markets than Thailand does, yet in both cases, banks were more active than in most developing countries, providing debt financing to a number of commercial firms. In both cases, the banks and commercial firms had little interest in rigidly fixed exchange rates. The banks both states did, however, have significant holdings of dollar-denominated debt. In the case of Mexico, the government also held significant external debt. In both cases, banks and other firms made tightly connected financial industrial groups, and the banking system was concentrated in structure, giving the largest banks political clout. The banking system was also becoming fragile in both states before the crisis. Banks had connections to parties in the governing coalition in Thailand, and in Mexico peak associations of banks and businesses negotiated directly with the government, but in both cases banks had channels of political influence. The stories of exchange rate crises in Thailand and Mexico do of course have several differences in their mitigating factors, such as differences in their electoral cycles, the political coalition-building of their governments, and international pressures. The evidence of similar processes of financial intermediation at work in shaping exchange rate policy, however, is more evidence (along with the statistical tests) that the financial intermediation hypothesis has generalizability across diverse contexts.

Notes

[1] See Lustig, 1998, Kessler, 1999, and Garrido, 2003 for the historical details.

[2] Technically, only the selling rate depreciated by 2.4% when the crawling band regime began. The buying rate remained fixed until March 15, 1992. After that date, it also depreciated by 2.4% per year.

[3] For attempts to perform statistical tests that do not use the IMF classification system, but unfortunately give inconclusive results, see the Appendix.

[4] See the publication by the Mexican Bankers' Association, 1991. See also comments from Mexican financial executives in *El Financiero*, 21 November 1991, p.15 and 13 February 1992, p.3, plus *El Norte*, 14 August 1992. These comments are cited in Kessler, 1999, p.95.

[5] Based on author's calculations.

[6] For an example of official arguments by government officials, see Banco de Mexico, 1995, pp.36-37 and Aspe, 1993, pp.44-46. For an example of government officials defending this position even after the crisis, see Gil-Diaz and Carstens, 1997. A report by Wessel, et. al. in the *Wall Street Journal* (6 July 1995, pp.A1 & A4) argues that this position was very much the position of Pedro Aspe, then the Finance Minister and the chief of Mexico's economic policy.

[7] See House Committee on Small Business, *Hearings on NAFTA and Peso Devaluation: A Problem for U.S. Exporters?*, Statement of Representative John LaFalce, 20 May 1993.

[8] See Wessel, et. al., *Wall Street Journal*, 6 July 1995, pp.A1 & A4 and D'Amato, 1995, pp.381-384.

[9] The insider accounts for this paragraph come from Wessel, et. al., *Wall Street Journal*, 6 July 1995, pp.A1 & A4.

Chapter 6

Peru

Thailand and Mexico represent cases of states exposed to high capital mobility maintaining a pegged exchange rate for several years due to the pressure from its banking and commercial sectors. But what happens in situations in which the banking sector is weak and financial intermediation is low? According to the financial intermediation hypothesis, such states should be able to abandon pegged exchange rates more quickly in the face of international pressures. Peru, a state not included in the sample used for the statistical tests, is an example of this dynamic. Due to government ownership, heavy regulation, and a period of hyperinflation, the Peruvian banking sector has been underdeveloped, leading Peru to having weaker banks and less overall financial intermediation than most states in Latin America. After almost thirty years of crawling pegs, Peru also officially adopted floating exchange rates in 1990, as part of a neo-liberal reform package. Peru dropped its formal promises to peg earlier than most states in the sample, whose time frame ranges from 1987 to 1998.

This chapter will argue that, even though Peru held a lot of external debt, the largely public ownership of the external debt, dollarization, and the weakness of the banking system gave few interest groups incentive to prefer a pegged exchange rate compared to Thailand or Mexico. Most external debt in Peru was publicly-held rather than privately-held in the 1980s, meaning that few private banks or firms had an interest in maintaining a peg to prevent the cost of debt service from increasing. After experiencing hyperinflation, the many Peruvians switched from holding domestic currency to dollars in their bank deposits. The government's exchange-rate policy thus became less relevant for dollar-holding Peruvians. Furthermore, the weakness of the Peruvian banking system prevented the accumulation of private dollar-denominated debt and prevented a strong lobby for exchange-rate stability from developing. After heterodox economic strategies contributed to hyperinflation in the late 1980s, government had depleted most of its foreign exchange reserves and most private groups supported some sort of political change. Hyperinflation, rooted in persistently monetarized budget deficits, eroded the government's ability to maintain a credible peg. In advising Peru how to structure a neo-liberal stabilization program, the IMF and World Bank advised the Peruvians to adopt a floating exchange rate and reduce its budget deficits. Given little domestic pressure for a peg, the government had wide latitude to adopt a floating exchange rate, in contrast to the domestic political pressures on the governments of Thailand and Mexico.

This chapter is structured much like the chapters on Thailand and Mexico. The next section summarizes the exchange-rate policy of Peru since the 1950s. The third section describes some of the main economic influences on the ERR, such as Peru's history of inflation, its relatively closed economy, and its pattern of foreign investment. The fourth section describes the underdeveloped state of Peruvian banks, and why disintermediation has been the norm. The fifth section reflects on the analysis on the previous sections and draws conclusions on what preferences interest groups would have had for the ERR, and analyzes why most interest groups had little desire for a peg. The last section details the shift in government policy before and after 1990, when Peru switched from heterodox strategies and a peg to neo-liberal strategies and floating. The switch to floating had much to do with the state of reserves for international currency, the role of the IMF and the World Bank. Given the growing autonomy of the Fujimori government and what little resistance it faced to a floating exchange rate, Fujimori could respond to international pressures for a float more quickly than other governments could.

Exchange-rate policy in Peru

In the early 1950s, Peru was unusual in that it had a floating exchange rate. Most developing countries pegged their exchange rates in accordance with Bretton Woods' par-value system. Peru, however, chose a floating exchange rate after it had a bad experience with fixed exchange rates with the 1940s. Alone among Latin American countries, Peru did not adopt exchange-rate controls immediately after the Great Depression (Pasco-Font and Ghezzi, 2001, p. 252). To insulate itself from capital movements, Peru chose a floating exchange rate instead.

Peru, however, depended heavily on exports for economic growth. In 1954, Peru adopted a pegged exchange rate, in part to help maintain exchange-rate stability. From 1954 to 1990, Peru would implement a series of pegged exchange-rate regimes. What were common to this period were a persistent depreciation of the real exchange rate and cycles of boom and bust culminating in periodic balance-of-payments crises. Following a crisis, the government would impose an austerity program. Thanks to some combination of higher prices for exported commodities and increased international lending, the balance of payments would improve. As the economy boomed, domestic spending and imports would increase, putting pressure on the balance of payments again. Another crisis would result. All six Peruvian governments from 1963 to 1990 had to struggle with balance of payments problems (Beckerman, 1989, p. 105). In all of these cases, however, the government would adhere to some form a pegged exchange rate, changing it only insofar as to alter the form of the peg (from adjustable to crawling or vice versa) or to adjust the rate of crawl.

Pegging continued in this period even through shifts in economic strategy. In the late 1970s, inflation had been stubbornly and persistently 60% per year for some time (Beckerman, 1989, p. 122). After the stabilization program of

1978, Peru had a current account surplus, which increased Peru's international reserves and thus its total money supply, contributing to inflation. In the 1980 election, Fernando Belaunde, whom the military had deposed in 1968, won the presidency due to his reputation as one of the most consistent opponents of the unpopular military government. He offered an orthodox program designed to "get prices right." Belaunde's government began to do away with export subsidies, tariff protection, interest rate regulations, and high reserve ratios in banks. It did not, however, restrain government expenditures, which alarmed some economists who saw the expenditures as the primary cause of inflation (Hamann and Paredes, 1991, p. 9). The Belaunde administration hoped that adjustment to a free market pricing would control inflation in the long run (Beckerman, 1989, pp. 122-123). The World Bank and Inter-American Development Bank approved of the neo-liberal program and extended about $200 million in credit a year shortly after 1980 (Beckerman, 1989, p. 123). Foreign banks provided another $850 million in new credit.

The Belaunde government assumed that the favorable terms of trade that it inherited would continue indefinitely. Unfortunately, the world economy would slip into recession in the early 1980s and developed countries cut their spending on foreign imports. On top of that, El Nino whether patterns hit Peruvian agriculture and fishing badly in 1983 (Hamann and Paredes, 1991, p. 9). The government accelerated the crawl of the exchange rate to engineer a devaluation, and inflation accelerated with it (Pasco-Font and Ghezzi, 2001, p. 256). In September 1984, the central bank began to pre-announce the devaluation rate weeks in advance in hopes of reducing the uncertainty of its exchange-rate policy (Beckerman, 1989, p. 126). By 1985, the economy was caught in a spiral of inflation and devaluation and many called the Belaunde government's experiment with orthodoxy a failure.

Alan Garcia, the new and charismatic leader of the APRA party, won the presidency in the 1985 election. Garcia's administration launched a distinctly heterodox and social democratic program (Hamann and Paredes, 1991, p. 9). The Garcia administration lowered taxes and raised government spending. The government fixed prices of key domestic products which also tamed inflation in the short run. Garcia also argued that external debt payments had become too oppressive and limited further payments. The government cut itself off from further foreign borrowing. To limit the erosion of foreign currency reserves, the government forced the exchange of dollars deposits into local currency. The government also limited the servicing of medium and long-term external debt to ten percent of export revenues (Larrain and Sachs, 1991, pp. 228-229). Unfortunately, these measures did not stop a significant loss of foreign exchange reserves in the late 1980s.

Shortly after taking office, the Garcia administration also reformed the exchange-rate system (IMF, *EAER*, 1986, p. 412). The government introduced a new currency, the sol, early in 1985. A dual exchange rate was implemented. Most transactions, such as export payments and conversion of dollar deposits, were conducted at an official fixed peg of 13,908 soles to the dollar. Other transactions, such as those for travel or personal remittances, were conducted at a free-market exchange rate. The government later introduced a new currency called the inti and added two more exchange-rate classifications to create a multiple exchange-rate system (IMF, *EAER*, various years). The government hoped that the multiple exchange rates would not only prevent the erosion of foreign currency reserves, but also anchor the Peruvian currency to a low-inflation currency (Pasco-Font and Ghezzi, 2001, p. 256).

The heterodox program was a disaster. In 1986, the rate of inflation did go down. Since the government engaged in deficit spending and refused to borrow from abroad, however, it increasingly resorted to printing money. The inflation rate later soared to 114% per month (Velarde, 1994, p. 140). Hyperinflation ravaged the economy, and the financial system nearly collapsed. For some, the episode demonstrated that heretodox programs need to rest on solid social democratic coalitions of organized labor, which Garcia did not have. Thus he resorted to incomplete stabilization packages to shore up dwindling support (Pastor, 1992). For neo-liberals, hyperinflation demonstrated the flaws in state-led approaches. By 1990, voters cared less about the causes and more about setting some new direction in policy.

Alberto Fujimori won the election in 1990 promising to impose a gradual approach to economic adjustment. But when in office, Fujimori jettisoned his original platform in favor of orthodox shock therapy, the platform of his defeated opponent, Mario Vargas Llosa (Velarde, 1994, p. 141). Fujimori's administration removed price controls after giving a one-time bonus to public servants and engineering a one-time increase in the minimum wage. A tax increase helped put the public budget back in balance. The Fujimori government also announced that it would resume payments on external debt withheld by the Garcia administration. Most importantly, the government swore off the monetization of the public debt and raised interest rates to combat hyperinflation and attract capital for investment. The Fujimori government also overturned years of import substitution strategies, lowered tariffs, and removed many import restrictions.

The exchange-rate system was reunified (IMF, *EAER*, 1991, p. 385). The government also introduced a new currency in 1991, the Nuevo Sol (new Sol). In most disinflation programs, however, governments often try to impose a highly credible peg to anchor the domestic currency to a low-inflation foreign currency. Fujimori, by contrast, floated the exchange rate and relied on restrictive fiscal and monetary policies to restrain inflation. What is notable in Peru's case is how it switched to floating in a macroeconomic crisis, before an exchange-rate crisis has a chance to erupt and without the foot-dragging that typified the governments of Thailand and Mexico.

With the central bank now focusing on strict monetary targets, the real exchange rate in Peru appreciated. Thanks to the appreciating sol, the current account deficit grew in 1991, but the capital inflows financed the deficit and still allowed the central bank to accumulate $550 million in foreign currency reserves in the last half of the year (Velarde, 1994, p. 146). The growth in capital inflows slowed the reduction of inflation, but by 1995 consumer price inflation fell to almost 11% and remained there for a few years after (IMF, *IFS*, various years). Peru's reserves have thus been growing in most of the years since the Fujimori reforms.

Some economists, however, can credibly object that the reality of exchange-rate movements belied the government pronouncements of pegging before 1990 and floating after 1990. According to Reinhart and Rogoff (2003b), Peru's exchange rate had been "freely falling" since September 1975 until November 1993. Freely falling exchange rates are characteristic of states with high or hyperinflation. If so, it helps to explain why the shift to an official float engendered little resistance. If the exchange rate was not actually stable under an official peg, it does not lose any stability in abandoning it. Moreover, Reinhart and Rogoff argue that from November 1993 to March 1999, Peru had a de facto crawling band against the dollar. Peru thus exhibited a "fear of floating" after inflation is tamed. According to Yeyati and Sturzenegger (2003), however, Peru had an intermediate regime from 1983 to 1990, and could be classified as either an intermediate regime or a float from 1990 to 2000. Yeyati and Sturzenegger's method, however, does not expressly take inflation into its cluster analysis. Descriptions of the de facto ERR strongly depend on the method used, although considering that Peru suffered from strong inflation, the characterization of a "freely falling" exchange rate prior to 1993 is apt.

Economic conditions in Peru

As with the other cases, it pays to put the economic conditions of Peru in perspective before examining the politics of exchange-rate policy. Inflation, trade patterns, and foreign investment shall be examined in turn. No major changes in these variables explain why Peru switched from pegging to floating when it did.

Inflation

The Peruvian economy has struggled with persistent, high inflation for several years. From 1954 to 1973, when Peru had a pegged exchange rate and mostly followed a liberal and export-based model of development, inflation normally remained below 10% a year. Troubles began in the mid-1970s, with the world economy suffering from inflation and oil shocks and Peru having switched to an import substitution model of development. While consumer price inflation was 9.5% in 1973, it climbed to 16.9% in 1974, then 23.6% in 1975 and up to a height of 66.7% in 1979 (IMF, *IFS*, various years).

The military regime that instituted the import substitution program gave way to a democratic regime. Inflation and balance-of-payments difficulties encouraged the electorate to support a change of economic strategy, and in 1980 they elected the neo-liberal Belaunde administration. Unfortunately, inflation only got worse. After a dip in inflation in 1980 and 1982, inflation soared to 111.65% in 1983. Inflation remained over 100% for the next couple of years (IMF, *IFS*, various years, see Table 6.1). Despite the Belaunde administration's goal to "get prices right," it failed to rein in the government spending that over-stimulated the economy (Beckerman, 1989, p. 122-123). The government, faced with strong competition in municipal elections, hoped to use government spending for the sake of electoral gains (Pastor, 1992, p. 114).

The failure of the neo-liberal program encouraged the swing to Garcia's heterdox program in 1985. As was mentioned above, Garcia hoped to contain inflation with price controls, but increased the government deficit and monetized the debt. After another dip in inflation from 1986 to 1987, hyperinflation exploded from 1988 to 1990. In 1988, inflation was running at 668.0%, climbing to 3392.8% in 1989, and 7489.0% in 1990 (see Table 6.1). In both the Belaunde and Garcia administrations, the crawling peg did not combat inflation but accommodated it.

The Fujimori government focused on the main source of the inflation, the public finances. With a commitment to an orthodox macroeconomic program and with significant popular support for policies to end the hyperinflation, the Fujimori government was more willing and able to raise taxes and lower government spending. Inflation gradually fell to 11.1% in 1995 (IMF, *IFS*, various years). The high inflation of the 1980s and its reduction in the early 1990s largely explain why Reinhart and Rogoff classified Peru's de facto exchange-rate regime as freely falling until 1993. Inflation rates alone, however, do not determine what the official exchange-rate regime will be. Rigidly fixed or pegged exchange rates may be helpful but not necessary for reducing inflation, and Peru demonstrated that even a country with an official floating exchange rate regime could reduce inflation.

GDP and Foreign Trade

Does trade exposure or GDP explain Peru's ERR? The evidence for the case of Peru fits the trade hypothesis of official exchange-rate regimes fairly well. Peru has never been a developed economy or one of Latin America's largest economies. Brazil, Mexico, and Argentina have had larger GDP's for many years (World Bank, *WDI*, various years). But GDP alone hardly explains the persistent use of pegged regimes until 1990, as Peru did not suddenly become a developed economy in the 1980s. What is more important is that Peru has never had much exposure to international trade. Peru's exports and imports were equivalent to 30-42% of GDP between the years of 1975 and 1985.[1] From 1985 to 1995, Peruvian exports and imports were never more than 30% of GDP (See Table 6.1). By the time Peru decided to float its currency in 1990, trade exposure in Peru was equivalent to 24.6% of GDP. Peru's trade exposure is lower than most other middle-income countries. For example, the countries used in the statistical tests have an average trade exposure of 94.75%.

Table 6.1 Economic data on Peru

Year	Real GDP (millions of national currency)	Real GDP Growth (%)	Inflation (CPI)	Exchange Rate (inti or soles /US $)	Trade Exposure
1980	100166.67	4.76	59.48	2.89E-07	41.60
1981	105315.95	5.14	75.41	4.22E-07	36.00
1982	102976.19	-2.22	64.49	6.98E-07	36.07
1983	92857.14	-9.83	111.65	1.63E-06	39.13
1984	97588.65	5.10	109.40	3.47E-06	35.03
1985	100000.00	2.47	163.78	1.10E-05	39.26
1986	110397.55	10.40	77.40	1.39E-05	28.25
1987	119269.10	8.04	86.30	1.68E-05	22.95
1988	108771.93	-8.80	668.38	1.29E-04	28.62
1989	96330.28	-11.44	3392.82	2.67E-03	25.90
1990	92517.01	-3.96	7489.04	0.19	29.61
1991	94680.85	2.34	409.03	0.77	26.67
1992	94339.62	-0.36	73.40	1.25	27.96
1993	98717.95	4.64	48.67	1.99	28.76
1994	111286.68	12.73	23.80	2.20	28.90
1995	121000.00	8.73	11.11	2.25	30.66
1996	123423.42	2.00	12.00	2.45	31.24
1997	131932.77	6.89	8.04	2.66	32.80
1998	131517.26	-0.31	7.32	2.93	31.88
1999	132765.20	0.95	3.47	3.38	31.92
2000	136917.89	3.13	3.76	3.49	33.84

Source: Figures calculated using IMF data, drawn from *International Financial Statistics*, various years.

Table 6.2 More economic data on Peru

Year	Money Multiplier	Credit Ratio	Capital Mobility	TED /GDP	TED/ Exports
1980	2.02	0.74	n.a.	n.a.	n.a.
1981	2.16	1.06	n.a.	n.a.	n.a.
1982	2.16	1.03	n.a.	n.a.	n.a.
1983	2.10	1.05	n.a.	n.a.	n.a.
1984	1.94	0.83	n.a.	n.a.	n.a.
1985	1.61	0.59	n.a.	n.a.	n.a.
1986	1.74	0.66	n.a.	n.a.	n.a.
1987	1.76	0.58	n.a.	n.a.	n.a.
1988	1.93	0.65	n.a.	n.a.	n.a.
1989	2.32	0.85	n.a.	n.a.	n.a.
1990	2.44	0.81	n.a.	n.a.	n.a.
1991	2.91	1.24	n.a.	61.8	617.65
1992	2.61	1.30	2.66	59.3	587.63
1993	2.75	1.50	3.07	63.9	630.51
1994	2.50	1.70	2.28	53.5	521.50
1995	2.52	1.93	0.44	47.9	458.97
1996	2.55	2.12	0.26	45.2	427.19
1997	2.81	2.37	n.a.	31.9	275.00
1998	3.48	3.04	n.a.	34.4	339.81
1999	3.64	2.98	n.a.	37.8	318.70
2000	3.54	2.81	n.a.	35.9	273.25

TED = total external debt
n.a. = not available

Sources: Money multiplier, credit ratio, and capital mobility figures calculated using data from IMF's *International Financial Statistics*. Total external debt figures drawn from the Central Reserve Bank of Peru, which does not supply data before 1991.

The structure of Peru's exports is tilted toward primary rather than manufactured products. In 2000, Peru's total exports totaled just over $7 billion. Of that, almost $3.3 billion came from mineral exports. Fishing and agricultural exports accounted for $1.8 billion. Industrial and other non-traditional exports accounted for $1.4 billion. Oil and its derivatives accounted for $402 million of exports (Central Reserve Bank of Peru, 2001, p. 38). According to some economists, Peru is a good example of a dependent economy (Pastor, 1992, p. 110). Years of import-substitution policies have done little, however, to restructure Peru's exports. Consequently, high commodities prices in world markets would allow Peru to increase its reserves, while low commodities prices would produce current account deficits and provoke devaluations (Dancourt, 1999, pp. 58-59).

But given the economy's relative isolation, Peru could float its currency with little of the disruption to domestic prices that would have afflicted most countries. The decline of trade exposure over time also helps to explain why Peru was more inclined to switch to a float after 1990, and more importantly, to maintain the float. But what the level of trade exposure does not help to explain is the exact timing of the ERR change. Trade exposure was below 30% all during the Garcia administration of 1985-1990, as it was during the Fujimori administration, yet the Garcia administration adhered to the crawling peg. A complete explanation still requires a political story to explain why the Fujimori government adopted a floating exchange rate when it did.

Capital Mobility and Foreign Investment

Under the Garcia administration, capital controls restricted capital movements (IMF, *EAER* 1989, pp. 374-377). Capital outflows required government approval, as did new foreign investments. Repayments of publicly-held external debt were suspended for a time. While foreign-currency accounts were allowed in Peruvian banks, banks could not loan against these funds. With a new neo-liberal program, the Fujimori government removed many of these restrictions (IMF, *EAER* 1992, pp. 381-382). Peru did not restrict capital outflows, although new investments required some percentage of participation from domestic investors. Banks could hold foreign-currency accounts, a hedge against inflation, and loan funds on the basis of these accounts.

The removal of capital controls seems to have increased capital mobility for Peru. Table 6.2 lists the capital mobility indicators for the years 1992 to 1996. The indicator for 1992 represents the average deviation of interest rates from parity from 1988 to 1992. Interest rates were 266.0% off from what they would have been if capital were completely mobile. By 1996, the indicator is down to 25.6%, indicating that capital is relatively more mobile after open capital markets operate from 1992 to 1996. The capital mobility indicator is sensitive to high inflation, so the capital mobility indicator is capturing the convergence in Peruvian and American interest rates as Peruvian hyperinflation is tamed. It also stands to reason, however, that as investors are increasingly allowed to move capital in and out of Peru, and as inflation drops, investors arbitrage interest rates as they have done in other countries. In both Mexico and Peru, capital controls prevent international transactions and the fear of high inflation reduces the incentives investors have to invest. As the Fujimori and Salinas governments tame inflation and remove capital controls, investor confidence revives and investors take advantage of capital mobility to arbitrage interest rates.

Peru, however, switches to a floating exchange rate at the same time that the government removes its capital controls. Mexico only adopted a floating exchange rate some years after it removes its capital controls, and then only under pressure. It may be tempting to think that the Peruvian government might have been consciously applying the hollowing-out thesis to its exchange-rate policy, anticipating that higher capital mobility might create trouble for a pegged exchange rate, and so it adopted a floating exchange rate as part of the policy package. But considering that most of the literature on the hollowing-out thesis only appears in the mid-1990s, after Peru adopts a float, it is unlikely that Peruvian decision-makers were consciously concerned with the warnings of the hollowing-out thesis. The Peruvian government may have been worried that high inflation combined with fewer capital account restrictions could have led to capital flight and a drain on foreign exchange reserves. The experience of Mexico from 1989 to 1993, however, demonstrates that a state with a history of high inflation can have few capital controls and a pegged exchange rate and not experience capital flight, if the government takes credible steps to tame inflation. Mexico, of course, experienced a financial panic in 1994, but that was because investors feared a devalued currency, not resurgent inflation.

Even with a more open capital account, though, Peru does not receive as much foreign investment as its neighbors do. Nevertheless, Peru saw foreign investment grow in absolute terms shortly after Fujimori implemented his program. In 1991, capital account inflows were $38 million dollars. By 1995, capital account inflows stood at just over $3 billion. Capital account inflows have since slowed down to $1.1 billion in 2000 (IMF, *IFS*, various years).

Much of the new foreign investment has been direct investment. In 1990, FDI inflows were $41 million. FDI inflows were just over $2 billion in 1995 and $680 million in 2000 (IMF, *IFS*, various years). Direct investment helped create a new constituency for exchange-rate policy. Foreign owners of Peruvian business assets had a vested interest against depreciation in the Peruvian sol, since these owners profited from remittances, and remittances were more valuable with an over-valued exchange rate (Iguiniz, 1998, p. 32). Since foreign direct investment proliferated only after capital restrictions were removed, however, foreign investors do not explain why Peru officially switched to a float in 1990, but can help explain why Peru maintain de facto exchange-rate stability after 1990.

Since, as will be detailed below, Peru has little in the way of securities markets and nothing in the way of derivatives markets, most capital account transactions that are not direct investment are in the form of loans rather than portfolio investment. Moreover, the government, not private banks and businesses, has historically been the main recipient of foreign loans. In the late 1960s and 1970s, the Peruvian government borrowed heavily from abroad to finance government projects (Dancourt, 1999, p. 56), only later to be caught in a balance-of-payments crisis in 1975 and 1976. 89% of the money banks lent to the government in the 1970s was denominated in dollars (Devlin, 1981, p. 162). Thanks to the lending boom and debt crisis, from 1973 to 1986 public external debt was significantly more than private external debt. By 1982, public external debt was $6.8 billion while private external debt was $1.7 billion (Central Reserve Bank of Peru, quoted in Beckerman, 1989, p. 117). By 1989 the ratio of Peru's external debt to its exports was 420%, higher than all other Latin American countries except Nicaragua, Argentina, and Bolivia (Larrain and Sachs, 1991, pg. 228).

Multilateral lending agencies provided some of the loans to the government, but much of the government's debt financing came from bilateral sources and, increasingly, from foreign private banks. In the 1975-76 balance-of-payments crisis, the government owed $259 million to multilateral agencies, but owed $825 million in bilateral agreements and $1.32 billion to foreign private banks. By 1982, the government owed $949 million to multilateral agencies, $1.2 billion in bilateral agreements, and almost $2 billion to foreign private banks (Central Reserve Bank of Peru, quoted in Beckerman, 1989, p. 117). Thus, the government held a greater stock of dollar-denominated debt before the switch to floating than private banks did and foreign banks had more direct lending ties with the government than with Peru's private banks. Multilateral lending agencies, however, performed the important function (by approving new loans) of signaling to private international banks when Peru was an acceptable risk after experiencing a crisis.

After Fujimori implemented a neo-liberal program and inflation declined, foreign investors became interested in Peru again. As in Mexico, private agents only became the primary recipients of foreign loans after the government reduced its budget deficit and removed capital controls. From 1994 to 1997, banks received more in foreign loans than the government did, which they did not do before 1990.[2] Peru also received foreign portfolio investment, both in the form of equity and debt, now that capital controls were not a barrier, although direct investment and bank loans still counted for more (IMF, *IFS*, various years). The government meanwhile increased repayments on its external debt and took on less debt as a result of tighter budgets. Total external debt both relative to GDP and exports declined after 1990 (see Table 6.2), improving Peru's credibility with the international community.

Comparisons with other cases help to summarize the main points about Peru's foreign investment patterns and their relation to exchange-rate policy. In Thailand, private actors held most of the stock of external debt in the years before the Asian financial crisis. In both Peru and Mexico, the government held at least two-thirds of the stock of external debt before each of these states floated.[3] In Latin America, of course, governments borrowed heavily in the 1970s and spent much of the 1980s and some of the 1990s paying back debt, while Thailand did not. Mexico opened up to foreign private investment while maintaining its peg and thus foreign investors became stakeholders in Mexico's exchange-rate policy. Peru, however, floated before receiving significant amounts of private inflows and thus foreign investors and private banks holding external debt played much less of a role in the policy change.

The financial system

Low levels of financial intermediation characterize Peru's financial system, especially compared with other developing countries like Thailand or even other Latin American countries like Mexico, Brazil, or Argentina. Like Colombia, which will be detailed in Chapter 7, Peru has a modest banking system and little in the way of capital markets. Government regulation stunted the development of the banking sector in the 1980s. Only after neo-liberal reforms in the 1990s did banks in Peru begin to grow, but Peru's banking sector is still not as strong as Mexico's. Much of the growth in banks during the 1990s, however, depended on inflows of foreign bank loans described in the previous section.

In the 1980s, commercial banks and development banks dominated Peru's banking sector. Commercial banks accounted for only 33.9% of the assets of all financial institutions in 1987, one of the lowest percentages in Latin America. Just over half of commercial bank assets were in the hands of government-owned banks, while domestic private banks accounted for less than half (Morris, et. al, 1990, p. 2). The rest of Peru's financial assets (66.1%) were in the hands of development banks, which direct credit mostly to agriculture, housing, and targeted industries, along with other forms of non-commercial banking such as pension funds or regional banks (Morris, et. al, 1990, pp. 2-3). The government controlled many of these development banks, making most of the banking sector in Peru publicly controlled in the 1980s. The Velasco government had nationalized much of the banking system in the 1970s. In 1987, President Garcia attempted to nationalize what banks remained in private hands as part of a program to encourage further investment and gain leverage of Peru's business groups, a program that was blocked in the courts (Pastor, 1992, p. 126).

In addition to government ownership of most of the banking sector, the government also employed extensive regulations on the banking sector to achieve political goals, such as high reserve requirements and low interest rate ceilings. In 1987, an average of 58% of demand, savings, and time deposits in commercial banks were kept on reserve with the central bank (Morris, et. al, 1990, p. 46; Rojas-Suarez and Weisbrod, 1995, p. 18). High reserve requirements were one of the few tools the government had to try to combat inflation, as Peru did not have a well developed market for public debt. The central bank offered better interest rates on reserves, which in turn encouraged banks to keep their capital in accounts with the central bank rather than lend it (Rojas-Suarez and Weisbrod, 1995, p. 18). Peru's high requirements were strikingly higher than most other Latin American countries, which had lowered reserve requirements to encourage lending in the 1970s. As a consequence, high reserve requirements limited bank lending in Peru in the 1970s and 1980s and commercial and development banks had a higher than average ratio of capital to assets going into 1982 (Rojas-Suarez and Weisbrod, 1995, p. 18). Peru also had fewer non-performing loans (NPL's) than other states if only because it had fewer total loans.

Nevertheless, high reserve requirements arguably laid some of the groundwork for a problematic monetary expansion in the 1980s. High reserve requirements limited the extent to which banks offered loans, and this may have contributed to the erosion of abilities in evaluating lending risks over time. As the Garcia administration expanded domestic credit after 1985, loans grew and with them the growth of NPL's (Rojas-Suarez and Weisbrod, 1995, p. 23). The central bank paid little regard to credit risks while expanding lending. Inflation turned into hyperinflation in 1988. Interest rates became even more negative and the official financial system lost even more access to savings, causing a crisis in Peruvian finance.

The government also maintained interest rate ceilings, typically to encourage lending for domestic production. Low interest rates and high inflation, however, produced negative real interest rates that discouraged savings and capital accumulation. The government also imposed credit quotas to geographical regions within Peru and to specific industrial sectors (Hamann and Paredes, 1991, p. 57). Consequently, the banking system did not encourage the most efficient allocation of capital. Informal credit markets grew to offer dollar-denominated accounts and interest rates that would attract deposits (Hamann and Paredes, 1991, p. 57; World Bank, 1989, p. 83). While documentary evidence on informal financial markets was difficult to establish, the nominal rate of return for dollars in 1987 was higher than the deposit rate for Peruvian inti and the rate of inflation. This caused upward pressure on the black market rate for dollars and indicated a strong demand for black market banking operations (World Bank, 1989, p. 83).

The effects of interest rate ceilings, directed credit, and high reserve ratios show up in the low measures of Peruvian financial intermediation in the 1980s (see Table 6.2). The money multiplier was at 2.16 in 1982 and falls to 1.76 in 1987 and 1.93 in 1988, well below 5.55, the average in the statistical sample used in chapter 3. The credit ratio followed a similar path, beginning at 1.03 in 1982 and falling to 0.58 in 1987 and 0.65 in 1988. For other developing states examined in the statistical tests, the average credit ratio was 4.45. Other measures of financial intermediation, such as the ratio of M2 to GDP also show how disintermediated Peru's financial system was compared to other developing states. M2/GDP in Peru begins at 12.7% in 1980 and falls to a low of 9.9% in 1985 before rising to 12.8% in 1987. For most Latin American states, M2/GDP averages between 20.0% and 22.4% during that period (Morris et. al, 1990, p. 10). Latin American financial systems, furthermore, were already relatively disintermediated compared to the rest of the world in the 1980s.

After the neoliberal reforms of the 1990s, financial intermediation in Peru begins to improve, but still remains below averages in other states. The money multiplier rose from 2.44 in 1990 to 3.54 in 2000. Change in the money multiplier was volatile in the hyperinflationary years of the late 1980s and the contractionary years of the early 1990s. After 1994, however, growth in the money multiplier continued at a slow and steady pace (Central Reserve Bank of Peru, 1998, p. 52). After the banking reforms and the loosening of reserve requirements, most of the growth in money multiplier in the 1990s was due to increased preferences for using cash in financial intermediation rather than changes in reserve requirements (Central Reserve Bank of Peru, 2001, p. 72). The credit ratio rose from 0.81 in 1990 to 2.87 in 2000. Much of the credit to the private sector was denominated in dollars, as described below (Central Reserve Bank of Peru, 2001, p. 73). Neo-liberal reforms allowing for market interest rates and allocation of credit based on profit considerations, along with reductions in inflation improved real interest rates and financial intermediation. Peru, however, still relied on foreign lending and investment more than domestic savings during the 1990s.

Thanks to the dollarization of the financial system (the substitution of foreign currency for domestic currency) in the 1980s and 1990s, this reliance on foreign investment reduced worries among the domestic banks about external debt repayment. As inflation ate away at the purchasing power of Peruvian currency and the role of the cocaine trade grew in Peru's economy, more and more Peruvians began to use U.S. dollars. Foreign currency deposits grew from 46% of all bank deposits in 1982 to 61% in 1984 (Rojas-Suarez and Weisbrod, 1995, p. 18). After 1994, Peruvians began to spend and deposit dollars saved up during the inflationary years and more foreign investment poured in (Dancourt, 1999, p. 64). By 1996, 75% of all deposits and 74% of all loans were denominated in foreign currency (Iguiniz, 1998, p. 32). Thanks to dollarization, the central bank saw a considerable accumulation in net international reserves and the expansion of domestic credit to the private sector led to the increase in foreign liabilities for non-financial firms (Dancourt, 1999, p. 64). Moreover, the dollar-denominated debt Peruvian banks owed to foreign banks carried little exchange-rate risk when most domestic lending was also denominated in dollars.

Dollarization imposed significant restraints on the central bank's ability to use exchange-rate policy. According to the Mundell-Fleming model, the central bank retains control over the supply of domestic currency with a floating exchange rate, and loses control with a fixed exchange rate, given that capital mobility was rising in Peru. In 1990, Peru switched to an official float, but in practice it was little different from a crawling peg after 1993 (Reinhart and Rogoff, 2003). The problem for the central bank was that even with truly independent float, the dollarization of three-quarters of the financial system left only one quarter of the financial system under the control of the central bank. The supply of dollars would respond to conditions for international capital movements outside the central bank's control, meaning that the central bank could not control the aggregate supply of credit. The foreign liabilities of banks and non-bank firms also makes it difficult for the central bank to intervene in foreign exchange markets by engineering a devaluation or a real exchange rate depreciation, as this makes debt repayment more difficult (Dancourt, 1999, pp. 64-65).

Peru's banking sector in the 1980s was not as concentrated as more developed systems in Thailand and Mexico. As was mentioned above, commercial banks held only 33.9% of financial assets in 1987, while most of the assets were in the hands of public development banks. The development banks served many different sectors and regions of the country, preventing assets from becoming concentrated in a few banks (see Morris, et. al, 1990, p. 3). From 1987 to 1990, the number of banks grew. The reforms of the Fujimori period, however, tended to promote concentration, and the number of banks fell from 23 to 17 between 1990 and 1993 (Iguiniz, 1998, p. 31). But by 1996, the number of banks had rebounded to their original level.

Peru has also never had well-developed capital markets. At the end of 1989, before the move to floating exchange rates, the capitalization of Lima's stock market was $931 million. Even in January 1998, well after Fujimori's reforms increased savings and investment, capitalization amounted to $17.4 billion, which was too small to allow Peru to rank in the top forty stock markets of the world (IFC, 1999, p. 272). Argentina's stock market, which ranked 31st that year, had a capitalization of $45.3 billion. The total value of shares traded was $90 million in 1989 and $352 million in 1998. In 1998, the total value of shares traded in Mexico was $33.8 billion and $15.1 billion in Argentina in 1998 (IFC, 1999, p. 24 & 272-3). Low interest rates, the lack of transparency in corporate reporting, and the lack of protection for minority stockholders explains some of the underdevelopment in the stock market during the 1980s (Hamann and Paredes, 1991, p. 57). Peru also did not have markets for trading government bonds or other forms of public debt in the 1980s. Consequently, Peru has relied mostly on its underdeveloped banking system for financing.

Banks, business, and politics

The Peruvian banking system, then, had no power to lobby against a shift to floating exchange rates in the early 1990s. Financial intermediation in the formal banking sector was low, giving the banking system a weaker role in the economy. The private commercial banks were a fraction of the banking system, sharing the field with publicly-owned commercial and development banks. Combined with relatively low levels of concentration in the banking system compared to Thailand and Mexico, Peruvian commercial banks faced more difficulties organizing for collective action. Moreover, banks could not organize to resist the interest rate regulations or high reserve requirements that stunted the growth of banking. Nor did the domestic banks have much interest in lobbying for the maintenance of a pegged exchange rate. As was mentioned above, Peru received fewer foreign loans than other Latin American countries did and the hyperinflation of the late 1980s scared off many foreign investors. Consequently

Peruvian banks were not laboring under a heavy burden of dollar-denominated debt.

What role, if any, did other interest groups or institutions play in the formation of exchange-rate policy? Foreign banks had exercised influence over Peruvian economic policy in the 1960s and 1970s, but that influence had waned by the 1980s. Peru's government once relied on foreign bank loans to finance budget deficits. Against economic troubles in the late 1960s, a military coup in 1968 brought a government nationalization program. The new government avoided going to the IMF and negotiated with foreign private banks to refinance their loans. The foreign banks agreed to do so only under condition that the new government keep to a strict repayment schedule and avoid contracting new debt in the near future (Devlin, 1981, p. 161). At the time, the foreign banks were more concerned with debt servicing and the nationalization program than with Peru's exchange-rate policy. In the early 1970s, however, foreign banks began to lavish funds on developing countries as the banks acquired access to petrodollars and banks became more interested in lending to Peru after oil was discovered in the country (Devlin, 1981, p. 162; Pasco-Font and Ghezzi, 2001, p. 253). Despite the earlier restrictions on the government, foreign banks extended credit to Peru without condition from 1972 to 1975, allowing the government to refinance its debt again (Devlin, 1981, p. 166). Banks became more cautious after 1976 when Peru experienced another devaluation. During the 1970s, Citibank used its clout to acquire more rights to the domestic banking market and Chase Manhattan used its clout to wring a concession over tax law for a client mining corporation (Riner, 1982, p. 14). When the Garcia government suspended debt repayment in the late 1980s, however, foreign banks were mostly concerned with repayments. The government turned to domestic sources of finance, making it less dependent on foreign banks, reducing their influence over policy.

Did manufacturing industries lobby for a specific ERR? Between 1981 and 1985, manufacturing accounted for about 36% of Peru's GDP, which fell to a range between 15 to 17% from 1990 to 2003 (World Bank, WDI, various years). Considering that the average percentage for manufacturing is 19.5% for the countries used in the statistical tests, Peru had a relatively strong manufacturing sector for a developing country, which falls to just below average during and after the Fujimori administration. On the surface, it seems that manufacturers should have been pressuring for a floating exchange rate during the 1980s.

Alberto Pasco-Font and Piero Ghezzi (2001), however, perform statistical tests on the manufacturing hypothesis that Frieden and Stein (2001) proposed. Pasco-Font and Ghezzi take a more nuanced approach to the hypothesis and argue that manufacturing interests will prefer a flexible and depreciating exchange rate if trade protection is low and a fixed and appreciating exchange rate if protection is high, since protection orients manufacturing to a domestic market. They run an ordered-logit test on time-series data from Peru, whose exchange-rate history since 1950 includes adjustable pegs, crawling pegs, free fall, managed and independent floating. Their independent variables include proxies for the share of GDP produced by manufacturing and a variable that interacts manufacturing's share of GDP with the average tariff rate to account for the manufacturing sector's preferences under different levels of protection. According to their results, when tariffs are high, a greater share of manufacturing correlates with some form of fixed exchange rate. Indicators for mining or agricultural exports do not have a significant correlation with the ERR. Pasco-Font and Ghezzi (2001, p. 273) note that with the military government of the late-1960s, the nationalization program dismantled private export groups, preventing exporters of primary products from having an organized voice. Presumably then, manufacturing interests had their interests addressed with the protective tariffs of the late 1980s and the flexible exchange rate of the early 1990s after the Fujimori government lowered tariff barriers. Admittedly, time-series statistical tests with data from one country do not provide evidence that the manufacturing firms lobbied the government for these policies or that any such lobbying was the critical factor in the government's decisions. Pasco-Font and Ghezzi do, however, provide some case study evidence that Peru's move from floating to a pegged exchange rate in the late 1950s was partly the result of a movement to industrialize the country according to an ISI paradigm (2001, pp. 270-271).

Democracy and the politics of central banking, however, do not adequately explain the transition to a floating exchange rate. According to the Polity IV database, Peru had a democracy and policy score of 7 and 8 respectively out of a possible 10 in the years from 1980 to 1991, which include the freely elected Belaunde and Garcia administrations, and the first year of the Fujimori administration. Peru's polity score drops to -3 in 1992 as Fujimori instigated an autogolpe (palace coup) by closing the legislature and firing members of the Supreme Court, in order to remove resistance to his plans to strengthen the military. In 1993, Fujimori introduces a new constitution that allows for elections but strengthens executive power, which raises Peru's polity score to 1. Just based on these events, it seems as if Peru should have made a transition from a floating exchange rate to a pegged exchange rate instead.

The heart of the transparency hypothesis, however, is the claim that states choose between independent central banks and fixed exchange rates as mechanisms for establishing credibility in fighting inflation. The problem with the Peruvian case is that Peru did not credibly employ either mechanism to fight inflation in the 1980s. According to Cukierman, the rate of turnover in central bank governors in Peru was 0.33 from 1950 to 1989, or about one change every three years, the highest rate of all four countries studied in this book. Peru had six different central bank governors between 1980 and 1992.[4] Mid-level staff, which held relatively conservative views on monetary policy, found that they had to answer to a small clique of heterodox policy planners (Pastor, 1992, p. 127). Central bankers were monetizing fiscal deficits in the late 1980s, especially after the Garcia administration cut itself off from foreign lending. Exchange rates were officially pegged during this time, but subject to numerous devaluations. Anti-inflationary credibility collapsed as hyperinflation ravaged the economy in the late 1980s.

Fujimori's tight monetary policy after 1990 might have been an opportunity to improve central bank independence and signal a determination to improve credibility and creditworthiness. The autogolpe, however, demonstrated that Fujimori had little desire to release the central bank or any government functions from political control.

Domestic politics and international pressures

Why then did Peru adopt a float when it did? As with Thailand and Mexico, the pressure to float came from international sources. With Thailand and Mexico, however, the international pressures were those described in the hollowing-out thesis, the pressures of capital mobility overwhelming a government's ability to defend its peg. Peru adopted its float at the same time that it opened its financial market to international capital. International pressure to float came instead from the World Bank, which recommended a float as part of a comprehensive overhaul of the Peruvian economy. The Garcia administration, which had restricted foreign loan repayment, had demonstrated that the Peruvian government could resist pressures from multilateral lending agencies. By 1990, however, no domestic groups or institutions were defending the pegged exchange rate, and consequently international pressures had no resistance in determining ERR policy. Why? The reasons for the absence of domestic counter-pressures are more understandable when examining the political foundations of the Garcia administration, the 1990 election, and the first year of the Fujimori administration.

Garcia came to power in 1985 due to his charisma and his ability to appeal to different social classes (Mauceri, 1996, pp. 60-61). By 1985, Peru was still suffering from inflation and economic stagnation, and many Peruvians blamed Belaunde's neoliberal economic policies. Alan Garcia led a movement to revive the APRA party after a painful defeat in 1980, quickly rising to prominence on the basis of his rhetorical abilities and the close relationship he had with the party's founder, Victor Haya de Torra, before Haya de Torra died. Garcia's youth and charisma played well in an election campaign against the older and unpopular Belaunde. APRA's populist message had competition from the more radical United Left (Izquierda Unida). But while the United Left campaigned for redistribution, Garcia presented APRA as a force for unifying business and labor against foreign demands for debt repayment and government corruption. He also spoke of investment for business as well as government help for the poor. Thus of all the leftist leaders, Garcia was the least offensive to the middle class and had a wider appeal.

Consequently, for the first two years of his administration Garcia designed his economic policies along a heretodox strategy to move away from the neo-liberalism of the Belaunde administration and crafts the strategy to have appeal to both labor and business groups. To please labor groups, Garcia engineered increases in wages and farm incomes. This he also hoped would raise aggregate demand to combat poor economic growth (Pastor, 1992, p. 125). To please business groups, the government reduced its investment, ostensibly to release capital for private investment. Garcia introduced multiple exchange rates to encourage imports of machinery and also encourage exports (Mauceri, 1996, p. 62; Beckerman, 1989, p. 134). Garcia also introduced a package of tax credits, subsidies, and lower interest rates to stimulate private investment. In return, businesses were expected to reinvest their profits and produce a cycle of investment that would sustain an economic take-off. According to Philip Mauceri (1996, p. 62), the tax credits and subsidies also worked in practice to supply clients with favors and encourage business to support the regime. Garcia also engaged in regular talks with the twelve largest business groups, called the "twelve apostles" in order to persuade them that wage increases need not be a threat to their interests and cement a working relationship with business interests (Pastor, 1992, p. 126; Mauceri, 1996, p. 63).

Representatives of business and labor, however, had little input into the economic policymaking process. Garcia surrounded himself with small group of technocratic advisors who drew up plans without consultation from business or labor groups. Garcia and his team would often reveal policy in bold, surprising moves to the public (Thorndike, 1988). Bureaucrats who disagreed with Garcia's measures, such as those in the central bank, often carried out their directives with "less than full enthusiasm" (Pastor, 1992, p. 127). Such a decision-making style also alienated labor groups, some of which followed the United Left's call to strike in May 1987 to protest stagnating wages and Garcia's relations with business groups (Pastor, 1992, p. 126; Mauceri, 1996, p. 63).

Garcia, furthermore, alienated business interests shortly afterward. Garcia had become increasingly upset with what he saw as the slow pace of reinvestment in the Peruvian economy. In July 1987 Garcia suddenly announced his attempt to nationalize the remaining private banks as a way of stemming capital flight and acquiring leverage over the "twelve apostles." Unfortunately for Garcia, the surprise move ruptured his relations with the business community without improving his standing with workers and the poor (Beckerman, 1989, p. 136; Pastor, 1992, p. 126; Mauceri, 1996, p. 66). United Left supported nationalization in principle but criticized what it saw as the potential for APRA to abuse power. The middle class and right-wing parties, by contrast, campaigned to invalidate the nationalization of the banks in the courts and cast Garcia as a totalitarian threat in the media.

Meanwhile, tax cuts and poor tax collection hurt the government's revenues. To cover the government's expansionist program of spending, the government could not borrow much from a weak banking sector and, thanks to the limits on external debt repayment, could not borrow from abroad either (see World Bank, 1989, p. xv). The government increasingly resorted to printing money, which turned inflation into hyperinflation despite government price controls, alienating business and the mass public further. By the first seven months of 1988, the annual rate of inflation was 535% (World Bank, 1989, p. xv) increasing further in 1989. In the logic of the election hypothesis, governments fear offending voters with a loss of purchasing power in the run up to an election, so governments tend to avoid devaluations or floatations during that time. These circumstances do not apply to the Peruvian election of 1990, however. Hyperinflation had already eroded the purchasing power of those who held Peruvian currency and citizens responded by dollarizing their economy. Whether or not the economy could have benefited from a true exchange-rate stabilization program, in most people's view the pegged exchange rate did nothing to fight hyperinflation. Consequently, neither the middle nor working class provided a constituency for defending a peg.

The contenders for the Peruvian presidency included APRA's Garcia, attempting to defend his job from a weakened position. United Left campaigned on a more hard left position and had the advantage of support from labor unions that could mobilize votes. Both parties, however, competed with left-wing Shining Path guerillas for the support of the poor, and confronted a prevailing mood of frustration with traditional parties among ordinary voters. On the right, the novelist Mario Vargas Llosa represented the Democratic Front (Fredemo) coalition, preaching a "shock therapy" that would re-introduce a comprehensive neo-liberal strategy quickly. Alberto Fujimori, then a relatively unknown bureaucrat backed by a party of his own making (Cambio 90), proposed a more gradual neo-liberal program. Fujimori's campaign slogan was "work, honesty, and technology" and part of his appeal was the vagueness of his policy proposals in contrast to the stricter ideological specifics offered by Vargas Llosa (Graham, 1994, p. 4; Crabtree, 1998, p. 15).

Private banks, commercial firms, and the middle-class predictably threw their support to right-wing candidates after the rupture of relations with Garcia. Most parties, including APRA, recognized a need to reduce tariffs and subsidies, rationalize the tax system, and allow the exchange rate to fall (Iguiniz, 1998, p. 28), they largely differed on the questions of timing and emphasis. For banks and business interests, the most important issues concerned economic strategy and the bank nationalization program, rather than exchange-rate policy.

In the first round of elections, Vargas Llosa came in first, with Fujimori second. In the second round runoff, Fujimori's relatively more centrist program attracted more support from leftist and centrist voters, and he won with 56.5% of the vote (Graham, 1994, p. 4; Mauceri, 1996, p. 73).

Once in office, Fujimori quickly implemented the kind of shock therapy program he had argued against in the campaign. Notably, he also made a floating exchange rate part of his anti-inflation policies. Many inflation stabilization programs utilize a rigidly fixed rate to a low-inflation anchor currency, such as Argentina's currency board or Ecuador's monetary union with the U.S. Why did Fujimori choose to employ a floating exchange rate? A 1989 World Bank report of the Peruvian economy probably influenced Fujimori's choice. At the time, Fujimori needed to negotiate with the IMF for relief from external debt payments and the IMF drew on World Bank research to formulate its prescriptions for Peru (Iguiniz, 1998, p. 29). The World Bank report argued that both a floating exchange rate and a crawling peg were viable regimes. But the authors concluded that given the loss of government control over fiscal and monetary variables plus depleted reserves of foreign exchange, "a floating rate would probably be a superior and more credible policy approach" (World Bank, 1989, p. xx). According to some observers, Fujimori had few options once in office (Graham, 1994, p.4; Mauceri, 1996, p. 80-81; Crabtree, 1998, p. 16). The IMF and international financiers would only re-invest in Peru if Fujimori implemented an orthodox stabilization program, and the lack of foreign exchange reserves and credibility among investors made a new pegged exchange-rate policy unworkable. Floating while tightening fiscal and monetary policy was the only option left.

Fujimori had considerable autonomy within Peru to impose a neo-liberal program without major opposition. First, many people expected that hyperinflation would require harsh measures and were willing to accept some short-term economic pain for a chance at long-run stability and growth. Second, the terrorism of the Shining Path guerillas in Peru may have made protests against the government suspect in the eyes of some, making many wary of taking to the streets (Graham, 1994, p. 4). Third, political parties in Peru had been weakened (Graham 1994, p. 4; Mauceri 1996, pp. 82-83). As mentioned above, APRA and the United Left had a difficult time commanding popular support. Vargas Llosa and the Democratic Front could not broaden their appeal beyond the urban middle class. Fujimori's political party was simply a vehicle for his election. The weaknesses of the poltical parties were a double-edged sword for Fujimori. On the one hand, the weakness of the opposition gave Fujimori less resistance to his policies. On the other hand, Fujimori did not have a political party that he could use to build long-term political support, leaving him potentially politically isolated.

Without a strong political party, Fujimori relied at first on his broad electoral support and his support from technocratic advisers and business to implement his programs. The majority of both houses of the legislature belonged to opposition parties, and provided what political resistance he got in the first years of his rule. As Fujimori got more resistance from the legislature, he relied more and more on the military to govern (Mauceri, 1996, p. 81). In 1992, Fujimori and his military allies overthrew the democratic order and instituted a new authoritarian government. Interestingly, Fujimori did not rely on institutional measures such as independent central banks or a powerful domestic financial sector to maintain credibility among international investors, but simply relied on his reputation as a neo-liberal reformer. Considering that his shock therapy program and palace coups were deviations from his campaign promises, this seems to indicate that Fujimori gained credibility simply for paying the costs of adjusting the economy to a neo-liberal program. The floating exchange rate and the neo-liberal program continued well into the 1990s without political resistance while Fujimori exercised authoritarian rule. The central bank reduced inflation through a policy of monetary targets during his rule. So while Peru officially maintained a policy of floating during this period, the relatively slow growth of the domestic money supply in both Peru and the U.S. encouraged little change in the real exchange rate for most of the 1990s. Peru could maintain an exchange rate that was little different from a crawling peg, a policy that has advantages in bringing price stability to a highly dollarized economy.

Conclusions

Peru switched to a floating exchange rate in 1990 largely due to a combination of international pressure from multilateral lending agencies and a change in political administration. Hyperinflation in the late 1980s prompted much of the pressure from multilateral lending agencies for a neo-liberal program and a willingness in the public to shift support to anti-incumbent parties in the 1990 election. Included in the neo-liberal program was a shift to a floating exchange rate. Thanks to dollarization, a floating currency had little effect on those with dollar-denominated assets. Domestic banks in the late 1980s and 1990s faced little exchange-rate risk as they both borrowed and lent in dollars. Peru's private sector had little outstanding external debt compared to other Latin American states in any case. For those working with Peruvian currency, the freely falling value of the exchange rate was the major concern, and whether the currency was officially pegs or floating mattered little to the value of the currency. The banking sector was also less developed and less organized than in other states. Thus the banking sector had little reason and little power to oppose the move to a float. Many manufacturers had their interests accommodated with the high tariffs of the 1980s, and when those were abolished, the floating exchange rate and inflation targeting helped to steady the real exchange rate. Given the political weakness or lack of interest concerning the exchange rate among most interest groups and political parties in Peru, the introduction of a floating exchange rate faced little opposition in Peru in the early 1990s.

Other hypotheses discussed here do not contribute as much to the explanation. Peru's small GDP does not justify a float, but its relatively small exposure to trade does make floating a viable option in the eyes of many economists. Peru's insulation from foreign trade, however, has persisted through several administrations and does not explain the timing of the shift. Increasing capital mobility does not explain the shift, as Peru opened up its financial markets to capital mobility only as it adopted the float. The hollowing-out thesis, however, does help explain why increasing capital mobility in the 1990s did not provoke an exchange-rate crisis in Peru, as Peru had no peg that could lose credibility.

Aside from economic variables, democracy and elections also fail to explain adequately the switch to floating. Even though Peru was a democracy in the 1980s, it displayed little evidence of an independent central bank or commitment to combating inflation. Meanwhile, it officially maintained a pegged exchange rate. An elected Fujimori administration worked to combat hyperinflation and introduced monetary targets and a floating exchange, but the floating exchange rate persisted in spite of a palace coup and any damage this caused to Fujimori's credibility. Peru's 1990 election was also a rare case where an election provided politicians with little incentive to defend a peg, as hyperinflation was eroding the value of the currency and the peg was not ameliorating the problem for many voters.

Notes

[1] Data for trade exposure is calculated from IMF data in *International Financial Statistics*, various years.
[2] The data is listed under "Other Investment Liabilities" in the capital account. See IMF, *IFS*, various years.
[3] This information can be found in World Bank, *Global Development Finance*, various years.
[4] This information is drawn from the De Haan and Kooi's (1998) data.

Chapter 7

Colombia

In the three previous chapters, the cases followed the logic of the financial intermediation hypothesis. Thailand and Mexico persisted in pegging even when this put them in danger of an exchange-rate crisis. In Peru the financial system was less developed and politicians faced less resistance in introducing a floating exchange rate. But many developing countries have small banking sectors and yet have pegged for a substantial time. Many Muslim states in the Middle East, such as Jordan, Saudi Arabia, Syria, Iraq, and Iran have pegged their currencies to the U.S. dollar or to the IMF's Special Drawing Rights, but have underdeveloped financial markets. All of these countries, except Jordan, earn much of their foreign exchange through oil exports, which are denominated in U.S. dollars in world markets. Hence, many of these states have an incentive to peg their exchange rates in order to maintain price stability. More importantly, all of these states have little or no exposure to international capital markets. Their reserves of U.S. dollars are not exposed to sudden changes in the demand for currencies. Consequently, hollowing-out pressures and the costs of pegging have remained small for these states, and it is easier for them to continue pegging. This indicates why the financial intermediation hypothesis applies best to states with some exposure to international capital markets.

Besides oil-dependent Middle Eastern states, other states such as Colombia and Sri Lanka have also maintained a peg for many years despite having underdeveloped banks. Colombia in particular is a puzzle, having maintained a peg or a band from 1967 to 1999. First, whether Colombia is exposed to high capital mobility depends on how it is measured. Colombia's underground economy of narcotics is probably responsible for confusing measurements of capital flows in and out of Colombia. But to the extent that Colombia is exposed to high capital mobility, why did it maintain a peg until 1999 when it did not have a strong banking sector advocating a peg?

Colombia presents two different stories of a state that maintained intermediate exchange rate targets far longer than one might predict. In the first story, which lasts from 1967 to 1994, three conditions reduced the likelihood of exchange-rate crises in Colombia. These conditions allowed Colombia to withstand hollowing-out pressures when capital was mobile. First, Colombia had capital controls on foreign exchange until the early 1990s. These controls did not necessarily reduce capital mobility in Colombia, but as long as capital flows were bypassing the official channels, the central bank and the official exchange rate were insulated from some of the volatility in currency trading. Second, the ERR the Colombians employed after 1994 was a crawling band with a wide margin. Third, until the mid-1990s, Colombia's foreign exchange reserves managed to grow fairly consistently, allowing it to absorb sudden shocks to the foreign exchange market. On those occasions when currency markets tested its exchange-rate commitments, Colombia had the foreign-exchange reserves needed to survive the test.

Most of the resulting exchange rate politics in Colombia during this period focused on the value of the exchange rate rather than the choice of exchange-rate regime. From 1967 to 1991, the political system supported a crawling peg that usually depreciated the real exchange rate. This policy was the result of a closed two-party political system that catered to export industries such as the coffee industry. As Colombia's industry diversified and the political system opened up to new interest groups, a new political foundation allowed a shift to a policy of real exchange-rate appreciation and neo-liberalism.

The second story begins in 1994, as the government maintains a crawling band in the face of growing hollowing-out pressures. As it opens up to capital flows and the real exchange rate appreciates, Colombia falls into a familiar trap of attracting destabilizing capital inflows. Once a recession developed and investors lost confidence in Colombia and its peso, the government faced a test of its resolve to maintain the band, until the government finally adopted a managed float in 1999. Banks were less involved in pressuring the government to maintain the band, but instead other conditions concerning elections and credibility were relevant here. Colombia demonstrates the limits of the financial intermediation hypothesis.

The following sections detail the argument outlined above. The second section details capital mobility and exchange-rate policy in Colombia in an effort to examine the elements of the puzzle. The third section examines trade exposure, GDP, and financial intermediation, which can help explain the persistence of pegging in other states but not in Colombia. The fourth section will examine the three factors listed above, illegal capital flows, the crawling band, and foreign exchange reserves, which do explain its ability to avoid hollowing-out pressures until 1994. The final sections will examine the political foundations underlying exchange-rate policy in Colombia. They examine how Colombia moved from a crawling peg that gradually devalued the peso to a crawling band regime that let the peso appreciate, and how the crawling band eventually fell apart.

The nature of the problem

Capital Mobility

Table 7.1 lists measures for capital mobility in Colombia along with measures for other economic variables. Colombian data on interest rates only begins in 1986. This yields indicators for capital mobility for ten years under analysis here, from 1990 to 1999.[1] The available calculations for Colombia show that interest rates for

Table 7.1 Economic data on Colombia

Year	Real GDP Growth	Inflation (CPI)	Exchange Rate (pesos/ US $)	Trade Exposure	Capital Mobility
1985	2.16	24.04	142.31	26.33	n.a.
1986	6.57	18.88	194.26	30.83	n.a.
1987	5.06	23.30	242.61	29.87	n.a.
1988	3.80	28.11	299.17	30.14	n.a.
1989	3.49	25.84	382.57	31.82	n.a.
1990	4.55	29.14	502.26	35.39	23.1
1991	2.02	30.39	633.05	35.25	24.4
1992	3.86	27.03	759.28	33.47	24.4
1993	5.42	22.61	863.07	35.19	24.1
1994	5.91	23.84	844.84	35.92	24.5
1995	5.15	20.96	912.83	35.50	24.3
1996	2.03	20.24	1036.69	36.04	23.3
1997	3.50	18.89	1140.96	35.60	22.3
1998	0.57	20.36	1426.04	35.91	23.1
1999	-4.20	11.22	1756.23	36.15	21.3

All figures are in percentages except for the exchange rate.

Sources: International Monetary Fund and World Bank.

90-day deposits in Colombia diverged from interest rates on similar deposits in the U.S. by an average of 24.5% by 1994 to 21.3% by 1999. These figures are well above the five percent average typical for the other states measured using this indicator. It may simply be that like the Middle Eastern states, Colombia has been able to peg for a long time because the global financial system imposed relatively few costs on it. Five-year averages in the divergence of interest rates did not decline by much during this period. Note a couple of caveats, however. First, the five-year averages, which are designed to smooth out fluctuations in the business cycle, mask the sharp decline in Colombian deposit rates during the recessionary years of 1998 and 1999. Lower interest rates may have been a result of higher capital mobility, deliberate attempts to stimulate the economy, or both. Second, the Mexican capital mobility indicator was 14.8%, well above the five percent average and yet global financial pressures still sparked a crisis in Mexico.

Most importantly, a test of capital mobility prior to 1990 suggests that Colombia has in fact had high capital mobility for some time. Jorge Garcia Garcia and Sisira Jayasuriya (1997, pp. 30-31) performed an ordinary least squares regression to find the major determinants of the domestic interest rate from 1951 to 1986. They regressed nominal domestic interest rates as a function of foreign interest rates (either U.S. Treasury bill rates or London Eurodollar rates), the domestic inflation rate, and the rate of devaluation in the exchange rate. Their results show that from 1951 to 1967, when Colombia had an adjustable peg, inflation was the main determinant of nominal domestic interest rates. From 1967 to 1986, however, when Colombia had a crawling peg, a one- percent change in foreign interest rates yielded a corresponding change in domestic interest rates by almost two percentage points. A one- percent increase in inflation or the rate of devaluation, however, yielded an increase of less than one percent in the domestic interest rate. The results suggest that after 1967 capital mobility increased and thus changes in foreign interest rates provoked changes in domestic interest rates more often. Garcia Garcia and Jayasuriya attribute the growth in capital mobility to economic growth, increased trade, better communications, better dissemination of information in the marketplace, and the inability of the government to isolate Colombia from international capital markets.

Exchange Rate Policy

From 1950 to 1967 Colombia employed a fixed exchange rate and multiple exchange-rate system. The government frequently devalued the peso to combat balance of payments crises even though they were unpopular. The government imposed import and capital controls and unified the exchange-rate system in November 1966 to deal with one of these balance of payments deficits (Garcia Garcia and Jayasuriya, 1997, p. 9). All foreign exchange transactions now had to go through the Banco de la Republica, the central bank. The government barred Colombians from holding foreign currency at home or abroad. Imports and exports now required licensing. Such restrictions on trade and international capital flows would be the norm until the neo-liberal reforms of the 1990s.

In 1967 the government established a crawling peg and returned to form by devaluing (Garcia Garcia and Jayasuriya, 1997, p. 10). After the debt crisis of 1982, foreign credit became largely unavailable and exports became harder to sell in a worldwide environment of recession. The government accelerated the rate of crawl to address balance of payments deficits and from 1983 to 1991 the government continually let the real exchange rate depreciate (see Banco de la Republica, 1992, p. 94). The gradual devaluation of the peso benefited coffee producers, producers of Colombia's main export, giving the government an influential ally in support of its exchange-rate policy.

Policies of real exchange-rate devaluation contributed to the sustained moderate inflation of 20% to 30% from 1973 to 1990 (see table 7.1). Prior to 1973, inflation tended to be low but volatile. After 1973, inflation was stable but stubbornly higher. Consistent devaluation gave the government wide latitude for expansion of the money supply (Carrasquilla, 1995, pp. 4-5). Monetary expansion allowed the government to finance fiscal deficits, allowing the government to reap gains through its seigniorage rights. Monetary expansion generated inflation, costing private agents purchasing power. Effectively, this transferred purchasing power from private agents to the government, commonly known as an "inflation tax." Normally the persistence of the inflation tax generates resentment among private agents, and they respond by exchanging domestic currency for foreign currency, which is currency substitution. But Colombians did not substitute currency in significant amounts. Alberto Carrasquilla argues many private agents tolerated the inflation tax for two reasons (Carrasquilla, 1995, pp. 5-6). First, as just mentioned, it redistributed wealth in favor of exporters, primarily coffee exporters. Second, widespread use of wage indexing and interest-rate indexing for mortgages limited the damage inflation made to real incomes. This made the monetary expansion and the crawling peg more palatable to workers and peasants.

With the Gaviria administration (1990-1994), Colombia turned decisively to a neo-liberal development strategy designed to fight inflation and open the economy to international trade and capital markets. The shift in strategy included changes in exchange-rate policy that culminated in the establishment of a sequence of crawling bands in 1994. Inflationary and heterodox policies had several long-run costs. First, inflation reduces consumption and productivity growth in the long-run (Carrasquilla, 1995: 7-8). According to World Bank reports, Colombia's growth rate of manufacturing output dropped from 6.1% to 4.9% between 1977 and 1987 (cited in Hallberg and Takacs, 1992, p. 263). Second, inflation hurt Colombia in the competition to attract foreign investment to Latin America. From 1989 to 1992, Colombia averaged a typical 28.9% for inflation, while Chile averaged 21.1% inflation and Mexico 21.5% inflation (Lora, 1994, pp. 1-2) and Chilean and Mexican figures were dropping. Many of Colombia's neighbors had undertaken austerity measures to combat inflation, and by 1990 Colombia had lagged behind in these efforts. Third, a closed economy frustrated the diversification of the industrial base (Hallberg and Takacs, 1992, pp. 262-263).

A number of reforms were introduced beginning in the late 1980s. To open the economy to trade, the Barco administration (1986-1990) began to remove quantitative restrictions on imports and replace them with tariffs. Later, the Barco and Gaviria administrations reduced tariffs and streamlined the tariff structure (Banco de la Republica, 1992, p. 92; Hallberg and Takacs, 1992, pp. 268-276; Lora, 1994, pp. 3-4). To open the economy to capital flows, capital controls were gradually removed.[2] The Gaviria administration made the Banco de la Republica formally independent of government control in 1992 (Banco de la Republica, 1992, pp. 60-61; Carrasquilla, 1999, p. 205). As the government removed capital controls, the central bank gradually reduced its efforts to sterilize capital flows (where the central bank injects or removes domestic currency to offset capital outflows or inflows) as capital mobility makes sterilization less effective (Carrasquilla, 1995, p. 12). As a result, the central bank gained more independence from the government while increasingly losing autonomy over monetary policy to international capital markets.

In 1991, the government abolished the crawling peg and replaced it with the rudiments of a crawling band system (see IMF, *EAER*, various years; Banco de la Republica, 1992, pp. 97-100; Carrasquilla, 1995, p. 13). After June 1991, the Banco de la Republica did not conduct foreign-exchange transactions with the non-financial private sector, but only public agencies and financial intermediaries. Commercial banks and financial intermediaries became the only authorized intermediaries for the foreign exchange market. In place of the crawling peg, the government instituted a system in which Colombians were required to surrender their foreign currency to the Banco de la Republica. In exchange, the central bank would sell private agents a security called an exchange certificate (certificado de cambio) for the equivalent amount in U.S. dollars. A private agent then had three choices. First, the agent could redeem the exchange certificate for dollars after one year. Second, the agent could also sell the exchange certificate to the Banco de la Republica for 87.5% or more of the certificate's value prior to the date of maturity. Third, the agent could sell the exchange certificate in the currency market at the market exchange rate. By selling exchange certificates, the central bank was still sterilizing the full amount of capital inflows, but through the foreign exchange market rather than the domestic money market. Furthermore, by selling dollars at a rates between 100% of foreign currency earnings (after one year) and 87.5% of foreign currency earnings (up to one year), the central bank effectively imposed an exchange-rate band on the foreign exchange market. Private agents had no incentive to buy and sell exchange certificates for pesos above and below those limits.

In January 1994, the government replaced the exchange certificate program with a formal crawling band regime (see IMF, *EAER*, various years, and Carrasquilla, 1995, pp. 14-15). The Banco de la Republica began with the market exchange rate for the peso and the dollar. The central bank then pledged to intervene in the currency markets if the exchange rate traded at plus or minus 7% of that value. The central bank would announce the limits of the exchange-rate band ten days in advance. The whole band crawled at the rate of 11% per annum. Beginning December 12, 1994, the central bank announced a revaluation in the exchange-rate band and increased the rate of crawl to 13.5%. The Banco de la

Republica would occasionally alter the rate of crawl for the exchange-rate band. Whatever the rate, the rate of crawl was less than the rate of inflation, meaning that the Colombia shifted from a policy of depreciating the real exchange rate to one of appreciating the real exchange rate, which when combined with a more open economy restrained inflationary pressures.

Unfortunately, the appreciating exchange rate also contributed to an increasing current account deficit. Foreign credit was more available thanks to neo-liberal policies and the reduction of inflation, but it helped to finance public sector a spending binge and more imports. The credit bubble burst and banks failed, but the government adjusted the exchange rate before any crises hit. At first the government devalued the band and then it later floated the peso in September 1999. The government has been operating a managed float ever since.

Three unsatisfying hypotheses

Why did Colombia manage to maintain some form of exchange rate commitment (a peg or band) from 1967 to 1999? A higher level of trade exposure, a lower level of GDP, or a higher level of financial intermediation should normally be part of the explanation for a long run of pegging. Unfortunately, levels of trade exposure and financial intermediation in Colombia would lead one to predict that Colombia would have abandoned pegging a long time ago. The GDP hypothesis would lead to a correct prediction, but would not address the question of why a small economy such as Colombia maintained a peg while other economies of a similar size have chosen to switch to floating much earlier.

Trade Exposure and GDP

A look at the figures for trade exposure (see Table 7.1) demonstrates that Colombia has never had much exposure to trade. From 1986 to 1990, trade exposure in Colombia remained around 30%. After the neo-liberal reforms in 1990, trade exposure grew to 33-36%. This level of trade exposure is low by the standards of most Latin American countries. Granted, Argentina and Brazil both had trade exposure that fell between 10-20% during the 1980s and 1990s, and Mexico's trade exposure fell between 30-40% until 1995. But these are the largest economies in Latin America, with sizable domestic markets. Colombia is one of the smaller economies. Most of the smaller economies in Latin America have levels of trade exposure higher than Colombia has. From 1985 to 1997, Bolivia's trade exposure ranged from 42 to 52%, Chile's ranged from 55 to 66%, Ecuador's ranged from 45 to 62%, Paraguay's ranged from 48 to 87%, and Venezuela's ranged from 40% to 60%. Colombia is relatively isolated from (legal) world trade compared to its neighbors and should therefore be less likely to maintain a pegged exchange rate.

Sales of narcotics, of course, are not included in calculations of Colombia's exports or GDP. If narcotics traffic were somehow to be included in the national accounts of Colombia, trade exposure would be higher, but the question is by how much. Estimates of how much profit Colombia earned from illegal trade in 1990 range from $1 billion to $7 billion (cited in Whynes, 1992, p. 335). Considering that the nominal GDP of Colombia was approximately $40.3 billion in 1990, the narcotics trade could have added between 2.4% to 14.8% to the level of trade exposure, which is closer to other small Latin American economies. But even revised trade exposure figures would still mean that Colombia has a moderate level of trade exposure for a middle-income country. Some middle-income states like Malaysia have trade exposure near or above 100% of GDP.

As in the case of Thailand, Colombia's small economic size helps to explain the persistence of pegged exchange rates. Unlike Mexico, which ranked as the world's 12th largest economy in 1999, Colombia was more typical of middle-income countries, being the 37th largest economy in the world that year (World Bank, 2000). The economy grew by an average of 4.6% per year between 1950 and 1993 (Garcia Garcia and Jayasuriya, 1997, p. 20). While the rates of real GDP growth varied from year to year, Colombia grew at a more consistent rate than many Latin American countries, with few years in recession (see Table 7.1), but its slow productivity growth often meant that GDP growth was sluggish. Colombia also had a population of 41.5 million people in 1999, the third most populous state in Latin America after Brazil and Mexico (World Bank, 2000). Colombia's relatively large population has thus given it a lower GDP per capita.

Small economies tend to be associated with dependence on imports, lack of diversification in exports, and trade concentrated with one major economy. Except for the dependence on imports, most of these conditions apply to Colombia. Hence it is not surprising that Colombia has maintained a pegged exchange rate for so long. However, the size of the economy alone does not explain two facts. First, many small economies other than Colombia chose to employ alternatives to pegging years before Colombia did. Why did Colombia maintain a peg when similarly situated economies often chose to float? Second, Colombia quit encouraging real exchange-rate depreciation in 1994 and encouraged real exchange-rate appreciation instead. As shall be argued below, while Colombia's small economy gives it benefits from pegging, insulation from hollowing-out pressures have allowed Colombia to peg its exchange rate for longer than other economies of similar size.

Financial Intermediation

Financial intermediation is also not the explanation for the persistence of pegged exchange rates in Colombia. Neither the banking sector nor the domestic capital markets in Colombia are very strong. While Colombia tends to rely more on bank credit than capital markets for the financing of commercial firms, many years of financial repression have retarded the growth of the banking sector. Hence, the banking sector never became a formidable lobbying group as it did in Thailand.

Before launching an analysis of banking in Colombia, it should be noted that Colombia has no significant capital markets. Colombia has three stock exchanges, in Bogota, Medellin, and Cali (IFC, 1999, p. 173). Not one of them ranks among the top forty in the world, regardless of whether they are listed in terms of market capitalization, value of shares traded, or the number of listed companies (IFC, 1999, p. 24). Even their combined strength would not put them in the world's top forty stock markets. In 1998, the three Colombian stock exchanges combined listed a total of only 163 companies. This is a small figure considering that the Stock Exchange of Thailand listed 418 companies that year and Thai finance is mostly based on bank credit. The total market capitalization of the three Colombian exchanges was 20.7 trillion pesos, or $13.3 billion in 1998, equivalent to 14.7% of GDP that year (IFC 1999, p. 173). By contrast, the market capitalization of Mexico's stock market was equivalent to 23.3% of its GDP in 1998. The value of the shares traded in 1998 was 2.2 trillion pesos, or $1.5 billion, meaning that investors traded 9.6% of the shares that year (IFC 1999, p. 173). Inflation and corporate tax policy have made debt financing more attractive than equity financing over the past few decades (Garcia Garcia and Jayasuriya, 1997, p. 29). The securities market, however, is also underdeveloped. As of 1990, 90% of the total transactions in the securities market involved bonds issued by the central bank or paper issued by public agencies (Garcia Garcia and Jayasuriya, 1997, p. 29).

Relatively more corporate financing takes place through bank lending. Financial intermediaries in Colombia include commercial banks, financial corporations (equivalent to investment banks), savings and loan associations, and commercial finance companies (which finance durable goods purchases) (Banco de la Republica, 1992, p. 57). Private commercial banks are clearly the largest group of financial intermediaries. At the end of 1998, the commercial banks had 41.7 billion pesos in assets, accounting for 53.9% of the total assets in the Colombian financial intermediaries. Publicly-owned banks accounted for 12.7% of the total assets that year, financial corporations accounted for 8.8%, savings and loan associations accounted for 17.8%, and commercial financial companies accounted for 6.7% (Banco de la Republica, 1999, pp. 155-156).

The indicators for the Colombian financial intermediation, however, are not strong compared to other middle-income states (see Table 7.2). From 1978 to 1985, the money multiplier grows from 1.58 to 2.16, and the credit ratio grows from 0.95 to 1.64. Part of the change in the money multiplier, however, was a direct result of the change in reserve requirements. The period of stagnant growth in financial deepening also lasts until 1992, as the money multiplier remains between 2.0 and 2.16, while the credit ratio remains between 1.3 and 1.8. After 1994, foreign investment flows into Colombia again and the banking system becomes more active. By 1999, the money multiplier grew to 4.0 and the credit ratio grew to 3.21. The late 1990s growth in the banking system, however, was slower and less robust than in Mexico. From 1988 to 1992, the Mexican money multiplier grew from 1.90 to 6.43 and the credit ratio grew from 1.63 to 6.27 (see Table 5.2). For most of the past 25 years, Colombia has had a relatively repressed financial system compared to its Latin American neighbors.

Table 7.2 More economic data on Colombia

Year	Money Multiplier	Credit Ratio	Total Foreign Debt/GNI	Total External debt/Exports
1978	1.576	0.946	n.a.	n.a.
1979	1.508	0.942	n.a.	n.a.
1980	1.686	1.161	n.a.	n.a.
1981	1.842	1.263	n.a.	n.a.
1982	1.877	1.336	n.a.	n.a.
1983	1.955	1.421	n.a.	n.a.
1984	1.973	1.413	n.a.	n.a.
1985	2.156	1.642	n.a.	n.a.
1986	n.a.	n.a.	n.a.	n.a.
1987	2.011	1.362	n.a.	n.a.
1988	2.014	1.539	n.a.	n.a.
1989	n.a.	n.a.	n.a.	n.a.
1990	2.125	1.710	45.1	181.0
1991	1.986	1.464	n.a.	n.a.
1992	2.128	1.518	n.a.	n.a.
1993	2.218	1.805	n.a.	n.a.
1994	2.489	2.122	27.7	178.3
1995	2.808	2.646	28.0	182.7
1996	3.115	2.886	31.0	199.3
1997	3.552	3.272	30.5	201.8
1998	4.802	4.619	34.3	225.4
1999	4.009	3.214	42.1	217.2

Figures for debt are in percentages.

Sources: International Monetary Fund and World Bank.

Colombian banking regulation during the 1970s and 1980s was extensive. The government had a long history of regulating interest rates, mandating high reserve requirements, directing credit to favored projects, requiring banks to hold certain investments in their asset portfolios, and extracting an inflation tax through monetary expansion (Garcia Garcia and Jayasuriya, 1997, p. 28; Clavijo, 1992, p. 96-97). In 1975, the government also "Colombianized" the financial sector by requiring that all foreign firms transform themselves into joint ventures in which Colombians held controlling interest in the firm (Barajas, et. al., 1999, pp. 8-9). The government gradually reduced the complexity and requirements of banking regulation during the 1970s and 1980s. While deregulation did not fully liberalize the banking sector, it did increase financial activity. In 1974 and 1975 for example, the Lopez Michelen administration reduced reserve requirements, raised the ceiling on deposit rates, deregulated lending rates, and reduced the use of directed credit (Garcia Garcia and Jayasuriya, 1997, p. 29). The same government, however, barred foreign entry into the financial sector and mandated negative real interest rates for the savings and loan associations (Garcia Garcia and Jayasuriya, 1997, p. 29).

During the 1980s, the government not only regulated banking but also dominated the operation of the banking sector. What private banking did operate was typically in the hands of a few firms. A few private conglomerates controlled most of the financial institutions in the 1970s. By 1980, 20% of Colombia's financial institutions owned 60% of bank assets, 65% of financial corporation assets, and 55% of the financial system's total assets (Garcia Garcia and Jayasuriya, 1997, p. 28). But after the debt crisis that began in 1982, the government nationalized four out of the nine largest banks in Colombia (Montes-Negret, 1996, p. 101). While the government did not nationalize the entire banking sector, publicly-owned banks accounted for 63% of the banking sector's total assets by the end of 1987 (Montes-Negret, 1996, p. 101; Clavijo, 1992, p. 95). Ownership of what privately-owned financial institutions still operated remained concentrated in the hands of a few. The five largest financial conglomerated owned half the equity of commercial banks and other financial intermediaries at this time (Montes-Negret, 1996, p. 101). The concentration of assets in the hands of the government and a few conglomerates, along with regulations restricting foreign competition, restricted competition among domestic banks.

In 1990, the Gaviria administration introduced major financial reforms to complement the liberalization of international trade (Lora, 1994, p. 10). The government privatized four commercial banks and two finance corporations that were nationalized after the 1982 debt crisis. Banks were allowed to merge or be liquidated. Some new financial institutions were also created. The government removed restrictions on what financial services financial institutions could provide, allowing universal banking. The government also removed restrictions on international investment, a policy shift that will be described in more detail below. After privatization and the opening of the banking sector to foreign competition in 1990, however, domestic financial conglomerates faced a different market environment. Publicly-owned banks accounted for only 10.3% of the banking system's assets in 1998 (Barajas, et. al., 1999, p. 14). But as noted above, the growth in Colombian financial intermediation was slower compared to other emerging markets that liberalized their financial sectors, such as Mexico.

Since international investment was restricted until 1990, and incrementally liberalized after 1990, the private sector in Colombia did not have a significant external debt burden until the late 1990s. Table 7.3 summarizes information on Colombian external debt from 1990 to 1997. Colombia's external debt is small in absolute terms compared to external debt in Thailand and Mexico, but in relation to the Colombian economy the debt burden became a little ominous. Total external debt in Colombia ranged from 30% to 45% of GDP during the 1990s. These figures were not as high as those of Thailand from 1994 on, but Mexico's total external debt was equivalent to 34.4% of its GDP in 1994 (see Tables 4.1 and 5.2).

Most of the external debt in Colombia in the 1990s was private non-guaranteed debt. In 1994, private non-guaranteed debt in Mexico was 18.0% of long-term external debt, and 12.5% of total external debt (World Bank, 1999, p. 376). Private non-guaranteed debt in Colombia reached these levels beginning in 1994 and grew thereafter. Furthermore, 92.5% of the private, non-guaranteed external debt in Colombia was in the form of bank loans in 1997. Bonds only accounted for 7.5% of the private, non-guaranteed external debt (World Bank, 1999, p. 157). Even most of the private non-guaranteed debt in Mexico in 1994 took the form of bonds rather than bank loans, and Mexico has a stronger system of bank-credit financing.

Thanks to the sudden boom in foreign lending after the slow start Colombia made in building a financial system, credit markets became unstable by 1998. In September 1998, non-performing loans (NPL's) were 13.2% of all loans and as the recession intensified NPL's reached 24.0% (IMF, 1999b, p. 11). Strikingly, Colombian banks had hedged much of their external debt against foreign exchange rate risk and thus the devaluation and floation of 1999 caused less damage than the collapse of the credit bubble did (IMF, 1999b, p. 11). Banks, however, were indirectly exposed to exchange rate risk through their ties to domestic firms. As of September 1998, commercial banks invested 39.3% of the loan portfolios with some form of business firm, be it in the agriculture, industry, mining, commerce, or service sector (Banco de la Republica, 1999, p. 157). Many of these Colombian corporations had acquired unhedged dollar-denominated debts during the 1990s (IMF, 1999b, p. 11). Juan Manuel Santos, then the finance minister, optimistically estimated that cleaning up the costs of the failing banking sector would amount to 6% of GDP (*Economist Survey*, 2001, p. 15).

In late 1998 and early 1999, the government took a number of steps to prevent the weakness of the financial sector from developing into a wider crisis (IMF, 1999b, p. 11). FOGAFIN, the government's agency for insuring and rescuing financial institutions, sold bonds to bank shareholders which the shareholders used to recapitalize the banks. In June 1999, the government also strengthened the financial sector reform law to give government agencies more

Table 7.3 External debt in Colombia

Year	PND	LTD	TED	PND /LTD (%)	PND /TED (%)	TED /GNI (%)	TED/ Exports (%)
1990	1,113	15,784	17,222	7.1	6.5	45.0	181.0
1994	3,091	17,448	21,940	17.7	14.1	27.7	178.3
1995	5,553	19,503	25,048	28.5	22.2	28.0	182.7
1996	8,162	23,016	28,900	35.5	28.2	31.0	199.3
1997	10,746	26,041	31,800	41.3	33.8	30.5	201.8
1998	10,101	27,105	33,338	37.3	30.3	34.3	225.4
1999	10,239	30,713	34,678	33.3	29.5	42.1	217.2

PND = Private Non-guaranteed Debt
LTD = Long-Term Debt (the total of public and private long-term debt)
TED = Total External Debt (the total of all external debt, both public and private, long-term and short-term)
All figures for external debt in millions of U.S. dollars.

Source: World Bank, *Global Development Finance* (Washington, DC: World Bank, 2001).

authority to address banking problems earlier. Interestingly enough, when foreign investors tested the government's foreign exchange rate band, the government chose not to defend the band at whatever the cost, but devalued, and when investors were not satisfied with devaluation the government floated the peso. Compared to the foot-dragging in Thailand and Mexico, the Colombian government took early steps to prevent more serious banking and exchange rate crises.

Colombia, then does not fit the financial intermediation hypothesis well for two reasons. First, Colombia's banking sector is not as strong as the banking sectors in Thailand or Mexico. Years of heavy regulation have stunted the growth of banks in Colombia. Even the privatization and deregulation of the Gaviria administration did not lead to full liberalization, and thus the growth in the banking sector has been slow, as demonstrated in its financial intermediation statistics. And yet Colombia maintained a crawling peg or band from 1967 to 1999. The second reason, as mentioned above, was that Colombian banks did a comparatively better job of hedging their external debt against foreign-exchange risk. Consequently, banks depended less on the exchange rate band for their financial health. Instead of focusing on trade exposure, GDP size, or financial intermediation, the answers to Colombia's long run of pegging lie elsewhere.

Three conditions mitigating hollowing out pressures

To understand what other explanations might account for the persistence of pegging in Colombia, it is helpful to revisit the assumptions of the hollowing-out thesis. In countries with low levels of capital mobility, the demands for foreign exchange from international capital markets are less likely to overwhelm the central bank's reserves of foreign exchange. Nor are the demands for domestic currency from international investors likely to provoke so much monetary expansion as to cause inflation. Hence, in an environment of low capital mobility, a government could persist in pegging the exchange rate with little risk of an exchange-rate crisis or an excessive monetary expansion. As discussed above, many Middle Eastern states are examples. In an environment of high capital mobility, however, governments are exposed massive capital movements from international capital markets. Sudden capital outflows or inflows measuring in the billions of currency units can provoke exchange-rate crises or politically intolerable monetary expansions. Furthermore, resort to capital controls, interest rate adjustments, and international lending to mitigate international capital movements may not work or may only cause other problems (Eichengreen, 1994). Since the risks and costs of pegging rise as capital mobility grows, the rational choice for a government to make is to replace pegging with a less risky and less costly exchange-rate regime.

The hollowing-out argument, though, depends on the costs and risks of pegging an exchange rate in an environment of high capital mobility. In the cases of Thailand and Mexico, the costs and risks of pegging were significant.

Colombia, however, has been subject to three conditions that allow it to avoid most of the risks and costs that other middle-income countries incur while pegging their exchange rates. First, from 1975 to 1991, capital controls have shielded the Banco de la Republica from massive capital inflows and outflows that could destabilize the exchange-rate system in Colombia. A black market for foreign currency has diverted much of the capital movements in the broader foreign exchange market from the Banco de la Republica. Second, the crawling bands that Colombian authorities have employed since 1991 have allowed much flexibility in the peso-dollar exchange rate. Third, Colombia has managed to maintain large reserves of foreign exchange over many years, which improved the credibility of the central bank's exchange-rate commitment. Thanks to these three conditions, Colombia has been able to maintain a peg for much longer than most middle-income countries.

Capital Controls and the Black Market for Foreign Exchange

As was mentioned above in the section on financial intermediation, the government imposed a broad array of capital controls in Colombia, in order to prevent the kinds of balance-of-payments crises Colombia experienced in the 1960s (Barajas, et. al., 1999, p. 7; Garcia Garcia and Jayasuriya, 1997, p. 10). Restrictions on the capital account were critical to the operation of the peg. Foreign direct investment was gradually restricted beginning in the 1960s. Decree Law 444 of 1967 mandated that the Banco de la Republica conduct all exchange-rate transactions (IMF, *EAER*, various years). The government vested the National Planning Department (DNP) with the sole authority to approve foreign direct investment in Colombia. While the new laws did not restrict foreign direct investment, in practice the DNP approved no new foreign direct investment in finance or public utilities for several years (Barajas, et. al., 1999, p. 7).

Capital controls tightened further with the establishment of the Andean Pact, a trade bloc formed in 1970 among Bolivia, Chile, Colombia, Ecuador, and Venezuela for the purpose of promoting trade within South America. The Andean Pact's strategy of import-substitution encouraged the tightening of capital controls. Colombia placed limits on the reinvestment and remittance of profits for foreign firms (IMF, *EAER*, various years). Foreign firms were also required to become joint ventures after no more than fifteen years if they wished to operate within the Andean Pact (Barajas, et. al., 1999: 8). At the time, Colombia opted out of requiring banks to become joint ventures. But in 1975 it reversed itself and required banks to become joint ventures within three years, with controlling interest held by Colombians. After the 1982 debt crisis, some politicians attempted to liberalize foreign direct investment in banks, but the attempts failed in Congress (Barajas, et. al., 1999, pp. 10-11). The government chose instead to recapitalize banks using public funds (Montes-Negret, 1996, pp. 102-106).

Foreign portfolio investment and foreign bank loans were similarly restricted during the 1970s and 1980s. By 1990, foreign investment in mutual funds incorporating Colombian equity and debt securities required the approval of the National Planning Board. Any foreign capital invested in these mutual funds could only be repatriated five years after the creation of the fund (IMF, *EAER*, 1991, p. 114). Foreign bank loans to private agents in Colombia had to be for a minimum of five years. The interest rates for foreign bank loans had a maximum of 2.5% over the New York prime rate or the LIBOR (IMF, *EAER*, 1991, p. 114). As mentioned before, regulations also prohibited Colombian nationals from holding foreign currency or exporting their capital abroad to invest in foreign assets or to hold foreign bank accounts.

In 1991, the government liberalized the capital account along with domestic banking regulations (IMF, *EAER*, 1992, pp. 114-115). The Andean Pact removed restrictions on foreign direct investment and the remittance of profits. Foreign investment was allowed up to 10% of ownership in almost any sector of the economy. By 1994, foreign firms were allowed to own 100% of a sector (IMF, *EAER*, 1995, p. 118). Foreign ownership, however, was still prohibited in the defense and waste disposal industries. Colombia allowed foreign firms to own 100% of a bank in 1990. Repatriation of foreign capital in a mutual fund was now allowed after one year. Colombian nationals were now allowed to export capital abroad. On the other hand, loans from foreign banks still retained their restrictions on the dates of maturity and interest rates. These restrictions were gradually reduced over the next few years. By 1994, regulations required temporary, non-remunerated deposit of a portion of the loan, depending on the length of maturity. By 1998, these restrictions were reduced and streamlined and only 25% of a foreign bank loan needed to be on deposit for twelve months (IMF, *EAER*, 2000, p. 221).

Capital controls are significant, first because they discourage foreign investment in Colombia and the investment of Colombian capital abroad through official channels, thus requiring fewer foreign exchange transactions from the central bank. Second, capital controls, in conjunction with the Colombian underground economy, have encouraged a significant black market for foreign exchange transactions. This black market has been the channel for billions of dollars of foreign exchange transactions, diverting foreign exchange activity from the Banco de la Republica, effectively relieving the central bank of some of the pressure of maintaining the official exchange rate. The black market for foreign exchange helps explain an anomaly, namely how a country with such strict capital controls during the 1970s and 1980s could exhibit such statistically significant levels of capital mobility in regression tests by Garcia Garcia and Jayasuriya.

The black market is partly a result of the internationalization of Colombian banks after the Colombianization of the banking system in 1975 (Montes-Negret, 1996, pp. 100-101). Colombian banks established a number of offshore branches and subsidiaries, particularly in Panama, where regulatory supervision was minimal. An export boom in Colombia provided domestic banks with the foreign exchange they needed to establish banks abroad. The subsidiaries also borrowed from international banks, sometimes legally, sometimes illegally, with parent banks in Colombia guaranteeing the loans. By establishing offshore subsidiaries, Colombian banks could avoid the domestic regulations against combining commercial and investment banking and the regulations restricting banks to a capital-liability ratio of 1:10. In Panama, the ratio reached as high as 1:20. Colombian authorities did not recognize how large the risks of unregulated offshore banking were, risks that later contributed to the 1982 debt crisis in that country. Nor did the authorities recognize the volume of exchange-control violations. By the end of 1986, Colombian banks had established three branches, eighteen affiliates, and twenty-three subsidiaries abroad. This offshore banking serves as a channel for a foreign-exchange market outside the purview of the Banco de la Republica (Grosse, 1992, p. 1197). Besides bankers, stockbrokers, traffickers in contraband and those who engage in small-scale transactions on the street also participate in the black market for foreign exchange (Grosse, 1992, pp. 1196-1197).

Estimating the volume of the black market is difficult, of course, since no official figures are kept. But estimates can be made using estimates of net capital flight in and out of Colombia, which represent unofficial capital movements (see Gunter, 1992). Analysts have developed two basic methods of estimating net capital flight. One adds together the net omissions and errors in the balance of payments with reported short-term capital exports by the private non-bank sector (Cuddington, 1986). The other subtracts from gross foreign debt the total of the current account balance, direct investment, and changes in foreign exchange reserves (BIS, 1989; Erbe, 1985). Frank Gunter modifies these latter estimates to include misinvoicing of exports and imports and changes in the valuation of Colombia's external debt (Gunter, 1992, pp. 357-362). By Gunter's estimates, Colombia had average unofficial net capital outflows of approximately $100-200 million per year from 1982 to 1990 (Gunter, 1992, p. 356).

Net capital flight, however, only indicates the balance of all of the unofficial inflows and outflows of capital, not the volume of the capital inflows and outflows separately. Estimates of the narcotics trade provide an estimate of the capital inflows. Robert Grosse (1992), an economist who has written on the black market for foreign exchange in Colombia, estimates that 60% of the supply of foreign currency in the black market in the 1990s came from the narcotics trade and other contraband activities. The other 40% comes from other contraband activities, remittances from Colombians emigrants to their families, and from Colombian businesspeople returning flight capital from abroad (Grosse, 1992, p. 1197). Although estimates of the average revenue for the narcotics industry in Colombia could range from $1 billion to $7 billion, more than one study estimates that the average revenue was about $2.5 billion per year in the 1980s (see Borrero, 1989; Sarmiento, 1991). Some of this money may have gone to people and places outside of Colombia, to pay the narcotics distributors or coca producers. The amount that actually reached Colombia could have been anywhere from half ($1.25 billion) to the full figure ($2.5 billion). Add to these figures a rough accounting for other illegal trading and remittances, and unofficial foreign-exchange inflows were probably between $2.08 billion and $4.17 billion per year in the 1980s. These figures represent much of the supply of foreign exchange in the black market.

Importers who wanted to buy foreign exchange outside official channels and private agents who wanted to hold foreign currency assets provided the unofficial capital outflows and the demand for black market currency. Strict capital controls gave these people incentive to purchase foreign exchange on the black market. Offshore banks and other black market operators have access to foreign exchange generated from unofficial capital inflows. Those who seek foreign exchange then purchase foreign currency and send it abroad. If Gunter's estimates of net capital flight are right, then unofficial capital outflows were approximately between $2.18 billion and $4.37 billion in the 1980s.

To put these unofficial capital flows in perspective, note that the Banco de la Republica had $4.5 billion in international reserves at the end of 1990 (Banco de la Republica, 1992, p. 105). Shifts in the supply and demand for foreign exchange in the black market could have made a significant difference to the level of foreign-exchange reserves had the transactions gone through the Banco de la Republica, although in practice they did not. Even if the estimates of the volume of the narcotics trade or the portion of narcotics revenues repatriated to Colombia were inflated, the currency trade in the black market would still drain a significant portion of the foreign exchange market away from the central bank. Unofficial capital flows of only $1 billion would still represent millions of dollars in transactions every day not flowing through the official exchange market. As the narcotics trade grew throughout the 1990s, the supply of foreign exchange for the black market grew with it, as did the central bank's stock of foreign reserves. But as the capital account was liberalized and Colombians were allowed to hold foreign currency and other dollar-denominated assets, the black-market demand for currency probably dropped. It would be hard to estimate how much foreign exchange the black market supplied and Colombians acquired in the 1990s.

Colombia is an unusual case in that it has been the hub of the cocaine trade for such a long time. Much of the coca is grown in Peru and Bolivia and made into coca paste in those countries. The coca paste has historically been shipped to Colombia, processed into its final forms there, and then distributed to North America and Europe (Gunter, 1992, p. 365). Colombian dealers have usually been in the position of directing much of the world's cocaine trade. Mexican drug dealers have taken over a greater share of the narcotics industry, but this has only developed in the past few years as the Colombian government has continued its war on drug traffickers. Since Colombia was the focus of so much of the narcotics trade in the 1980s and early 1990s, Colombia had supplies of unofficial foreign exchange earnings not available to other developing countries. Consequently Colombia's black market for foreign exchange was probably larger relative to its economy than in most other developing countries in which the black market simply serviced traditional capital flight.

Bandwidth

The broad width of the crawling bands that Colombia has employed since 1991 is another reason why hollowing-out pressures have been less threatening to government exchange-rate commitments. With the exchange certificates (also known as the CCAMB regime), Colombia effectively had an exchange-rate band of 12.5%. When the Colombians instituted a new crawling band in 1994, they had an exchange-rate band of 14%, with an exchange rate able to vary within plus or minus 7% of a central exchange rate. These margins for the exchange rate made interventions to defend exchange-rate commitments rare until 1997. As is shown in Figure 7.1, exchange-rate fluctuations only required central-bank intervention on two occasions prior to 1995 when exchange-rate movements reached the floor of the exchange-rate band, during December 1993 and December 1994. In these cases the Banco de la Republica readjusted the band. Most central bank interventions have been executed to adjust the exchange rate within the band. Either the central bank has tried to neutralize the effect of large public sector transactions in the current account or has intervened to dampen the effects of temporary economic shocks on the nominal exchange rate (Carrasquilla, 1995, p. 15). While the exchange-rate bands did not eliminate exchange-rate intervention in the early 1990s, they did allow the central bank to dispense with active sterilization.

Nevertheless, if international capital movements are large enough, they can test the margins of any exchange-rate band. The period from 1995 onward was more problematic. Beginning in October 1995, the exchange rate would hover around the upper or lower limit of the band for the next few years. This required more intervention and in September 1998 and June 1999 Colombia devalued its band to try to relieve pressure on the exchange rate band. Unfortunately, investors kept selling the peso, and the government dispensed with the band in September 1999.

A comparison with Mexico serves as a case in point. Mexico's crawling band had an ever-widening width. While the floor of the exchange-rate band remained constant, the ceiling depreciated at the rate of 2.4% per year (Banco de Mexico, 1995, pp. 36-38). The width of the band thus kept widening. From 1991 to 1993, the exchange rate rarely moved near the margins of this band. Mexico's troubles began when the exchange rate hit the ceiling of the crawling band and would not budge for several months. Banks and others did not want the government to devalue, so to please them the government spent its reserves and those reserves fell throughout the year. In Colombia, however, the Banco de la Republica had more flexibility in adjusting the exchange-rate band since the Colombian peso was threatening to appreciate beyond the floor of the exchange-rate band in 1993 and 1994. Adjustments in the band allowed for continued real exchange-rate appreciation, which in turn helped to contain inflation. Since the reduction of was inflation the government's highest priority at the time, few government officials had reason to oppose an adjustment of the exchange-rate band. Only when the exchange rate hovered around the ceiling of the band, beginning in late 1997 and continuing for about a year, was the government forced to choose among the options of spending reserves, devaluing, and floatation.

The HOT argues that crawling bands are simply unsustainable when in an

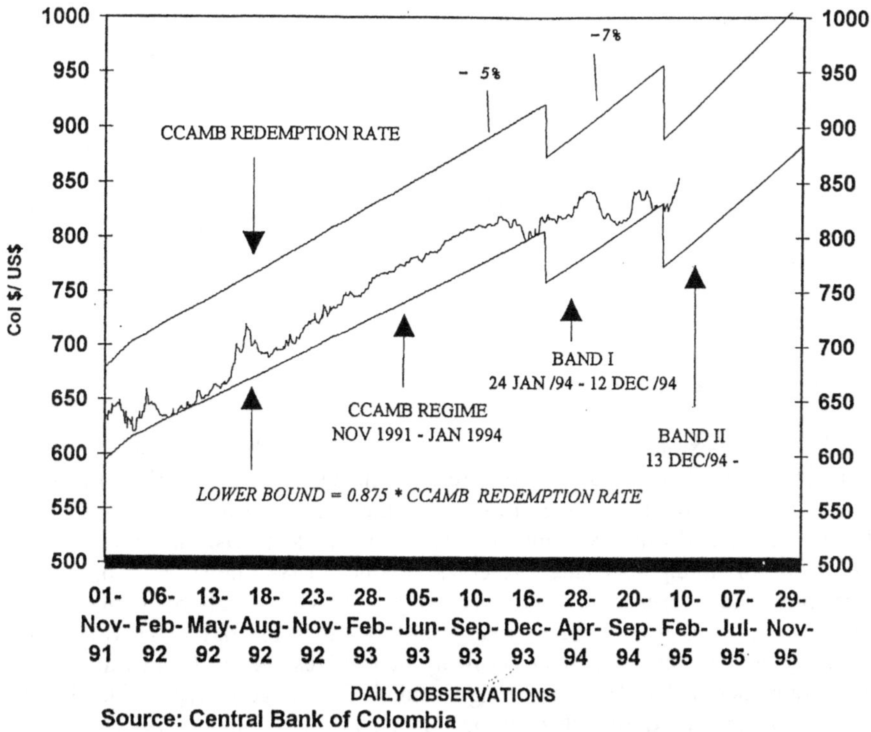

Figure 7.1 Exchange-rate bands for the Colombian peso, 1991-1994

Source: Carrasquilla, 1995, p. 16a, drawn from Banco de la Republica data.

environment of high capital mobility (Eichengreen, 1994). John Williamson (2000) disagrees, arguing that crawling bands or other target zones are no more prone to misalignments or crises than the corner solutions are. Much seems to depend on whether the spot exchange rate floats within the band on hovers near the edges. If the spot exchange rate floats within the limits of the band, Williamson (2000, p. 23) seems to be right to argue that the band shapes market expectations for the forward exchange rate and improves government credibility, as it did during the early 1990s in Colombia. But if the spot exchange rate hovers around the limits of the band for long periods, as it did later in the 1990s, it attracts the short-term investors who bet on whether the band will remain as it is, forcing the central bank to make tough decisions.

Stocks of Foreign Exchange Reserves

In addition to flexibility in monetary and exchange-rate policy, Colombia has been fortunate to have a growing stock of foreign-exchange reserves. Table 7.4 lists the stock of gross foreign-exchange reserves at the end of each year from 1975 to 1996. The worldwide recession of 1980 and the debt crisis in 1982 drained Colombia of foreign-exchange reserves. Since 1984, however, Colombia's foreign-exchange reserves have consistently grown. The rate of growth in foreign-exchange reserves from 1984 to 1991 was faster than the rate of growth in the economy, as demonstrated by the growing ratio of reserves to GDP. Balance-of-trade surpluses and inflows of foreign capital were largely responsible for the growth of reserves during this period (Banco de la Republica, 1992, p. 105). During the mid- and late 1980s, Colombia became an oil exporter and diversified into other products, losing its traditional reliance on the coffee industry. The new export industries contributed to several years of balance-of-trade surpluses, allowing the Colombians to earn dollars from abroad.

After 1991, liberalized foreign-investment laws helped generate further capital inflows throughout the 1990s, even as export boom slowed and the trade balance went into deficit from 1993 to 1998. In the end, the capital inflows and current account deficits were not sustainable. The capital inflows, however, were in excess of the current-account deficits for all but two years during this decade, and thus gross foreign-exchange reserves continued to grow. The reserves, however, did not grow faster than the economy after 1994. Thus in the early 1990s, a combination of neo-liberal policies, lower inflation, and strong foreign exchange reserves gave Colombia a new credibility among foreign investors. As reserves declined in relation to GDP after 1994, investors began to worry about the health of the financial sector and the government's ability to handle the civil war and the rule of law. As the spot exchange rate hovered near the limits of the band, the central bank had to spend more of its foreign exchange reserves.

Table 7.4 Foreign exchange reserves in Colombia

Year	Reserves (in millions of US $)	Reserves/GDP (%)
1975	632.6	4.83
1976	1,291.2	8.42
1977	2,032.8	10.44
1978	2,809.6	12.08
1979	5,030.1	18.00
1980	6,473.8	19.38
1981	6,078.5	16.70
1982	5,605.4	14.39
1983	3,512.0	9.07
1984	1,785.5	4.67
1985	2,197.3	6.30
1986	3,481.1	9.96
1987	3,416.3	9.39
1988	3,699.9	9.44
1989	3,862.4	9.77
1990	4,452.5	11.06
1991	6,334.5	15.27
1992	7,550.6	15.34
1993	7,670.1	13.75
1994	7,862.0	11.21
1995	8,205.0	10.18
1996	9,690.0	11.37
1997	n.a.	n.a.
1998	8397.0	8.16
1999	8198.0	9.47

Source: World Bank, *World Development Indicators*, (Washington, DC: World Bank, various years).

The politics of real exchange rate valuation

Colombia, then, had various conditions that allow it to maintain some form of pegged exchange rate in combination with high capital mobility. As a result, for a long time the focus on exchange rate policy in Colombia was on the value of the exchange rate rather than the choice of the exchange-rate regime. Colombia had a consistent policy of real exchange-rate depreciation from 1967 to 1991. After 1991, however, Colombia shifted course and encouraged real exchange-rate appreciation. Two reasons account for this shift, the opening of its political system to multi-party competition and shift in the preferences of non-financial firms from export-promotion to combating inflation.

Colombia has traditionally employed a two-party political system since the nineteenth century (Martz, 1992, p. 24). Colombia has also managed to avoid military rule for most of its history as an independent country. Colombia's two main parties, the Liberals and the Conservatives, have thus dominated Colombian politics for almost a century. The exception was during the brief military rule of General Gustavo Rojas Pinilla in the 1950s, established after a period of internal violence in Colombia. In 1957, the two parties returned to power under an arrangement called the National Front. Under the National Front, the two parties agreed to alternate occupation of the presidency and to establish parity in legislative representation and the division of cabinet ministries (Martz, 1992, p. 27). Jonathan Hartlyn and John Dugas describes the resulting political order as consociational, a form of democracy in which all of the major political groups are represented, and decisions are based on consensus rather than majority rule (Hartlyn and Dugas, 1999, p. 267; see also Lijphart, 1977). The principles of alternation in the presidency and parity in representation were allowed to lapse in the 1970s, but bipartisan control continued in the political system. In practice, Colombia had a two-party duopoly, in which people could vote for one of the two established parties but other parties and political movements were effectively barred from power (Martz, 1992, p. 28; Hartlyn and Dugas, 1999, p. 288).

Because the two parties engaged in little competition for power, they had little incentive to mobilize masses of voters in the 1960s and 1970s. Colombian politicians instead relied on patron-client relationships and the brokerage of political favors for the consolidation of their power (Hartlyn and Dugas, 1999, p. 268). Exchange-rate policy would thus reflect the preferences of vested interests in Colombia. One of the most important political clients was the coffee industry. Coffee was the dominant export industry in Colombia for decades. Coffee exports accounted for about 70% of total exports in the 1950s, a figure which declined to 40% of total exports by the early 1980s (Garcia Garcia and Jayasuriya, 1997, p. 22). Even though the coffee-growing region represented less than a quarter of the population and the GDP, it provided forty percent of the Ministers of Finance and central bank governors (Jaramillo, et. al., 2001, p. 204). The coffee industry had a preference for a depreciating exchange rate, since this increased peso earnings from dollar-denominated exports of its product. Moreover, the coffee industry did not have to rely on imported inputs. Other exporters, such as the growing oil and coal sectors, and firms that competed against imports also had preferences for real exchange-rate depreciation. Since the political system catered to elites more than the masses, the crawling-peg policy had solid political support, even if it did contribute to moderate inflation.

The bipartisan control of Colombian politics came under stress in the 1980s and was reformed in 1991. During the operation of the National Front, the traditional parties faced growing challenges to their authority. Labor unions organized strikes and resistance. Drug cartels exerted influence in the cities of Cali and Medellin as the cocaine trade boomed in the 1970s. Guerilla movements captured rural territories in Colombia. Violent conflicts between guerillas, drug cartels, right-wing militias and the government grew in intensity during the 1980s (see Hartlyn and Dugas, 1999, pp. 276-280; Martz, 1992, pp. 30-36). After a series of broken cease-fires and ineffective crackdowns, a consensus developed in favor of opening the political system to the guerilla movements and other voices of social protest. In 1990, President Cesar Gaviria threw his political weight behind the formation of a Constituent Assembly, an elected body that would accelerate constitutional reform. Elections for the Constituent Assembly gave less than half the seats to the traditional parties, making them unable to dominate the agenda (Hartlyn and Dugas, 1999, p. 281). The 1991 constitution established a number of reforms, including restraints on presidential power, democratic election of departmental governors and the vice-president, electoral reforms, and the abolition of all vestiges of parity in cabinet participation and legislative representation (Hartlyn and Dugas, 1999, p. 282).

Constitutional reform, however, did not directly inspire the neo-liberal economic reforms of the Gaviria administration. Some of the constitutional provisions were actually contrary to standard neo-liberal program, allowing government to infringe on property rights and mandating a devolution of government financing that increased the central government's budget deficit. While the constitution embraced a market economy, it also allowed government to constrain markets if policymakers deemed it to be in the broader interest of society (Hartlyn and Dugas, 1999, p. 272). The new constitution, however, still allowed the presidency discretion in determining economic policy. The opening or "apertura" in the political system also broke down the influence of old patron-client relationships as new voices participated in the political system.

As a result, the Gaviria administration had the opportunity to develop an economic policy based on new foundations of political support. By the 1990s, the coffee industry had declined to where it supplied only about 20% of Colombia's total exports, (Garcia Garcia and Jayasuriya, 1997, p. 22), but oil and coal had become major foreign exchange earners (*Economist Survey*, 2001, p. 15). These industries continued to prefer depreciation, but were appeased when the government tempered its free-market reforms with tariff or subsidy programs targeted specifically for their industries (Jaramillo, et. al., 2001, pp. 222-224). The neo-liberal program promised lower inflation and higher productivity. The crawling bands allowed for an appreciating real exchange rate. Appreciation hurt export industries but helped restrain inflation, which had a broader appeal to consumers and non-exporters.

The demise of the crawling band

How then did the crawling band fall apart in 1999? The transparency hypothesis may help to provide an answer but it is not clear. In 1963, the government nationalized the hitherto private Banco de la Republica, which maintained Colombia's gold standard. Until the apertura reforms of 1991, government officials made up the entire Board of Directors for the central bank. The new 1991 constitution made the central bank more legally autonomous, with a Board made of up members appointed by the government with staggered fixed-year terms (Jaramillo, et. al., 2001, pp. 208-209). The history of the bank's legal foundations implies that it was highly dependent from 1963 to 1991 and more independent after 1991. If so, then the crawling peg was Colombia's commitment to a given rate of monetary expansion in the years of limited democracy and central bank dependence. Colombia could more readily float after 1991 once it had established a new constitution and credibility for its newly independent central bank.

However, two caveats are in order. First, Colombia's moderate inflation for many decades could signal that it was not committed to any restrictions on monetary expansion using any commitment mechanism. But in defense of the government, even Colombia's moderate inflation was noticeably lower than the hyperinflation some of its neighbors experienced, and more consistent over time. Second, the legal dependence of the Colombian central bank during the period from 1963-1991 is also contradicted by Cukierman's behavioral measure of central bank independence (1992) which measures the turnover in central bank governors. After 1960, a central bank governor had an average tenure of 6.5 years, longer than in most Latin American countries (Jaramillo, et. al., 2001, pp. 209-210). This may indicate that central bank governors had more de facto independence from the government than apparent in the law, but it could also simply reflect the unusual stability of the Colombian state.

As far as some economists are concerned, the crawling band's appreciation laid the seeds of its own demise and the seeds of recession. Central bank officials tended to deny this, arguing that the devaluations were largely the result of expansionary fiscal policy and growing consumer spending.[3] In their view, the real appreciation of the exchange rate was in equilibrium and a response to foreign investment in a country with increased productivity and petroleum discoveries. Linda Kamas (2001), on the other hand, argues that the central bank actually maintained a misaligned exchange rate. The central bank kept interest rates high and this, combined with a crawling band with rate of depreciation slower than the rate of inflation, encouraged capital inflows. The capital inflows, combined with persistent government budget deficits, increased imports at a time when the real exchange rate appreciation hurt exports. The current account deficit worsened. Foreign investors were willing to invest in Colombia while inflation was down and productivity was growing, and thus Colombia could finance its current account deficits. The Colombian financial system however was weak and inadequately supervised and so it invested the foreign funds poorly (Economist Survey, 2001, pp. 13-14). Foreign investors eventually lost confidence as asset and property bubbles burst, insurgent activity shook the government, and the current account showed no signs of improving (see IMF, 1999b, pg. 5). Growth in real GDP slowed down to just 0.57% in 1998, for the first time in several years. When the capital inflows would no longer finance current account deficits, Colombia's authorities had to make the familiar but difficult choice of whether to defend, devalue, or float the exchange rate. The government devalued the crawling band in September 1998 and June 1999. These actions still did not relieve pressure on the band, and so in September 1999 the government finally let the exchange rate float.

After decades of being shielded from unstable capital flows, Colombia fell into the familiar trap of a persistently misaligned exchange rate, a rush of capital inflows, followed by a loss of investor confidence. Why did the government try to maintain the ailing crawling band from 1997 to 1999? The first devaluation came a few months after a presidential election, which is more evidence favoring the election hypothesis. After the election in mid-1998, however, the government's behavior needs further explanation. Private agents had less observable interest in the crawling band at this time. With the economy already in a recession, the struggle for lower inflation appealed to fewer people, although consumers lost purchasing power with the falling peso. Export and manufacturing industries would only benefit from the depreciating and more competitive exchange rate. The bankers' association opposed any move that would curtail real appreciation, low inflation, or capital inflows (Jaramillo, et. al., 2001, pp. 224-225). The financial intermediation hypothesis, however, is less relevant here. First, the banks had already hedged much of their external debt against exchange rate risk. The banking sector was already facing a crisis due to non-performing loans and a devaluation or floatation was not going to exacerbate the situation. Second, while indicators of financial intermediation were improving in the 1990s, Colombia's banking system was still weak and underdeveloped compared to other middle-income states and thus was not the powerful lobby that banking was in other states.

The reason that the government tried to maintain the crawling band after the 1998 elections seems to have more to do with anti-inflation credibility. After using the crawling band and high interest rates to bring down inflation in the early 1990s, the central bank seemed loath to give up that credibility. In contrast to the idea that independent central banks and pegged exchange rate are substitutes, the bank had based some of its credibility on the crawling band and floatation would have meant that it had to rebuild credibility through other means. Colombia's recession seems to have been another case where a government was holding to a policy that favored long-run anti-inflation performance even when in the short-term the real economy could have used some depreciation in the exchange rate.

Once the government finally did float the exchange rate, however, it faced little organized opposition from domestic constituencies.

Conclusions

Colombia demonstrates the limits of the financial intermediation hypothesis and what one needs to remember if one wants to apply it to other countries. First, from 1967 to 1994 Colombia is an example of a state that persisted in managing an intermediate ERR even though it had little bank-credit intermediation. If countries with little bank-credit intermediation maintain pegs or bands for longer than most middle-income countries, it is largely because they are not exposed to the hollowing-out pressures that have encouraged or forced other countries to abandon pegging. Many oil-rich states in the Middle East face little capital mobility and can thus retain a peg to the dollar to keep oil revenues stable. Colombia's case is more unique in that while it has a crawling peg from 1967 to 1991 it had capital controls. The capital controls did not prevent a lot of capital from being mobile, but offshore banking and a black market in foreign exchange helped to facilitate underground capital mobility. Consequently sizable capital movements did not endanger the central bank's reserves of foreign exchange. After 1990, Colombia abolished many of the capital controls and established crawling bands. The wide band of the exchange-rate regime was flexible enough to adjust to most international capital movements in an environment of high capital mobility, although the central bank had to adjust the bands at times. Growing international capital reserves helped to keep the confidence of international investors during the 1990s. In a number of ways, Colombia has historically been isolated from hollowing-out pressures. The financial intermediation hypothesis applies best when states face difficulty in maintaining a peg with mobile capital, but states must consider other concerns besides the threat from mobile capital.

After 1994, the situation changes and Colombia represents a different difficulty for the financial intermediation hypothesis. Colombia at this point has no significant capital controls, the spot exchange rate hovers near the limits of the band, and the central bank spends reserves to defend it. Without its normal protections from hollowing-out pressures, Colombia falls into a familiar trap. The crawling band, low inflation, and market-friendly policies encourage capital inflows and a widening trade deficit. When investors lose confidence and pull out their money and government officials must make hard choices concerning the ERR. In this particular case, the government defends the crawling band for over a year but the banking sector seems to contribute less to the explanation. The government faces an upcoming election and the central bank relies on the band as a source of inflation-fighting credibility. Colombia has reasons to maintain its ERR, but not the reasons given in the financial intermediation hypothesis. While bank-credit financial intermediation makes maintaining a peg or band more likely, and while the pressure of banking sectors is a common part of the explanation of pegging that later had to yield to an exchange-rate crisis, it is not the only possible condition that can encourage a government to maintain a peg or band. Colombia is an object lesson in how otherwise sufficient conditions are not necessary conditions.

Notes

[1] Since calculations did not range from 1987 to 1996, Colombia was not included in the dataset for the aggregate statistical tests in Chapter 3.
[2] The removal of capital controls will be detailed below.
[3] According to the Kamas' (2001) first endnote, the central bank made this point in a number of its publications. See Kamas, 2001, p. 164.

Chapter 8

Conclusions

Exchange-rate crises occur for a number of reasons. The 1990s saw a number of crises in developing countries in which a foreign private investment boom was followed by a sudden panic of foreign investors, causing the exchange rate to plunge. In many cases, economists blamed pegged exchange rates, arguing that they caused real exchange-rate misalignment and presented credibility problems. Defenders of the "hollowing out thesis" (HOT) argued that growing capital mobility made pegged exchange rates more difficult to maintain and therefore governments would increasingly use some form of rigid fixes or floats. As Mexico, Thailand, Malaysia, Brazil, and others faced exchange-rate collapse throughout the decade, and abandoned their pegs for floats, the HOT gained credence, even with officials in the IMF and the U.S. Treasury Department. The experiences of these developing countries beg the question why, if the environment of quicksilver, global capital made a pegged exchange rate so dangerous, did so many governments keep using them? Why did these governments not see the warning signs and start establishing monetary unions or floats earlier? Why did so many governments wait until a crisis erupted and had no other choice?

To answer this question, this book has investigated seven hypotheses concerning exchange-rate regimes. The objective was to refine and highlight the evidence for one hypothesis in particular, the claim that states with strong financial systems based on bank credit were more likely to maintain their pegged exchange rates. The hypothesis argues that a number of governments catered to the specific interests of their banks and/or feared a possible banking crisis. The next section of this book summarizes and analyzes the results of the statistical tests and the case studies for each of the hypotheses considered. The second section considers the implications for the development of theory in political economy. The last section details what implications the findings have for policy concerns.

The hypotheses

This book considered seven hypotheses concerning capital mobility, trade, GDP, manufacturing, government transparency, elections, and financial intermediation. This section will examine each in turn.

Capital Mobility

According to the statistical tests, the degree of capital mobility does not significantly influence the likelihood that a state will maintain a peg. In this case, negative results need some careful interpretation. The lack of significance could be because 1) the indicator does not measure capital mobility well, 2) the HOT is invalid or 3) the rational actor assumption behind the hypothesis is invalid.

Capital mobility is notoriously difficult to measure. Furthermore, the indicator used here measures differentials in interest rates, which is not the only approach to measuring capital mobility. Other approaches to measuring capital mobility involve indexes of capital controls (Quinn, 1997; Haggard and Maxfield, 1996) and measuring the correlation of domestic savings and investment (Feldstein and Horioka, 1980). Each method has its problems (Montiel, 1993). The interest-rate approach used here requires estimates of exchange rate expectations that are difficult to measure. Capital controls indexes do not capture all of the possible barriers to capital mobility, which include tax regulations and asymmetric information. Savings-investment correlations do not provide cross-section, time-series data for individual countries. More work could be done on improving the indicators, and devising a series of tests that investigate if all of the approaches provide consistent answers. In many tests of exchange rate policy and exchange rate crises, however, the indicator for capital mobility is a dichotomous variable coded 0 if capital controls are prevalent and 1 if capital controls are few (see Shambaugh, 2004, p. 288; Eichengreen, Rose, and Wyplosz, 2003, p. 145). The tests used here have the advantage of using a continuous variable that measures more than the legal barriers to capital mobility.

Could the HOT simply be invalid? The case studies imply that capital mobility definitely has a role in ERR decisions. Thailand, Mexico, and Colombia all experienced exchange rate crises in the 1990s. In each case, sudden capital outflows prompted the government to float the currency after several years of pegging. Without capital mobility, each of these states may have found it easier to maintain their pegs. What the cases demonstrate is that the HOT, by relying on the systemic variable of capital mobility, is primarily a theory of consequences. It argues that the costs of maintaining a credible peg rise as capital mobility rises. Thailand found it more difficult and expensive to ward off speculative attack in the mid-1990s as compared to previous years. Mexico used several billion dollars in reserves trying to defend its crawling peg in 1994. As a theory of consequences, capital mobility can be considered a structural variable, determining the benefits and costs of choosing different policy options (Andrews, 1994). The HOT helps explain why numerous crises have reduced the number of pegs in developing countries and why states rarely go back to a peg after experiencing a crisis.

Both Thailand and Mexico, however, had high capital mobility for years before their respective crises but continued to peg. Peru, by contrast, abandoned pegging commitments well before capital mobility reached those levels. If capital mobility was so dangerous, why did Thailand and Mexico not switch to a float earlier? A theory of the consequences of policy behavior is not necessarily a theory of the policy behavior itself. In other words, the costs of maintaining a peg do not by themselves determine whether or not a state will peg, unless a crisis hits and the costs of maintaining a peg are unbearable. The case studies indicate that governments are simply not often forward thinking when it comes to exchange rate policy and do not act with rational expectations concerning the effects of capital mobility. Increasing capital mobility will not automatically generate worries among government officials that the risks of a crisis are growing. Hence defenders of the HOT felt the need to warn governments about the dangers of footloose capital (Council on Foreign Relations, 1999). Furthermore, if growing capital mobility does not produce worries of the growing risk of crisis, it is no surprise that capital mobility has no direct effect on the choice of ERRs. Capital mobility may have an influence on ERR policy in the long run, acting as a harsh environment that weeds out misaligned pegs. Until crises hit, however, governments focus on other considerations in the short run. This begs the question of what those considerations are and what could be diverting governments away from considering the risks of sudden capital outflows.

Trade Exposure and GDP

When discussing factors that influence the choice of ERR, economists traditionally look to optimal currency area (OCA) theory, which argues that the desirability of an ERR depends on the structural characteristics of an economy, characteristics that shape the benefits and costs of different ERRs. The more an economy benefits from price stability in its interactions with other economies, the more desirable is a fixed exchange rate. The more isolated or rigid the internal market is, the more desirable is a floating exchange rate. Economists have identified a number of characteristics as potential factors in the determination of ERR, such as GDP per capita, the geographic concentration of trade, and the diversification of exports, but the evidence presented here examines the two most cited factors, trade exposure and the size of GDP. According to OCA theory, smaller, more open economies are more likely to fix their exchange rates.

Since GDP was collinear with other variables in the statistical tests, the variable was left out. The GDP hypothesis is only partly successful in the case studies, however. Thailand and Colombia, both small economies, do indeed peg for many years throughout the 1980s and 1990s. Mexico, however, adheres to a crawling peg throughout 1994, in spite of intense pressure from international investors and in spite of being one of the larger economies of Latin America and the developing world. Peru is a smaller economy than Mexico, but it floats its exchange rate earlier (although in practice its exchange rate is little different from a crawling peg.

The trade hypothesis fares better with the evidence presented here. In the statistical tests, trade exposure is significant when controlling for the credit ratio, but not significant when controlling for the money multiplier. These results are robust even when performing checks on the statistical tests. Thailand is a relatively open economy and a pegged exchange rate suited its economy. Peru, more isolated from the world economy, was more willing to adopt a float. Colombia, however, had similarly low levels of trade exposure, and continued pegging for longer. Mexico is the most difficult case for the trade hypothesis. During the 1980s and early 1990s, when Mexico had relatively little trade exposure, it pegged its exchange rate. After Mexico's peso crisis, it floated its exchange rate, and its trade exposure grew.

In several statistical tests not presented here (Rizzo, 1998; Poirson, 2001), trade exposure and GDP demonstrate significance as influences on ERR choices. The preponderance of evidence from these tests is enough to allow the conclusion that cases such as Mexico and Colombia are exceptions rather than the rule. One can explain many of the exceptions by noting two problems with OCA theory. First, economists identify a number of economic variables as influences on ERR (trade exposure, GDP, the geographic concentration of trade, etc.), and a number of economic objectives (such as price stability or economic growth) that a government could try to achieve with an ERR. The different structural characteristics of an economy may yield different and conflicting pressures for an ERR. Consequently, an ERR chosen to satisfy one economic objective may frustrate a lesser objective. In the case of Mexico, the crawling peg was designed to reduce inflation, and the government was less concerned about using the exchange rate to absorb adjustments for a relatively large, closed economy, as OCA theory would emphasize.

Second, OCA theory virtually assumes that governments are unitary actors whose only interest is the optimal performance of the aggregate economy. Hence, governments rationally choose to fix exchange rates when an economy depends heavily on exports and imports or has a small internal market. Governments, however, are perfectly capable of choosing sub-optimal policies or policies that favor some groups or sectors at the expense of the whole economy. What is still needed, even when OCA theory applies well, is a theory of how governments come to choose policy objectives and decide that certain ERRs would satisfy those objectives. Such theorizing helps to explain why governments adopt new ERRs when they do. OCA theory has difficulty explaining the timing of ERR changes since economic characteristics tend to persist for long period of time. Economic considerations such as capital mobility, trade exposure and GDP can identify equilibrium conditions, which is to say that they can help explain why some governments persist with an ERR once it is adopted. Political factors, however, help explain why governments may persist with ERRs in spite of countervailing economic conditions or facilitate a country's transition to a more economically viable ERR.

Manufacturing

Frieden and Stein (2001) argue that unless trade exposure is quite high, manufacturing interests in developing countries will prefer a floating exchange rate. A fixed exchange rate tends to produce appreciation in the real exchange rate over time, which hurts competitiveness. Hence, they hypothesize that the larger the manufacturing sector in a developing country, the more likely it is to adopt a floating exchange rate. The statistical tests presented here provide some support for this hypothesis. When controlling for the credit ratio, the size of the manufacturing sector is significant, and increases the likelihood that a state will abandon a peg. When controlling for the money multiplier, however, the variable is not significant. The significance of the manufacturing sector, when controlling for the credit ratio, is robust in the face of further tests. As mentioned in chapter 2, cross-section tests performed by Frieden , Ghezzi and Stein (2001) and hazard tests performed by Blomberg, Frieden and Stein (2002) also find evidence for the hypothesis.

The case studies, however, demonstrate that the argument behind this hypothesis requires three caveats. Frieden, Ghezzi and Stein (2001) discuss the first two caveats in their evaluation of their results. First, if the government protects manufacturing firms with high tariffs, such firms may concentrate on the domestic market, and thus have less interest in export competitiveness. Pasco-Font and Ghezzi (2001) argue that this is the case in Peru from the 1950s to the 1980s, and thus the manufacturing sector was not actively lobbying the government for a float. Second, if manufacturing firms rely heavily on imported inputs for production this will increase the incentives for those manufacturers to support a fixed exchange rate to help stabilize production costs. Third, if manufacturing firms owe dollar-denominated debt directly to foreign investors this will increase incentives to prefer a pegged exchange rate. The overall preferences of manufacturing firms for exchange-rate policy depend on the overall balance of firms' export sales, imported inputs, financial liabilities, and financial assets (see Walter, 2005). In Thailand, where the manufacturing sector is relatively large for a developing country, these caveats help explain why manufacturing firms did not lobby hard for the government to abandon the pegged exchange rate. In Mexico, where malquiladora plants proliferated after the government reduced restrictions on foreign direct investment, the reactions of manufacturing firms to the sudden decline in the value of the peso in 1994 were also mixed.

The caveats help to explain how the trade and manufacturing hypotheses could simultaneously achieve significant results, as they do here and in Frieden, Ghezzi, and Stein's (2001) results. The trade hypothesis implies that a strong export sector would prefer fixed exchange rates, while the manufacturing hypothesis implies that it would prefer floating exchange rates. If domestic manufactures use primarily domestic inputs for export production, then competitiveness is a strong concern. If manufacturers use a lot of imported inputs (making trade exposure higher), then price stability is more of a concern. If manufacturers are primarily oriented to the domestic market, however, then stability in export and import prices are less of a concern. Even a country with a small manufacturing sector may prefer a floating exchange rate to shift economic adjustments onto the exchange rate and away from the domestic goods sector.

The degree of export orientation, imported inputs, trade protection, and foreign indebtedness varies among manufacturing firms. This implies that while (all other thing being equal) manufacturing firms will prefer a competitive exchange rate, some manufacturing firms have more interest in competitiveness than others and some have significant offsetting interests in exchange rate stability. Consequently, the diversity of interests produces collective action problems for manufacturing firms should they wish to lobby the government. More case study research could be done at the firm and industry levels to discover firm preferences and the dynamics of lobbying on exchange-rate issues. More statistical research could also be done at a macro level to investigate how diverse firm preferences are.

Democracy and Transparency

Broz (2002) argues that states face a basic choice while establishing anti-inflation credibility, a choice between establishing an independent central bank and a fixed exchange rate. Private actors have difficulty in determining how truly independent central bank decision-making is. By comparison, private actors can easily see how well a government adheres to a fixed exchange rate. Broz goes on to argue that democracies, having more electoral competition, open media outlets and higher audience costs for decision-makers, can provide decision-makers with more incentive to protect central bank independence (CBI) and can give private actors more ability to monitor decision-makers. Authoritarian governments, which cannot provide credibility for CBI, must rely on fixed exchange rates instead. Broz thus hypothesizes that authoritarian governments are more likely to choose fixed exchange rates than democracies are.

The research presented here presents little evidence in favor of this hypothesis, but it does have support elsewhere.[1] The statistical tests using interactive variables do demonstrate significance for the indicator of democracy at the 0.10 level, but not at the 0.05 level. The tests that do not use interactive variables show no significance for the indicator. Broz finds significance for democracy at the 0.01 level, and Shambaugh (2004) finds significance at the 0.05 level, with tests that control for forms of financial intermediation. All of these tests use the same indicator drawn from the Polity IV database. Frieden, Ghezzi, and Stein (2001) find some significance for a dummy variable representing authoritarianism. The lack of significance in the tests presented here may largely be due to differences in samples used in the tests. Broz presents statistical tests using data from 109 countries, and incorporates both developed and developing countries in his dataset. Advanced industrial democracies often have high degrees of CBI and several years of experience in floating exchange rates. The findings are not simply the result of including developed states in the dataset, however. Shambaugh and Frieden, et. al. perform tests on data only from developing countries and also find significance for the variable. The lack of significance here could be due to a smaller sample size, a different specification of the statistical equation, or a different coding of ERRs than what Broz and Frieden et. al. use.

Aside from statistical evidence, however, the case studies provide troubling difficulties for the causal logic of the argument. First, it not clear that all developing-country governments strive for anti-inflation credibility. Some governments resort to printing money in order to satisfy domestic constituencies with government spending programs, to avoid taking the painful steps necessary to tax or borrow, because they are discounting the need to establish credit for foreign borrowing, or some combination of the three. Peru's experience in the 1980s is a case in point, where both the Belaunde and Garcia administrations restricted external debt repayment and refrained from restraining government spending or raising taxes to mollify key supporters. Colombia also tolerated persistently high inflation until the 1990s so that its export industries could benefit from consistent real exchange rate depreciation.

Second, it is not clear that governments treat fixed exchange rates and independent central banks as mutually exclusive options. Thailand has one of the more independent central banks in the developing world, with relatively consistent turnover in central bank governors regardless of who was in charge of the government or what form of government Thailand had. Maxfield (1997, pgs. 78-86) argues that Thai governments were more willing to defend central bank independence to maintain credibility with foreign investors. Nonetheless, Thailand also maintained a pegged exchange rate during most of the 1980s and 1990s, even though this limited the autonomy of the central bank. Colombia's central bank, another central bank with regular, relatively de-politicized turnover in leadership, relied on a crawling band and an appreciating currency to help maintain anti-inflation credibility in the 1990s.

Third, governments may sometimes employ a third alternative for combating inflation, income policy. In one sense, Mexico confirms the transparency hypothesis, as Mexico employed a crawling peg during the years of opaque and autocratic PRI rule during the Salinas administration, while maintaining a float after the relatively free and fair elections of 1994 and 2000. The crawling peg of the Salinas administration, however, was part of a negotiated bargain in which unions promised to restrain wage demands and businesses promised to restrain price increases if the government maintained an effective peg. The government chose a combined strategy of a pegged exchange rate and income policy to combat inflation after suffering the high inflation of the 1980s. Other Latin American states have employed income policy to varying degrees in order to combat inflation. Four cases are not enough to disconfirm a hypothesis. These cases, however, make it quite plausible that while democracy may correlate with floating exchange rates in developing countries, the transparency hypothesis may have misdiagnosed the causal process that links the variables.

Elections

Frieden and Stein (2001) also argue that governments are more likely to maintain a fixed exchange rate in the months before an election, for fear of offending voters with a loss of purchasing power. Devaluations and floatations are more common immediately after an election, which gives most governments more time to improve economic conditions before the next election. As with the manufacturing hypothesis, tests by Frieden, Ghezzi, and Stein (2001) and by Blomberg, Frieden, and Stein (2002) support this argument. On a related note, Leblang (2003) finds that an impending election makes a developing-country government more likely to defend rather than devalue an exchange rate. Shambaugh's tests (2004) do not find confirmation of this argument. Shambaugh, however, uses annual data that may not be detailed enough to capture the effects of elections, as these effects are often specific to certain months. The tests presented here use quarterly data, but also do not confirm the hypothesis. More puzzling is that the hazard ratios imply that elections increase the likelihood of abandoning a peg. Since the results are not significant, however, the results may be due to chance. The relatively smaller sample size may frustrate the ability of these hazard tests to test the election hypothesis. While variables such as capital mobility, trade exposure, and financial intermediation have different measures every quarter for each country, the number of elections in a sample of fourteen states is small. Furthermore, since the dataset must end with the year 1998, the dataset does not manage to include the abandonment of Brazil's crawling peg in early 1999, which followed an election. The tests by Freiden et. al. and Blomberg et. al. employ monthly data from a wide variety of developing countries, which is probably the most appropriate approach for testing this hypothesis.

The case studies provide extra support for the argument. Mexico persisted with its crawling peg in 1994 in part to appeal to middle-class and working class voters. As more than one scholar has noted (Kessler, 1999; Starr, 1999b) the crawling peg increased purchasing power for consumer imports. The botched devaluation and the consequent peso crisis came a few months after the election. Colombia devalued its crawling band a few months after a presidential election in 1998, finally abandoning the band in September 1999. In the Peruvian election of 1990, voters demonstrated little wish to see officials defend a pegged exchange rate, but this was a period of hyperinflation and the peg provided no discernable protection of purchasing power. In Thailand, the election hypothesis did not apply because no election was scheduled in 1996 or 1997 while foreign investors put pressure on the currency. The logic of the hypothesis seems to hold when examining individual cases.

Financial Intermediation

The main purpose of the statistical tests and the case studies was to investigate the effect that forms of financial intermediation had on the length of time that a government held on to a pegged exchange rate. Both the statistical tests and the case studies provide evidence for financial intermediation hypothesis, although they also demonstrate four limitations of the hypothesis.

The statistical tests provide support for financial intermediation hypothesis. Two different indicators of the strength of the banking system, the money multiplier and the credit ratio, are significant at the 0.05 level. The tests are fairly robust to checks on outliers. These results are consistent with Shambaugh's (2004) tests of forms of financial intermediation on ERRs. The two sets of tests have strengths that make up for the weaknesses in each, providing stronger support for the claim that scholars should control for financial intermediation when performing tests of ERR choice. Shambaugh's cross-section, time series logit tests include data from a wide number of developing countries from 1973 to 2000. His tests measure private bank lending and foreign portfolio lending as a share of GDP, and measure capital controls as a dummy variable. The hazard tests presented here concern a smaller sample of countries and time series, but use different indicators for financial intermediation and a more sophisticated indicator for capital mobility. Financial intermediation variables can be shown to have a wide applicability across developing countries and even when testing for a number of other relevant variables.

The case studies also demonstrate an underlying causal process for those states with strong banking sectors and a pegged exchange rate that the government maintained until an exchange rate crisis hit. Although Thailand and Mexico have different cultural and economic backgrounds, both countries have strong banking sectors. Bank credit forms the basis of Thailand's financial sector. In Mexico, capital markets are arguably as strong if not stronger than the banking sector, but the banking sector grew considerably after bank privatization, and Mexico developed one of the stronger banking sectors in Latin America. In both cases, three or four banks dominated the banking sector and banking operations were run much like a cartel. This helps the respective banking sectors organize for their interests in active bankers associations. Governments often protected their private banking sectors from foreign competition and strict accounting practices. In Thailand, this reflected the central role that banks played in Thai finance, while in Mexico these protections made banks more attractive for purchase in the process of privatization. The lack of accountability allowed non-performing loans to accumulate. Thanks to capital mobility, banks were also able to borrow significant sums of unhedged dollar-denominated debt. The unhedged external debt in both countries made banks sensitive to a devaluation or floatation, and, combined with their non-performing loans, susceptible to a crisis. In both cases, governments tried to defend their currencies despite pressures from worried and doubting investors. When the governments could no longer defend their currencies, exchange rate crises occurred, producing the very floating exchange rates and banking crises governments were trying to avoid.

Peru is a negative case in which a country faces international pressures to abandon a pegged exchange rate, but has no strong banking sector or interest groups that oppose the transition. In Peru's case the international pressure did not come from capital mobility, as capital controls and exchange restrictions were relatively tight under the Garcia administration. Consequently, domestic banks did not borrow extensively from abroad. After experiencing hyperinflation in the late 1980s, the World Bank recommended a floating exchange rate as part of a shock therapy package. The IMF would grant loans for the crisis contingent on these recommendations. Once in office, Fujimori implemented a shock therapy program with a floating exchange rate. Few domestic groups opposed the float. Many banks were in government hands. The private banks did not hold significant amounts of dollar-denominated debt, and what external debt the banks did have did not face much exchange-rate risk since much of their domestic lending was in dollars. Moreover, the manufacturing sector could benefit from a more competitive exchange rate, parties were weak and most voters simply wanted the government to rein in the hyperinflation. In Peru's case, it was easier for the government to move to a float without offending key interests. As a result, Peru abandoned its peg earlier than Thailand or Mexico did. Peru thus avoided the combination of capital mobility and misaligned pegs that damaged Thailand and Mexico.

Nevertheless, the financial intermediation hypothesis has its limits. If it is true that banks oppose a floating exchange rate when they hold dollar-denominated debt, then it is reasonable to argue that the interaction of a financial intermediation indicator and an indicator of foreign liabilities should be significant. The indicator for the level of foreign liabilities is not significant in any of the tests. Frieden, Ghezzi, and Stein (2001) also find no significance for the same indicator in their tests. The interaction of financial intermediation and foreign liabilities is also not significant. It could mean that the indicator for foreign liabilities, the amount of dollar-denominated debt divided by M2, is not the best measure of foreign liabilities and scholars should develop and test other measures. One possible explanation, however, is that the mere presence of foreign liabilities is not enough to convince a government to maintain pegged exchange rates. Those holding unhedged dollar-denominated debt may face collective action problems in articulating their preferences for a peg to the government. For example, some larger manufacturing firms in a developing country may have borrowed extensively from international banks, but many other manufacturing firms may not have, making the manufacturing sector more divided over exchange rate policy. Nor may governments be concerned with some private firms facing uncertain costs for debt repayment if other economic considerations take priority. An active banking sector, however, often has qualities that overcome these difficulties. With a concentrated and active banking sector, most of the largest banks will have borrowed extensively from abroad, giving the dominating banks similar interests in a peg and fewer collective action problems. Furthermore, if a state actively relies on bank credit for the financing of industry, threats to the balance sheets of banks could result in a banking crisis or a slowdown in lending. Either of these results would damage economic growth to a degree that repayment difficulties in other firms would not. While this explanation does not explain why interactive terms for financial intermediation and foreign liabilities are insignificant, it helps explain why the size of the banking sector is the more significant indicator.

Tests of the financial intermediation indicator on de facto exchange rate regimes (based on actual exchange rate behavior) are not significant (see Appendix). None of the hypotheses described above, however, demonstrate the expected results in these tests. Financial intermediation has a demonstrable effect on official exchange-rate policy, not the degree to which governments allow flexibility in foreign exchange. One can object that banks and other actors will rationally be more concerned with actual exchange rate behavior than with the promises of governments, especially if governments break those promises, but this objection must be considered in perspective. Economists have only recently developed techniques to determine the degree to which governments adhere to their stated exchange-rate regime and these techniques involve sophisticated econometrics. Banks and other private actors in developing countries have been limited in their ability to monitor their governments' adherence to their exchange-rate commitments. It is relatively simple to observe when exchange rates diverge from the government's stated peg or band, frequent announcements of devaluations, or the growth of a parallel exchange market. By contrast, if a government proclaims a floating exchange rate but operates a de facto peg, and that de facto peg is abandoned, this is more difficult to detect. Furthermore, an abandoned de facto peg involves fewer issues of credibility. While private actors may discount official government commitments when devaluations are frequent or people exchange currency in parallel markets, they often look to official exchange-rate policies, since they are the only guide to future exchange rate behavior that is easy to monitor. Hence when private actors lobby the government, they emphasize the official exchange-rate policy.

Banks also borrow significant amounts from abroad only when capital is mobile. When capital is immobile across borders, banks do not accumulate dollar-denominated debt. Mobile capital, however, can take several forms, such as foreign direct investment or portfolio investment, or go to governments or manufacturing firms instead of banks. Capital mobility is thus a necessary, but not sufficient condition for the financial intermediation dynamic to supply pressure to maintain a peg. Colombia illustrates this well. Banks in Colombia are weak compared to Thailand and Mexico, but it maintained a peg throughout the 1980s. Colombia faced few hollowing-out pressures due to the use of capital controls and informal financial markets that evaded capital controls, and thus the government avoided exchanging large amounts of foreign currency to meet demand. Many oil-producing Arab states also limit capital mobility, which allows their governments to continue pegging without being overwhelmed by demands for foreign exchange. Peru's capital controls and hyperinflation in the 1980s constrained capital mobility, so the international pressure to abandon a peg came from multilateral lending agencies, not private investors. In all of these cases, states have low rates of domestic savings, and without access to foreign savings banks are unable to develop significant levels of financial intermediation. Banks therefore do not become key interests in the formation of exchange rate policy. If capital is not mobile, though, states can maintain a peg without risking a crisis simply for lack of hollowing-out pressures.

The financial intermediation hypothesis does not imply that all exchange rate crises are the result of banks pushing for misaligned pegs. Colombia illustrates some of the other conditions that can encourage a misaligned peg. In the 1990s, the Colombian banking sector was still underdeveloped and what foreign borrowing banks did was often hedged, as banks had observed what happened in the Mexican peso crisis. The drive to maintain a peg came instead from the government's use of a crawling band as the foundation of an anti-inflation commitment. Colombia, now more diversified after decades of relying on a few commodities for export, now contained private actors more concerned with restraining inflation rather than improving competitiveness, and elected leaders interested in satisfying those demands.

Theoretical implications

In many balance-of-payments crises in developing countries in the 1970s and 1980s, the crises resulted from unsustainable government borrowing which encouraged imports and persistent balance of payments deficits. Pressure from the IMF, World Bank, the U.S. Treasury, and domestic interests led many developing countries to restrain government spending and open up their capital and goods markets. It was assumed that this neo-liberal consensus would not only reduce inflation and improve long-run economic growth, but reduce balance-of-payments and exchange-rate crises as well. In the 1990s, a new kind of balance-of-payments crisis developed in which capital mobility allowed foreign investment to finance more private investment in developing countries, only to exit quickly when balance of payments deficits and misaligned exchange rates seemed unsustainable. The research presented here emphasizes one particular dynamic in these crises. Capital mobility became a source of tension in countries like Thailand, Mexico, and Brazil. On the one hand, capital mobility, which provided access for more development finance, also provided the risk that foreign investors would place larger bets on the performance of an exchange rate peg. On the other hand, those states that relied on bank-credit for domestic financing found that their banks borrowed extensively from abroad and became sensitive to exchange rate fluctuations. Governments became caught in a bind, facing opposing pressures from currency market speculators and domestic banks, pressures that became more intense if other domestic interests besides banks favored a peg to reduce exchange rate risk or maintain purchasing power. Crises resulted as governments tried to maintain misaligned pegs to please domestic constituencies but increasingly found their ability to defend those pegs eroding.

Other scholars, mostly economists, have noted the role of dollar-denominated debt in these recent crises, but little work has been done to test the relevance of this claim with statistical tests. Little work has also been done to specify how such has a role in government decision-making and the political process. This book was written to fill those gaps. It also has implications for different strands of political economy literature, notably the debate on the HOT, the new literature on the political economy of monetary institutions, the "fear of floating," and the analysis of exchange-rate crises.

As stated above, the HOT is best conceived as a structural constraint on state behavior that does not determine choices. As capital mobility grows, the costs to the state of maintaining a peg grow in terms of enforcing captial controls, raising interest rates, and borrowing from abroad. An environment of mobile capital becomes a harsh environment in which states with pegged exchange rates pay higher costs. In a sort of Darwinian fashion, states abandon pegging as crises hit or costs become politically intolerable, and fewer states move from floating or rigid fixes to pegging. This begs the question of why some states persist in pegging despite the risks and costs. The theory advanced here analyzes exchange rate crises as the result of a tension between domestic and international variables, in this case a tension between the domestic pressures of banking interests and the Darwinian environment of capital mobility. The theory is part of a larger movement within international political economy research to emphasize the interaction between domestic and international level variables (Frieden and Martin, 2003). This sort of research inevitably builds on previous research that focused only on domestic or international level variables. In this case, the HOT detailed the consequences of choosing a pegged exchange rate and the long-term constraints on such a choice. The financial interemediation hypothesis, like many examples of recent research that emphasize domestic political factors, analyzes conditions governments consider when choosing ERRs in the short-run. Bringing the two together helps explain one dynamic behind some of the exchange rate crises in the 1990s, namely that governments chose to maintain pegs to appease domestic lobbies even though this choice was not sustainable in the long run. Moreover, capital mobility not only increases the cost of pegs but in some cases is a necessary ingredient for the foreign borrowing that gives banks an incentive to press for adherence to the peg. In this sense, capital mobility seems to be the foundation for contradictory and dangerous pressures in economic policymaking in ways that the proponents of the HOT had even not considered.

The research presented here has been empirical in its focus, analyzing why governments choose the ERRs they do. It has not been directed at the normative debate surrounding the HOT, the question of whether or not states should be pegging in today's environment of high capital mobility. Defenders of the HOT (Eichengreen, 1994; Goldstein 1995; Fischer 2001) have argued that capital mobility now makes pegging unsustainable, and that governments which continue to do it are tempting fate. Frankel (1999), a critic of this view, argues that "no single currency regime is right for all countries or at all times." Frankel emphasizes the central claim of OCA theory, that all ERR choices have economic benefits and costs, and these benefits and cost vary for each country and vary over time. The normative question revolves around weighing the costs of one ERR choice relative to the costs of the others. Frankel is right to argue that much of the debate about pegging has neglected discussion of what costs states incur from rigidly fixing or floating their exchange rates. In this book, I have granted that capital mobility is increasing the costs of pegging. Rigid fixes and floating, however, also come with costs such as prolonged adjustment during recessions or instability of prices. In the research presented here, cases like Thailand and Mexico demonstrate that some governments have focused on the costs of devaluation and floatation, while discounting the risks and costs of adhering to a peg. Following Calvo and Reinhart (2000), it seems that more economists should consider how the costs of dollar-denominated debt repayment, central to the "fear of floating," weigh against the costs of capital controls, high interest rates, and maintenance of investor credibility, central to the "fear of pegging." Such calculations seem to be more relevant to governments facing the possibility of exchange-rate crisis than proponents of the HOT have acknowledged.

The financial intermediation hypothesis also emphasizes a difficulty with the new political economy of monetary institutions, which analyzes fixed exchange rates and CBI as approaches to anti-inflation credibility. Conditions affecting the choice of monetary institutions are framed in terms of how they affect the tradeoff between anti-inflation credibility and policy flexibility (Bernhard, et. al, 2002). The approach has the advantage of analyzing how governments form a coherent monetary commitment strategy instead of looking at ERRs and central banks in isolation. Proponents of this approach allow that governments may establish monetary commitments for reasons other than anti-inflation credibility, but argue that anti-inflation credibility has been the emphasis in most states and the emphasis in most scholarly studies of monetary institutions. While it is true that credibility may be the goal for most exchange rate commitments, other motives may be decisive factors. Frieden (2002), for example, argues that interest-group debate over the adoption of European monetary union (EMU) pitted firms in tradable sectors, concerned mostly with exchange-rate stability, with firms in the non-tradable sectors, concerned mostly with monetary policy autonomy. In his analysis, anti-inflation credibility was not the main issue among interest groups. The financial intermediation hypothesis emphasizes that governments may maintain pegs more out of concern for foreign liabilities and the possibility of bank crashes than concern over inflation. Colombia's exchange rate crisis in 1999 demonstrated that the pursuit of anti-inflation credibility could lead to a crisis, and credibility was a key ingredient in the Mexican peso crisis. The Thai government was more concerned with protecting the banking sector, however, and concern for the banks rather than inflation helps explain the behavior of the Mexican government after the 1994 election. The time-inconsistency approach captures much of the considerations in government policymaking, but admittedly simplifies government objectives. A broader framework for theorizing must accept that a number of government objectives may influence exchange rate decisions.

The financial intermediation hypothesis also specifies a channel through which concerns about debt repayment can be articulated to the government. As mentioned above, Calvo and Reinhart (2000) argue that repayment of dollar-denominated debt is a concern behind the "fear of floating," but do not articulate a political mechanism through which government becomes sensitive to these concerns. Such mechanisms are evident for other economic policy concerns. As mentioned above, Frieden (1991, 2002) argues that different industrial sectors will articulate different concerns, price stability or competitiveness if they are tradables sectors and monetary policy autonomy if they are non-tradables sectors. Voters and investors can articulate anti-inflation concerns through elections and lobbying, respectively. The financial intermediation hypothesis locates the political articulation of debt repayment concerns in its most likely constituency, the banks. Other domestic constituencies, such as capital-market investors and manufacturing firms, may also borrow significant sums of dollar-denominated debt, but face more collective action problems in articulating these concerns to governments. The financial intermediation hypothesis thus puts prior examples of the fear of floating in a political context.

Finally, the financial intermediation literature fills a hole in the new literature on the political economy of exchange-rate crises. Some economists (Velasco and Cabezas, 1998; Kaminsky and Reinhart, 1999) note the connection between banking regulation or banking crises and exchange rate crises, but only describe the connection in terms of economic variables or regulatory policy. Other scholars have argued that political variables such as veto players (Haggard, 2000; MacIntyre, 2003), elections (Starr, 1999a; Leblang 2003) or partisan control of the government (Leblang 2003) have influences on the likelihood of crisis. Eichengreen, Rose, and Wyplosz (2003) have tested the role of government popularity only to find no evidence linking it to the likelihood of crisis. The research presented here makes the case that future research on exchange-rate crises should consider the political role of financial intermediation.

Predictions and recommendations

What future crises does the financial intermediation hypothesis anticipate? The hypothesis implies that high capital mobility, a strong private domestic banking sector, and pegged exchange rates can be a combustible combination under the right circumstances. Few middle-income developing countries today, however, have that combination, and those that currently do have mitigating factors that may prevent a crisis from occurring. Present circumstances may change and some countries may experience banking sector lobbying to maintain a peg, but for the time being it is unlikely. Future exchange rate crises are likely to occur for different reasons.

In the 1990s, Mexico, Thailand, South Korea, and Brazil were all open to capital mobility, developed strong banking sectors with extensive external debts and non-performing loans, and most of them insisted on pegging their exchange rates until investors panicked and forced a crash.[2] All four switched to floating exchange rates and refrained from re-establishing pegs. One of the consequences on the exchange rate crises of the 1990s was to clear away the pegged exchange rates from almost all of the emerging-markets with both high capital mobility and strong banking sectors. Several middle-income states still use pegs after the crises of course, but the vast majority of these states do not have strong banking sectors. This is apparent when surveying the states middle-income countries with populations over a million people in different regions of the world. In Latin America, most of the remaining pegs belong to Belize, Costa Rica, Honduras, Suriname, Uruguay, and Venezuela, none of whom have actively growing banking sectors. The populist politics of Venezuela are also likely to limit the influence of the financial sector on the government. In the Middle East, Egypt, Iran, Jordan, Morocco, Oman, Saudi Arabia and Syria all peg their exchange rates, in some cases because their economies are dependent on a dollar-denominated oil trade. A combination of government intervention and Muslim restrictions on lending at interest often prevents the development of strong private banking sectors, foreign portfolio investment or foreign bank lending. In Africa, Botswana and Swaziland have high figures for financial intermediation, but their economic development is focused on the diamond trade and they peg their currencies to the South Africa rand. Much of their pegging is due to their dependence on the South African economy. Hungary and Latvia are the primary examples of states that continue to use pegs in Eastern Europe, but in both cases the banking sector is underdeveloped and government officials treat their pegged exchange rates as stepping stones on the way to the adoption of the Euro. Current conditions may change, and states in Latin America particularly may try to encourage stronger banking sectors as a method of promoting investment and long-run industrial development. For now however, it is difficult to foresee where this may happen.

Until recently, the two states in East Asia that relied heavily on bank-based financing and maintained a peg were Malaysia and the People's Republic of China. Both altered their exchange rate policies in 2005 but continue to protect their exchange rates with capital controls. Both governments came to the same conclusion about the Asian financial crises: exposure to hot money puts an economy in danger. Malaysia was the one state with strong banking measures and a pegged exchange rate to re-establish a peg after succumbing to Asian contagion. The leader of Malaysia at the time, Dr. Mahatir Mohamad, blamed foreign investors for the crisis and imposed strict capital controls to prevent another crisis. Mahatir recently retired, and in 2004 a new election returned his successor, Abdullah Badawi, and his National Front coalition to power by a wide margin. Badawi has named a cabinet composed of many officials from previous Mahatir governments (*Economist*, 3 April 2004, p. 44). The new Badawi government shows little sign of diverging from the economic policies of Mahathir, making it likely that Malaysia will maintain capital controls into the foreseeable future.

China is unlikely to remove capital controls in the near future. The question of China's ERR is has been the subject of much debate. U.S. Treasury officials had demanded that China revalue or float its exchange rate, arguing that its decade-long policy of pegging to the U.S. dollar kept China's currency, the yuan, artificially low, helping to increase America's already extensive trade deficit. China has stated it wants to move the yuan to a floating exchange rate in the long term. On 21 July 2005 it revalued the yuan about 2% against the dollar and declared that it would peg the yuan to an undisclosed basket of currencies within a narrow band for the foreseeable future. Malaysia soon afterward declared that it would also no longer peg its currency, the ringgit, to the U.S. dollar (*New York Times*, 22 July 2005, p. A1). If China did float, its central bank would not need to purchase so many U.S. securities to maintain the exchange rate, relieving it from the pressure to accumulate reserves denominated in a declining dollar. Floating the yuan, however, would also disturb China's already shaky banking sector (*Economist*, 15 May 2004, pp. 67-69). While China has developed new capital markets in the past few years, capital markets that have grown remarkably quickly, the Chinese banking sector absorbs domestic savings equivalent to forty percent of GDP (*Economist Survey*, 8 February 2003, p. 11). Four-fifths of the lending from the four largest state-owned banks goes to state-owned enterprises (SOEs), which often lose money. The lending prevents bankruptcies and job losses but drains the economy of useful capital. Non-performing loans have piled up, but good estimates of how bad the problem is are predictably difficult to determine (*Economist Survey*, 20 March 2004, pp. 18-19). Given China's capital controls and its current account surplus, a sudden outflow of financial capital would not follow a float. Floating or revaluing the yuan, however, could allow the currency to appreciate. While this would make external debt repayment easier, it would attract a potentially unstable inflow of capital at a time when China is trying to restrain inflation. Appreciation in the currency might encourage an asset-price bubble and would also threaten China's export sector, threatening the stability of SOEs and their attendant banks. In this sense, state-owned financial intermediation is encouraging the maintenance of highly managed exchange rates, albeit according to a different causal logic than in Thailand and Mexico. Capital controls may prevent this situation from becoming an exchange-rate crisis, although China may still be exposed to a domestic banking crisis in the near future.

Bolivia is the only middle-income developing country that currently has high capital mobility, a growing banking sector, and a pegged exchange rate. Its interest rates on 90-day deposits (both those denominated in domestic currency and U.S. dollars) have been converging on U.S. interest rates for similar deposits. Bolivia's money multiplier and credit ratio have also been steadily increasing over the past few years.[3] Bolivia, however, has probably the most dollarized economy of any state short of those states like Ecuador and El Salvador that have formally adopted full dollarization (IMF, 2003, p. 15). This dollarization, like Peru's, was a reaction to a long period of hyperinflation. Consequently, Bolivian banks are not lending as much in domestic currency and are not so exposed to exchange-rate risk. Growing capital mobility and dollarization have effectively eradicated much of the government's control over much of the money supply, which now depends on the flow of dollars in and out of the country. While Bolivia officially pegs, its high degree of dollarization makes Bolivia's ERR little different from a rigid fix in practice. Banks, then, are unlikely to be responsible for pressure to maintain a fixed exchange rate and sudden outflows of capital are more likely to cause deflation than a devaluation.

Nevertheless, Bolivia's economy could become less dollarized over time, other Latin American states could begin to develop stronger private banking, or Malaysia and China could remove their capital controls. Policy actions taken now could prevent banks from contributing to future crises in these circumstances. It is tempting to think that if bank-credit financing encourages the maintenance of misaligned pegs, then perhaps governments should promote capital markets instead. Capital markets face more collective action problems in lobbying thus exposing governments to less direct political pressure. But capital markets, by themselves, may be no panacea. Mexico had some of the developing world's most sophisticated capital markets in the 1990s, but the bank privatization program allowed brokerages and financial companies to own many of the private banks, giving these investment firms incentive to favor a pegged exchange rate. One useful recommendation is establishing a particular kind of capital market, derivatives to hedge against exchange-rate risk. This would allow banks and commercial firms in developing countries to reduce their exposure to risk and distribute that risk among those more willing and able to accept and manage it. During the 1990s, few developing countries had markets for such derivatives. Only the banks and wealthiest firms in these countries could afford hedging instruments in international markets and many of them often did not bother to pay the costs. After the Mexican peso crisis, however, Mexican and Colombian banks were more likely hedge against exchange-rate risk, a trend that should be encouraged.

Additionally, governments should take steps to reduce concentration in the banking sector, or at least refrain from increasing concentration. Many commentators have advised that developing countries should only lift capital controls after the banking sector has been liberalized and decontrolled (McKinnon and Mathieson, 1981; Edwards, 1984; Eichengreen, 2003). They have also recommended that governments apply stricter accounting standards to banks to prevent the proliferation of non-performing loans. Many developing countries could benefit from banking sector liberalization and stricter accounting standards, but many of these recommendations do not address the political and institutional structures that promote inefficiencies and lax standards in the first place. Government policies that encourage bank-industry partnerships, consolidate banks for privatization, or limit foreign competition in the domestic banking sector may unwisely concentrate market share in few firms (although not always). Not only do these policies reduce competition in banking services, but they help a few banks become dominant and encourage domestic firms and individuals to depend on a few powerful banks. A small number of large banks find it easier to coordinate their lobbying and use their key role in investment to demand favors. While concentration is not the only reason accounting standards may be lax and non-performing loans grow, governments would have an easier time applying tougher standards to banks if individual banks were not as powerful.

Nevertheless, the present lack of countries that are likely to have the combustible combination of pegs, capital mobility, and strong banks in the future may imply that the time when banks were significant contributors to exchange-rate crises has largely passed. Banks were pushing governments in middle-income countries to maintain pegs in the 1990s and exchange rate crises did away with some of those pegs. Many middle-income countries with predominantly bank-credit financing now use managed floating. Exchange rate crises in the future are more likely to result from governments that pursue inflationary policies (as in Russia and Turkey) or anti-inflationary exchange rate policies that yield real exchange rate appreciation and persistent current account deficits (as in Argentina and Colombia). The latter problem indicates that exchange rate crises could occur even when governments adhere to rigid fixes or forms of managed floating. While capital mobility increases the risk that a pegged exchange rate will lead to a crisis, any ERR can be associated with a crisis. Since more and more developing countries have adopted managed floating, many of the next exchange rate crises will probably strike more states that intervene in currency markets.

Above, I argued that a difficulty with the new political economy of monetary institutions (Bernhard, et. al, 2002) was that it reduced the analysis of exchange rate regime determination to a tradeoff over time-inconsistency. The theoretical frameworks of scholars should allow that governments are not simply concerned with long-run anti-inflation credibility and policy flexibility to handle short-term growth problems. To the extent that anti-inflation mechanisms contribute to misaligned exchange rates and crises however, the new time-inconsistency approach will probably be more useful in identifying countries at risk of future crises than the financial intermediation hypothesis will be. Scholars working within the time-inconsistency approach, however, need to do more work identifying conditions applicable to developing countries that influence policies on ERRs and central bank independence and performing empirical research on developing countries. Nevertheless, this approach may still hold the most promising theoretical possibilities for identifying "warning signs" of misaligned exchange rates and exchange-rate crises in the future.

Such forecasts should not necessarily surprise us or indicate that research on the political influence of banks is useless. After the debt crises of the 1980s, scholarly attention focused on the causes and consequences of borrowing by developing countries and over-lending by international banks, and the effects of structural adjustment policies on growth and inequality in developing countries. Little of that research however, as valuable as it was, prepared anyone for the flight of private capital during the Mexican peso crisis or the Asian financial crisis. Scholarly research on these crises is not guaranteed to help us anticipate the next crises. Perhaps the last, ironic, lesson of the financial intermediation hypothesis may be that it is already time to look elsewhere for the causes of the next exchange-rate crises.

Notes

[1] In some of the tests I performed that control for levels of foreign exchange reserves and overvaluation of the exchange rate, the democracy indicator is significant at the 0.10 level and the hazard ratios for the indicator imply that higher democracy scores increase the likelihood of abandoning a peg. The indicator is not significant when controlling for growth in domestic credit or GDP per capita.

[2] In South Korea's case, however, the government heavily managed its floating exchange rate.

[3] Based author's calculations using IMF data.

Appendix

Chapter 3 reports the results of tests using a coding of ERRs based on the IMF's system of classifying official exchange-rate policies. Chapter 3 mentioned that other codings of ERRs are available, coding systems that do not rely on the declared policies of governments but on the movements of actual market exchange rates. This appendix describes one alternative system of coding ERRs, a process for adapting it as a dependent variable for hazard tests, and results of tests using this dependent variable. Unfortunately, the results are problematic, not just for the financial intermediation hypothesis, but also for all of the hypotheses discussed in this book. All of the variables in the tests fail to achieve significance except for the degree of foreign liabilities, but the hazard ratio for that variable is contrary to expectations. The last section of this appendix provides an analysis of what these test results may mean.

The Reinhart-Rogoff system

Carmen Reinhart and Kenneth Rogoff (2003a) developed an alternative method of coding ERRs designed to avoid the problems associated with official exchange-rate regime pronouncements. While their complete algorithm is too complex to report in detail here, some features that distinguish their method from the IMF's original system deserve to be mentioned. Their first step is to distinguish unified from dual exchange rate systems, arguing that most ERR classification systems fail to note how often states employ dual exchange rates. When market-determined exchange rates diverge significantly from official rates, Reinhart and Rogoff use the market exchange rates as the basis for classification. Second, they distinguish regimes with a pre-announced exchange rate target from those that do not and check exchange rate behavior to see if governments meet their targets. Third, if a state has no verifiable, pre-announced exchange rate target, the degree of volatility in the exchange rate over a five-year window determines the classification of the ERR. Fourth, they assign regimes to fifteen different classifications, including a category of their own invention, "freely falling." Freely falling exchange rates suffer from high inflation in their home states, as opposed to truly "freely floating" regimes in which the currency can either rise or fall in value.

To adapt the Reinhart-Rogoff method to a hazard model, I employ a new algorithm. Reinhart and Rogoff's data come in monthly form, except in some cases where exact dates are given for transitions between ERRs. When the identification of an ERR is not consistent over a whole quarterly period, the ERR adopted for most of the quarter determines how the quarter is coded. When Reinhart and Rogoff identify an ERR as a pre-announced exchange-rate target (whether that target is a peg or a band, adjustable or crawling), I code that state and quarter as a zero. De facto pegs or bands are also coded as a zero if Reinhart and Rogoff or the IMF record evidence of some sort of pre-announced target is associated with exchange rates.[1] Currency boards, managed floating, free floating and free falling represent corner solutions and are coded as a one. De facto pegs and bands with no pre-announced targets are also counted as a one, on the assumption that states have dropped any commitment to moderating the volatility of exchange rates. The HOT, remember, argues that capital mobility makes it difficult for states to *commit* to pegging. Using this system of coding pegs and non-pegs yields a different sample of states and a different observation period. Fifteen states fit the criteria of case selection described in chapter 3 and also had spells of de facto pegging observed from 1987 to 2000, although these were not the same set of states used in the chapter 3 tests.[2] Of the fifteen states that had a pre-announced, de facto peg between 1987 and 2000, ten abandoned their pegs for a float or free fall and five maintained their peg until the end of the observation period. Again, none of the states in the sample abandoned their pegs for a rigid fix.

Results of tests on actual exchange rate movements

I performed a second set of tests using the Reinhart-Rogoff data. These tests use hazard equations similar to those described and displayed in chapter 3, but with a different dependent variable. The indicators for the independent variables are the same as those described in chapter 3.

The descriptive statistics and correlation matrix for the tests are given in tables 9.1 and 9.2 respectively. Even with the use of a different sample of countries, the means for the independent variables are similar to the means in previous tests.[3] In the correlation matrix, the capital mobility indicator and inflation continue to have a high correlation, and GDP continues to have a strong correlation with trade exposure and the credit ratio. Otherwise, multicollinearity is not apparent.

The results of tests using an ERR indicator based on the Reinhart-Rogoff classification system do not support the financial intermediation hypothesis, but curiously they also do not support any of the hypotheses discussed in chapter 2. Table 9.3 shows the results of two tests using the Reinhart-Rogoff coding system. Equation V uses the money multiplier as the indicator for financial intermediation, while equation VI uses the credit ratio instead. The tests indicate that lower levels of capital mobility do reduce the likelihood of abandoning a peg, but the indicator is not significant. Nor unfortunately, are the either of the financial intermediation indicators. Curiously, however, none of the other economic and political variables cited in the other hypotheses, (trade exposure, GDP, size of the manufacturing sector, level of democracy, and the timing of elections) display any statistical significance either. The one exception is the foreign liabilities indicator, which is significant at the 0.05 level in equation V and significant at the 0.10 level in equation VI. Unfortunately, the tests indicate that a one percent increase in foreign

Table 9.1 Descriptive statistics for the tests using the Reinhart-Rogoff system

	Mean	St. Dev.	Minimum	Maximum
Money Multiplier	5.41	2.39	1.47	12.12
Credit Ratio	4.46	3.00	0.57	15.03
Capital Mobility	8.49	10.13	1.06	63.89
Foreign Liabilities	10.29	10.48	0.14	68.82
Inflation (log)	2.16	0.76	-1.34	4.83
Current Account	-1.24	6.60	-9.71	40.84
Trade Exposure	94.11	41.06	27.43	192.11
GDP (log)	4.15	0.77	2.65	5.72
Manufacturing	21.79	8.13	4.31	37.42
Democracy	4.97	6.02	-10.00	10.00
Elections	0.051	0.379	-1	1

Table 9.2 Correlation matrix for the tests using the Reinhart-Rogoff system

	CM	FLIA	INFL	CA	Trade	GDP	MM
CM	1.000						
FLIA	0.378	1.000					
INFL	0.582	0.173	1.000				
CA	-0.152	-0.197	-0.038	1.000			
TRADE	-0.477	-0.303	-0.295	0.221	1.000		
GDP	0.229	0.361	-0.206	-0.376	-0.569	1.000	
MM	-0.129	0.015	-0.230	0.252	-0.022	0.199	1.000
Credit	-0.022	0.317	-0.280	-0.145	-0.258	0.625	0.742
MANU	-0.046	0.082	-0.146	-0.333	0.378	0.052	-0.195
DEMO	0.127	0.063	0.069	-0.074	-0.409	0.228	0.098
ELECT	-0.010	0.002	-0.028	-0.019	-0.031	0.035	0.050
	Credit	Manu.	Demo.	Elect.			
Credit	1.000						
MANU	0.121	1.000					
DEMO	0.073	-0.481	1.000				
ELECT	0.054	-0.030	0.052	1.000			

Note: for a list of the abbreviations, see chapter 3, pp. 39-40. “MM” signifies the money multiplier, while “Credit” signifies the credit ratio.

Table 9.3 Results of tests using the Reinhart-Rogoff system

Variable	V	VI	VII	VIII
Capital Mobility	0.994 (0.055)	0.998 (0.056)	0.922 (0.092)	0.912 (0.104)
Foreign Liabilities/M2	1.061** (0.031)	1.057* (0.033)	1.073** (0.035)	1.086*** (0.034)
Inflation (log)	1.273 (1.688)	1.253 (1.661)	3.714 (8.178)	3.265 (7.419)
Current Account/GDP	0.932 (0.108)	0.932 (0.104)	0.824* (0.086)	0.810* (0.094)
Trade Exposure	0.992 (0.020)	0.992 (0.024)	0.967* (0.018)	0.964 (0.027)
GDP (log)	3.532 (3.370)	2.826 (2.528)	1.289 (1.116)	1.742 (1.621)
Money Multiplier	0.836 (0.154)		0.494** (0.174)	
Credit Ratio		0.952 (0.146)		0.611 (0.220)
Manufacturing Sector	0.951 (0.060)	0.961 (0.054)	0.966 (0.057)	0.981 (0.054)
Democracy	0.968 (0.126)	0.960 (0.115)	0.965 (0.057)	0.983 (0.070)
Elections	0.724 (0.815)	0.711 (0.750)	0.966 (1.138)	0.889 (1.128)
Log of time dependence (?)	0.306 (0.461)	0.286 (0.454)	0.980*** (0.321)	0.932** (0.391)
N	507	507	395	395
chi-squared	18.75	22.89	26.26	32.42
Prob>chi^2	0.043	0.011	0.003	0.000

* indicates significance at the 0.10 level
** indicates significance at the 0.05 level
*** indicates significance at the 0.01 level

liabilities relative to the broad money supply *increases* the likelihood of abandonment by about six percent. This is the opposite of what the financial intermediation hypothesis would predict. While this finding seems to falsify the financial intermediation hypothesis, it also presents a puzzle: why would an increase foreign indebtedness cause an increase in a state's chances of floating the exchange rate or letting the currency free fall? Floating or free falling currencies are only a threat to those in the state holding the debt and increasing foreign liabilities should only increase their preference for a de facto peg.

I performed other tests to check how robust these results are, with results not reported here. Tests that include an interaction variable for foreign liabilities and financial intermediation display no significance for the interactive variables and no indication that financial intermediation is significant in these equations.[4] Tests that drop the logarithm of GDP but include all of the other independent variables show the same lack of significance for all independent variables except foreign liabilities, indicating that multicollinearity is unlikely to be the source of the results.

Perhaps the method used to apply the Reinhart-Rogoff classification system to coding the dependent variable is problematic. As stated above, the tests in equation V and VI use a coding of the dependent variable in which only de facto pegs with some pre-announced exchange rate targets are coded as a zero, while all other regimes are coded as one (an instance of failure). The tests have been run using a different coding system, one in which all cases of de facto pegs and bands in the Reinhart-Rogoff system are coded as a peg, whether or not there is a pre-announced target, with results also not shown here. Only de facto floating and free falls are coded as a one. Using this third method of coding ERRs, I could identify a total of twenty countries with a de facto peg that satisfied the case selection criteria listed above. Of these twenty countries, ten ended with a float or a free fall and ten ended with states maintaining their de facto peg.[5] None of the spells ended with a state abandoning a peg for a rigid fix. The tests are not shown here but have identical results to equations V and VI. Foreign liabilities are significant and still indicate that more foreign liabilities increase the odds of abandonment. Financial intermediation and the other hypothesized variables are not significant.

Analysis

Why are the results so different with the Reinhart-Rogoff coding for ERRs? One plausible interpretation could begin by arguing that the Reinhart-Rogoff system of classifying ERRs is indeed superior to the IMF's original system. If so, then the results of equations V and VI demonstrate that we cannot discount the null hypothesis that financial intermediation has no real influence on ERR choices. Case studies aside, statistical testing has not demonstrated the general applicability of the financial intermediation hypothesis, and the results for foreign liabilities may call into question the logic of the hypothesis. But this would also imply that the Reinhart-Rogoff system calls into question not just the financial intermediation hypothesis but a wide body of theory on ERR determination. It is frankly disturbing that none of the indicators yield the predicted results, and more tests on ERR determination using the Reinhart-Rogoff system would be necessary to specify what the new system implies for a number of theories.

An alternative interpretation would, however, make two caveats. The first is that the IMF and Reinhart-Rogoff system do make different measurements. As stated above, the IMF system concerns official policies concerning exchange rates and official exchange rates, while the Reinhart-Rogoff system concerns actual exchange rate movements in (mostly) parallel exchange rate markets. One could argue that the financial intermediation and bank lobbying simply has more effect on official policies than the movement of exchange rates in non-official markets. Official ERR policies may or may not have an effect of actual market exchange rates. Perhaps political lobbying simply has a direct impact on official policies but is one step removed from determining patterns in market exchange rates.

Second, the case selection in the two datasets are different and may make much of the difference in the results. The tests using the IMF classification system include the cases of Belize, Egypt, El Salvador, and Papua New Guinea, while these cases must be dropped for the Reinhart-Rogoff tests reported above. In these four cases, the higher the level of financial intermediation, the longer they tended to peg. Meanwhile, the Reinhart-Rogoff tests do include Costa Rica, Mexico, South Korea, Sri Lanka, and Uruguay, while the IMF tests do not. In the cases of Costa Rica and Sri Lanka, low levels of financial intermediation did not prevent long stretches of de facto pegging. In equations VII and VIII display the results of hazard tests that leave out the Costa Rican and Sri Lankan data. Note that the money multiplier is significant, while the credit ratio is not. More variables achieve some level of significance in these tests than in equations V and VI. While tests that deliberately exclude data are not rigorously scientific tests, they may indicate that the lack of significance for financial intermediation on de facto ERRs may simply result from the fact that some states have low financial intermediation but have other reasons for maintaining a de facto peg. Here it is important to recall the specifics of the financial intermeditation theory presented in chapter 2. While high levels of financial intermediation encourage a banking lobby to borrow and press for pegging, when levels of financial intermediation are low, states face less domestic pressure to peg. But perhaps some states with weak banking sectors have alternative reasons for pegging. This is why chapter 7 investigates the case of Colombia, another state which has a relatively weak banking sector but maintained a crawling band for several years. Strong financial intermediation is by no means the only reason that states may persist in pegging, and perhaps the Reinhart-Rogoff tests include more states that have other reasons for pegging, reasons difficult to measure with quantifiable indicators.

One last point about the election hypothesis deserves to be made. In the tests shown above, the election indicator is not significant, but does have hazard ratios lower than one, implying that upcoming elections do lower the likelihood that a state will abandon a peg. This stands in contrast to the puzzling results of the IMF tests in chapter 3, which imply that upcoming elections increase the likelihood of abandoning a peg. The lack of significance for the election indicator in the Reinhart-Rogoff tests may in part be due to an anomalous outlier. In December 1999, Chile had a presidential election, while on 2 September 1999 Chile abandoned its pre-announced crawling band for a managed float (Reinhart and Rogoff 2003). The incumbent party actually won re-election in spite of the floatation. This episode is a rare example of an anomaly for the election hypothesis. I performed some further tests to find out what effect the anomaly had on the Reinhart-Rogoff tests, with results not shown here. If the Chilean floatation had occurred immediately after the 1998 election, then the election indicator would have been significant at the 0.01 level, regardless of whether the money multiplier or credit ratio was used. If the Chilean election had simply not occurred in 1998 but the government still floated toward the end of that year, the election indicator would still not have been significant. The first findings indicate that results for the election indicator may be sensitive to individual examples of elections, and different datasets might easily produce different results for the election hypothesis. Considering that the timing of elections mattered to the timing of ERR changes in Mexico and Peru, perhaps the election hypothesis should be taken more seriously than the tests in chapter 3 imply.

Notes

[1] For example, in some cases a state has a pre-announced band, but Reinhart and Rogoff report that the de facto band is actually wider than the state's claims. They thus classify such regimes as de facto bands even though the state has a pre-announced target.

[2] 2000 was the last year for which data on all of the independent variables was available. The cases in this sample were Algeria, Botswana, Chile, Costa Rica, Ecuador, Guatemala, Jamaica, (South) Korea, Malaysia, Mauritius, Mexico, Sri Lanka, Swaziland, Thailand, and Uruguay. Brazil also had a spell of pre-announced, de facto pegging according to Reinhart and Rogoff, but hyperinflation caused Brazil to have such extreme values for the capital mobility indicator that the case became an outlier responsible for false reports of significance for the capital mobility indicator. The results reported here use data that do not include Brazil.

[3] The mean for the capital mobility indicator does not match the mean for capital mobility described in chapter 3 since Brazil was dropped from the dataset in these tests.

[4] Unfortunately, Wald tests are not available on equations using Huber/White standard errors, but the full equations with interactive variables do not show chi-squared scores significantly higher than hazard models that lack the financial intermediation and interactive variables.

[5] Reinhart and Rogoff's data continue to 2001, while the data in these statistical tests ends in 2000. This admittedly means that five of the spells suffer from problems of "right censoring," but the right censoring is randomly distributed in the sample.

Bibliography

Adams, Cristina, 1995, "Treading Water," *Mexico Business*, Vol. 1, No. 6, March, pp. 45-48.

Aghevli, Bijan B., Moshin Khan, and Peter J. Montiel, 1991, *Exchange-Rate Policy in Developing Countries: Some Analytical Issues*, IMF Occasional Paper No. 78 (Washington, DC: IMF).

Alfa, S.A. de C.V., 1997, *Annual Report 1996* (Mexico City: Alfa).

Andrews, David, 1994, "Capital Mobility and State Autonomy: Toward a Structural Theory of International Monetary Relations," *International Studies Quarterly*, Vol. 38, No. 2, June, pp. 193-218.

Anek Laothamatas, 1992, *Business Associations and the New Political Economy of Thailand: From Bureaucratic Polity to Liberal Corporatism* (Boulder, CO: Westview Press).

Aspe, Pedro, 1993, *Economic Transformation the Mexican Way* (Cambridge, MA: MIT Press).

Austen-Smith, David, and John R. Wright, 1992, "Competitive Lobbying for the Legislator's Vote," *Social Choice and Welfare*, Vol. 9, pp. 229-257.

Baily, Martin, Diana Farrell, and Susan Lund, 2000, "The Color of Hot Money," *Foreign Affairs*, Vol. 79, No. 2, March/April, pp. 99-109.

Bamrud, Joachim, 1995, "The U.S. Corporate Reaction," *U.S./Latin Trade*, Vol. 3, No. 2, February, p.29.

Banco de Mexico, 1991, *The Mexican Economy* (Mexico City: Banco de Mexico).

Banco de Mexico, 1995, *The Mexican Economy* (Mexico City: Banco de Mexico).

Banco de Mexico, 2001, official website, available at http://www.banxico.org.mx.

Banco de la Republica, 1992, *Colombia: Economic Structure 1992* (Bogota: Banco de la Republica).

Banco de la Republica, 1999, *Indicadores Economicos Colombia* (Bogota: Banco de la Republica).

Bancomer, S.A., 1998, *Annual Report 1997* (Mexico City: Bancomer).

[Note: *Bangkok Post* articles are arranged according to date and page, and a "B" on the page number indicates the business section.]

Bangkok Post, 1997, "Speculators Routed, but War Far From Over," 16 May, pp. B1 & B12.

Bangkok Post, 1997, "Investors Edgy Over Impact of Suspension," 1 July, p. 1.

Bangkok Post, 1997, "Helping to Safeguard Customers of 16 Firms," 1 July, p. B1.

Bangkok Post, 1997, "Boost Its Value Instead – Olarn," 2 July, pp. 1-2.

Bangkok Post, 1997, "Foreign Interest in 16 Ailing Firms," 2 July, p. B1.

Bangkok Post, 1997, "Bold Move, and the Best Way Out," 3 July, p. 1.

Bangkok Post, 1997, "Pain to Herald Gain: Chaos Reigns in Commercial Banks," 3 July, pp. 1-2.

Bangkok Post, 1997, "Private Sector Praise Despite Loss on Foreign Loans," 3 July, p. B12.

Bangkok Post, 1997, "Retail Oil Prices Likely to Rise Half-Baht/Litre," 3 July, p. B12.

Bangkok Post, 1997, "Tax Relief Likely to Ease Debt Burden," 3 July, p. B12.

Bangkok Post, 1997, "Automotive Sector Dealt Serious Blow," 4 July, p. B3.

Bangkok Post, 1997, "Floating Baht Given Credit for Cheaper Thai Rice," 4 July, p. B3.

Bangkok Post, 1997, "Exporters Start Doing Their Sums," 4 July, p. B12.

Bangkok Post, 1997, "Steel Goods Prices to Rise 15%," 5 July, p. 1.

Bangkok Post Economic Review, 1995, "Inflation Up Amid Volatility," 30 June, pp. 8-9.

Bangkok Post Economic Review, 1995, "Trying to Get the Balance Right," 30 June, p. 13.

Bangkok Post Economic Review, 1996, "BBC Crisis Rocks Authority," 2 July, p. 33.

Bangkok Post Economic Review, 1996, "Vijit Under Mounting Pressure," 2 July, p. 35.

Bank for International Settlements, 2004, *Triennial Central Bank Survey: Foreign Exchange and Derivatives Market Activity in 2004* (Basle, Switzerland: BIS) March.

Bank of Thailand, 2001, official website, available at http://www.bot.or.th.

Barajas, Adolfo, Roberto Steiner, and Natalia Salazar, 1999, "Foreign Investment in Colombia's Financial Sector," IMF Working Paper WP/99/150 (Washington, DC: IMF, November).

Barnes, William, 1997, "Profit Gone, but Hope Remains," *Asian Business*, August, pp. 26-27.

Bata Shoe of Thailand, 1997, *Annual Report 1997*, (Bangkok: Bata Shoe of Thailand).

Beckerman, Paul, 1989, "Austerity, External Debt, and Capital Formation in Peru," in *Paying the Costs of Austerity in Latin America*, ed. by Howard Handelman and Werner Baer (Boulder CO: Westview Press).

Benassy-Quere, Agnes and Benoit Coeure, 2000, "Big and Small Currencies: The Regional Connection," *CEPII Working Paper*, pp. 2000-2009.

Bernhard, William, J. Lawrence Broz, and William Roberts Clark, 2002, "The Political Economy of Monetary Institutions," *International Organization*, Vol. 56, No. 4, Autumn, pp. 693-723.

Bernhard, William and David Leblang, 1999, "Democratic Institutions and Exchange-Rate Commitments," *International Organization*, Vol. 53, No. 1, Winter, pp. 71-97.

Bird, Graham, 2002, "Where Do We Stand on Choosing Exchange Rate Regimes in Developing and Emerging Economies?," *World Economics*, Vol. 3, No. 1, January-March, pp. 145-167.

Blomberg, S. Brock, Jeffry A. Frieden and Ernesto Stein, 2002, "Sustaining Fixed Rates: The Political Economy of Currency Pegs in Latin America," Presented at the 98th Annual Meeting of the American Political Science Association, available at http://www.people.fas.harvard.edu/~jfrieden/.

Borrero, Oscar, 1989, "La Finca Raiz y la Economia Subterranea," *Camacol Seminario* (Bogota) 8 November.

Broz, J. Lawrence, 2002, "Political System Transparency and Monetary Commitment Regimes," *International Organization*, vol. 56, no. 4, Autumn, pp. 861-888.

Burgess, Katrina, 2003, "Mexican Labor at a Crossroads," in *Mexico's Politics and Society in Transition*, ed. by Joseph S. Tulchin and Andrew D. Selee (Boulder CO: Lynne Rienner) pp. 73-107.

Calvo, Guillermo A. and Carmen M. Reinhart, 2000, *Fear of Floating*, NBER Working Paper 7993 (Cambridge, MA: National Bureau of Economic Research).

Camard, Wayne, 1996, *Discretion with Rules?: Lessons from the Currency Board Arrangement in Lithuania*, IMF Paper on Policy Analysis and Assessment 96-1, (Washington, DC: International Monetary Fund).

Carrasquilla, Alberto, 1995, "Exchange Rate Bands and Shifts in the Stabilization Policy Regime: Issues Suggested by the Experience of Colombia," IMF Working Paper WP/95/42 (Washington, DC: IMF) April.

Central Reserve Bank of Peru, 1998, *Annual Report 1997* (Lima: Central Reserve Bank of Peru).

Central Reserve Bank of Peru, 2001, *Annual Report 2000* (Lima: Central Reserve Bank of Peru).

Chaffin, Joshua , 1995, "Mixed Blessings," *Mexico Business*, Vol. 1, No. 6, March, pp. 48-50.

Charoen Thanatat, 1997, "Fighting the Good Fight," *Asian Business*, July, pp. 28-30.

Charoen Thanatat, 1997, "Bad Loan: Scenario a Nightmare for Thai Banks," *Asian Business*, August, pp. 24-26.

Charoen Thanatat, 1997, "Companies with Foresight Weather Devaluation Storm," *Asian Business*, October, pp. 20-21.

Clavijo, Sergio, 1992, "Overcoming a Financial Crisis During Transition from a Repressed to a Market-Based System: Colombia 1970-89," in *The Colombian Economy: Issues of Trade and Development*, ed. by Alvin Cohen and Frank R. Gunter (Boulder, CO: Westview Press).

Cohen, Benjamin J., 1998, *The Geography of Money* (Ithica, NY: Cornell University Press).

Cooper, Richard, 1971, *Currency Devaluation in Developing Countries*, Princeton Essays in International Finance No. 86 (Princeton, NJ: International Finance Section, Department of Economics, Princeton University).

Cooper, Richard, 1999, "The Asian Crises: Causes and Consequences," in *Financial Markets and Development: The Crisis in Emerging Markets*, ed. by Alison Harwood, Robert E. Litan, and Michael Pomerleano (Washington, DC: Brookings Institution) pp. 17-28.

Corden, Warner Max, 2002, *Too Sensational: On the Choice of Exchange Rate Regimes* (Cambridge, MA: MIT Press).

Council on Foreign Relations, 1999, "The Future of the International Financial Architecture," *Foreign Affairs*, vol. 78, no. 6, pp. 169-183.

Crabtree, John, 1998, "Neo-Populism and the Fujimori Phenomenon," in *Fujimori's Peru: The Political Economy*, ed. by John Crabtree and Jim Thomas (London: University of London Institute of Latin American Studies) pp. 7-23.

Crockett, Andrew, 1994, "Monetary Policy Implications of Increased Capital Flows," in *Changing Capital Markets: Implications for Monetary Policy: A Symposium Sponsored by the Federal Reserve Bank of Kansas City, Jackson Hole, Wyoming, August 19-21, 1994* (Kansas City, MO: Federal Reserve Bank of Kansas City).

Cuddington, J. T., 1986, *Capital Flight: Estimates, Issues, and Explanations*, Princeton Studies in International Finance, No. 58, (Princeton, NJ: International Finance Section, Department of Economics, Princeton University) December.

Cukierman, Alex, 1992, *Central Bank Strategy, Credibility, and Independence: Theory and Evidence* (Cambridge, MA: MIT Press).

Cukierman, Alex, Sebastian Edwards, and Guido Tabellini, 1992, "Seignorage and Political Instability," *American Economic Review*, Vol. 82, No. 3, June, pp. 537-555.

Cukierman, Alex and Steven B. Webb, 1995, "Political Influence on the Central Bank: International Evidence," *World Bank Economic Review*, Vol. 9, No. 3, pp. 397-423.

Cukierman, Alex, Steven B. Webb, and Bilin Neyapti, 1992, "Measuring the Independence of Central Banks and Its Effect on Policy Outcomes," *World Bank Economic Review* Vol. 6, No. 3, pp. 353-398.

D'Amato, Alfonse, 1995, "Report on the Mexican Economic Crisis" (Washington, DC: United States Senate).

Dancourt, Oscar, 1999, "Neoliberal Reforms and Macroeconomic Policy in Peru," *CEPAL Review*, Vol. 67, April, pp. 51-73.

De Haan, Jakob, and Willem J. Kooi, 1998, "Does Central Bank Independence Really Matter?: New Evidence for Developing Countries Using a New Indicator," Unpublished manuscript, November, available at www.eco.rug.nl/medewerk/dehaan/newtor2.pdf.

Devlin, Robert, 1981, "Transnational Banks, External Debt, and Peru: Results of a Recent Study," *CEPAL Review*, Vol. 14, August, pp. 153-184.

Diaz-Bonilla, Eugenio, and Hector E. Schamis, 2001, "From Redistribution to Stability: The Evolution of Exchange Rate Policies in Argentina, 1950-98," in *The Currency Game: Exchange Rate Politics in Latin America* ed. by Jeffry A. Frieden and Ernesto Stein (Washington DC: Inter-American Development Bank) pp. 65-118.

Doner, Richard, and Daniel Unger, 1993, "The Politics of Finance in Thai Economic Development," in *The Politics of Finance in Developing Countries*, ed. by Stephan Haggard, Cheng Lee, and Sylvia Maxfield (Ithica, NY: Cornell University Press).

Dornbusch, Rudiger, 1997, "The Folly, the Crash, and Beyond: Economic Policies and the Crisis," in *Mexico 1994: Anatomy of an Emerging-Market Crash*, ed. by Sebastian Edwards and Moises Naim (Washington, DC: Carnegie Endowment for Peace) pp. 125-140.

Dornbusch, Rudiger, and Alejandro Werner, 1994, "Mexico: Stabilization, Reform, and No Growth," *Brookings Papers on Economic Activity*, No. 1.

Dresser, Denise, 1997, "Falling from the Tightrope: The Political Economy of the Mexican Crisis," in *Mexico 1994: Anatomy of an Emerging-Market Crash*, ed. by Sebastian Edwards and Moises Naim (Washington, DC: Carnegie Endowment for Peace) pp. 55-79.

Dreyer, Jacob S. 1978, "Determinants of Exchange-Rate Regimes for Currencies of Developing Countries: Some Preliminary Evidence," *World Development*, Vol. 6, April.

Economist, 2004, "So Much for the New Broom," Vol. 371, No. 8369, 3 April, p. 44.

Economist, 2004, "Time to Hit the Brakes," Vol. 371, No. 8375, 15 May, pp. 67-69.

Economist Survey, 2001, "Drugs, War, and Democracy: A Survey of Colombia," Vol. 359, No. 8218, 21 April.

Economist Survey, 2003, "The Weakest Link: A Survey of Asian Finance," Vol. 365, No. 8367, 8 February.

Economist Survey, 2003, "A Cruel Sea of Capital: A Survey of Global Finance," Vol. 367, No. 8322, 3 May.

Economist Survey, 2004, "Behind the Mask: A Survey of Business in China," Vol. 370, No. 8367, 20 March.

Edison, Hali J. and Michael Melvin, 1990, "The Determinants and Implications of the Choice of an Exchange-rate System," in William S. Haraf and Thomas D. Willet, eds., *Monetary Policy for a Volatile Global Economy* (Washington, DC: AEI Press) pp. 1-44.

Edwards, Sebastian, 1984, *The Order of Liberalization of the External Sector in Developing Countries*, Princeton Studies in International Finance No. 156 (Princeton, NJ: International Finance Section, Department of Economics, Princeton University) December.

Edwards, Sebastian, 1996(a), "The Determinants of the Choice Between Fixed and Flexible Exchange-Rate Regimes," NBER Working Paper No. 5756 (Cambridge, MA: National Bureau of Economic Research).

Edwards, Sebastian, 1996(b), "Exchange Rates and the Political Economy of Macroeconomic Discipline," *American Economic Review*, Vol. 86, No. 2, May, pp. 159-163.

Edwards, Sebastian, 1997, "Bad Luck or Bad Policies?: An Economic Analysis of the Crisis," in *Mexico 1994: Anatomy of an Emerging-Market Crash*, ed. by Sebastian Edwards and Moises Naim (Washington, DC: Carnegie Endowment for Peace) pp. 95-124.

Eichengreen, Barry, 1994, *International Monetary Arrangements for the 21st Century* (Washington, DC: Brookings Institution).

Eichengreen, Barry, 2003, *Capital Flows and Crises* (Cambridge, MA: MIT Press).

Eichengreen, Barry, Andrew Rose, and Charles Wyplosz, 2003, "Exchange Market Mayhem: The Antecedents and Aftermath of Speculative Attacks," in Barry Eichengreen, *Capital Flows and Crises* (Cambridge, MA: MIT Press).

El Economista, 14 April, 1994, p. 48.

El Financiero, 1994, "Companies with Debts in Foreign Currency Take a Hard Hit," 21 December, p. 6.

Elman, Colin, 1996, "Horses for Courses: Why *Not* Neorealist Theories of Foreign Policy?" *Security Studies*, Vol. 6, No. 1, Autumn, pp. 7-53.

Erbe, S., 1985, "The Flight of Capital from Developing Countries," *Intereconomics*, Vol. 20, No. 6.

Falkus, Malcolm, 1995, "Thai Industrialization: An Overview," in *Thailand's Industrialization and Its Consequences*, ed. by Medhi Krongkaew (New York, NY: St. Martin's Press).

Feldstein, Martin and Charles Horioka, 1980, "Domestic Savings and International Capital Flows," *Economic Journal*, Vol. 90, No. 358, June, pp. 314-329.

Fischer, Stanley, 2001, "Exchange Rate Regimes: Is the Bipolar View Correct?" *Journal of Economic Perspectives*, vol. 15, no. 2, pp. 3-24.

Fleming, J. Marcus., 1962, "Domestic Financial Policies Under Fixed and Under Floating Exchange Rates," *IMF Staff Papers*, Vol. 9.

Flood, Robert P., 1979, "Capital Mobility and the Choice of Exchange Rate System," *International Economic Review*, Vol. 20, June, pp. 405-416.

Fomento Economico Mexicano, S.A., de C. V., 1997, *Annual Report 1996* (Mexico City: Femsa).

Frankel, Jeffrey A., 1993, "Quantifying International Capital Mobility in the 1980's," in Jeffrey A. Frankel, *On Exchange Rates* (Cambridge: MIT Press).

Frankel, Jeffrey A., 1999, *No Single Currency Regime is Right for All Countries or at All Times*, Princeton Essays in International Finance, No. 215 (Princeton, NJ: International Finance Section, Department of Economics, Princeton University) August.

Frankel, Jeffrey A., Sergio Schmukler, and Luis Serven, 2000, "Verifiablity: A Rationale for the Failure of Intermediate Exchange Rate Regimes," Paper prepared for the InterAmerican Seminar in Economics, Buenos Aires, 3-4 December 1999.

Frieden, Jeffry A., 1991 "Invested Interests: The Politics of National Economic Policies in a World of Global Finance," *International Organization*, Vol. 45, No. 4, Autumn, pp. 425-451.

Frieden, Jeffry A., 1994, "Exchange Rate Politics: Contemporary Lessons from American History," *Review of International Political Economy*, Vol. 1, No. 1, pp. 81-103.

Frieden, Jeffry A., 2002, "Real Sources of European Currency Policy: Sectoral Interests and European Monetary Integration," *International Organization*, Vol. 56, No. 4, Autumn, pp. 831-860.

Frieden, Jeffry A., Piero Ghezzi, and Ernesto Stein, 2001, "Politics and Exchange Rates: A Cross-Country Approach," in *The Currency Game: Exchange Rate Politics in Latin America* ed. by Jeffry A. Frieden and Ernesto Stein (Washington DC: Inter-American Development Bank) pp. 21-63.

Frieden, Jeffry A., and Lisa Martin, 2003, "International Political Economy: Global and Domestic Interactions," in *Political Science: The State of the Discipline* ed. by Ira Katznelson and Helen Milner (New York: W.W. Norton).

Frieden, Jeffry A., and Ernesto Stein, 2001, "The Political Economy of Exchange Rate Policy in Latin America: An Analytical Overview," in *The Currency Game: Exchange Rate Politics in Latin America* ed. by Jeffry A. Frieden and Ernesto Stein (Washington DC: Inter-American Development Bank) pp. 1-19.

Friedman, Milton, 1953, "The Case for Flexible Exchange Rates," in *Essays in Positive Economics* ed. by Milton Friedman (Chicago, IL: University of Chicago Press) pp. 157-203.

Garcia Garcia, Jorge and Sisira Jayasuriya, 1997, *Courting Turmoil and Deferring Prosperity: Colombia Between 1960 and 1990* (Washington, DC: World Bank).

Garrett, Geoffrey, 1998, "Global Markets and National Politics: Collision Course or Virtuous Circle?" *International Organization*, Vol. 52, No. 4, Autumn, pp. 787-824.

Garrett, Geoffrey, and Peter Lange, 1995, "Internationalization, Institutions, and Political Change," *International Organization*, Vol. 49, No. 4, Autumn, pp. 627-655.

Garrido, Celso, 1994, "National Private Groups in Mexico, 1987-1993," *CEPAL Review*, No. 53, August, pp. 159-175.

Garrido, Celso, 2003, "Mexico's Financial System and Economic Development: Current Crisis and Future Prospects," in *Confronting Development: Assessing Mexico's Economic and Social Policy Challenges*, ed. by Kevin J. Middlebrook and Eduardo Zepeda (Stanford, CA: Stanford University Press) pp. 89-122.

Ghosh, Atish R., Anne-Marie Gulde, and Holger C. Wolf, 1998, "Currency Boards: The Ultimate Fix?" IMF Working Paper WP/98/8 (Washington, DC: IMF) January.

Gil-Diaz, Francisco, and Agustin Carstens, 1997, "Pride and Predjudice: The Economics Profession and Mexico's Financial Crisis," in *Mexico 1994: Anatomy of an Emerging-Market Crash*, ed. by Sebastian Edwards and Moises Naim (Washington, DC: Carnegie Endowment for Peace) pp. 165-200.

Gilpin, Robert, 1987, *The Political Economy of International Relations*, (Princeton: Princeton University Press).

Glick, Reuven, Peter Kretzmer, and Clas Wihlborg, 1995, "Real Exchange Rate Effects of Monetary Disturbances under Different Degrees of Exchange Rate Flexibility: An Empirical Analysis," *Journal of International Economics*, Vol. 38, Nos. 3-4, pp. 249-273.

Goldstein, Morris, 1995, *The Exchange Rate System and the IMF: A Modest Agenda*, Policy Analyses in International Economics No. 39 (Washington, DC: Institute for International Economics) June.

Gould, David M., 1996, "Mexico's Crisis: Looking Back to Assess the Future," in *Changing Structure of Mexico: Political, Social, and Economic Prospects*, ed. by Laura Randall (Armonk, NY: M. E. Sharpe).

Graham, Carol, 1994, "Introduction: Democracy in Crisis and the International Response," in *Peru in Crisis: Dictatorship or Democracy?*, ed. by Joseph S. Tulchin and Gary Bland, Woodrow Wilson Center Current Studies in Latin America (Boulder, CO: Lynne Rienner) pp. 1-20.

Grosse, Robert, 1992, "Colombia's Black Market in Foreign Exchange," *World Development*, Vol. 20, No. 8, August, pp. 1193-1207.

Gruben, William and John H. Welch, 1996, "Distortions and Resolutions in Mexico's Financial System," in *Changing Structure of Mexico: Political, Social, and Economic Prospects*, ed. by Laura Randall (Armonk, NY: M. E. Sharpe).

Gunter, Frank R., 1992, "Colombian Capital Flight: 1982-90," in *The Colombian Economy: Issues of Trade and Development*, ed. by Alvin Cohen and Frank R. Gunter (Boulder, CO: Westview Press).

Haggard, Stephan, 2000, *The Political Economy of the Asian Financial Crisis* (Washington, DC: Institute for International Economics).

Haggard, Stephan and Sylvia Maxfield, 1996, "The Political Economy of Financial Internationalization in the Developing World," *International Organization*, Vol. 50, No. 1, Winter, pp. 35-68.

Hale, David D., 1997, "The Markets and Mexico: The Supply-Side Story," in *Mexico 1994: Anatomy of an Emerging-Market Crash*, ed. by Sebastian Edwards and Moises Naim (Washington, DC: Carnegie Endowment for Peace) pp. 201-245.

Hall, Michael G., 2002, "The Political and Institutional Sources of Exchange Rate Regime Choice," Ph.D Diss., University of California, Santa Barbara.

Hallberg, Kristin, and Wendy E. Takacs, 1992, "Trade Reform in Colombia: 1990-94," in *The Colombian Economy: Issues of Trade and Development*, ed. by Alvin Cohen and Frank R. Gunter (Boulder, CO: Westview Press).

Hamann, A. Javier, and Carlos E. Paredes, 1991, "The Peruvian Economy: Characteristics and Trends," in *Peru's Path to Recovery: A Plan for Economic Stabilization and Growth*, ed. by Carlos E. Paredes and Jeffrey D. Sachs (Washington, DC: Brookings Institution) pp. 41-79.

Hartlyn, Jonathan, and John Dugas, 1999, "Colombia: The Politics of Violence and Democratic Transformation," in *Democracy in Developing Countries: Latin America*, 2nd ed., ed. by Larry Diamond, Jonathan Hartlyn, Juan J. Linz, and Seymour Martin Lipset (Boulder, CO: Lynne Rienner Publishers) pp. 249-307.

Hefeker, Carsten, 1996, "The Political Choice and Collapse of Fixed Exchange Rates," *Journal of Institutional and Theoretical Economics*, Vol. 152, No. 2, pp. 360-379.

Heller, Robert H., 1978, "Determinants of Exchange Rate Practices," *Journal of Money, Credit, and Banking*, Vol. 10, August.

Henning, C. Randall, 1994, *Currencies and Politics in the United States, Germany, and Japan* (Washington, DC: Institute for International Economics).

Hewison, Kevin, 1989, *Bankers and Bureaucrats: Capital and the Role of the State in Thailand*, Monograph Series 34, Yale University Southeast Asia Studies (New Haven, CT: Yale University Press).

Holden, Merle, Paul Holden, and Esther Suss, 1979, "The Determinants of Exchange Rate Flexibility: An Empirical Investigation," *The Review of Economics and Statistics*, Vol. 61, August.

Honkapohja, Seppo, and Pentti Pikkarainen, 1994, "Country Characteristics and the Choice of Exchange Rate Regime: Are Mini-skirts Followed by Maxis?," in *Exchange Rate Policies in the Nordic Countries*, ed. by Johnny Akerholm and Alberto Giovannini (London: Centre for Economic Policy Research) pp. 31-56.

House Committee on Small Business, 1993, *Hearings on NAFTA and Peso Devaluation: A Problem for U.S. Exporters?*, Statement of Representative John LaFalce, 20 May.

Iguiniz, Javier, 1998, "The Economic Strategy of the Fujimori Government," in *Fujimori's Peru: The Political Economy*, ed. by John Crabtree and Jim Thomas (London: University of London Institute of Latin American Studies) pp. 24-40.

International Finance Corporation, 1999, *Emerging Stock Markets Factbook 1999* (Washington, DC: International Finance Corporation).

International Monetary Fund, 1999a, *Results of the 1997 Coordinated Portfolio Investment Survey* (Washington, DC: IMF).

International Monetary Fund 1999b, *Colombia: Staff Report for the 1999 Article IV Consultation*, IMF Staff Country Report No. 99/149 (Washington, DC: IMF) December.

International Monetary Fund, 2003, "Bolivia: Selected Issues and Statistical Appendix," IMF Country Report No. 03/258 (Washington, DC: IMF) August.

International Monetary Fund, various years, *Annual Report on Exchange Arrangements and Exchange Restrictions* (Washington, DC: IMF).

International Monetary Fund, various years, *International Financial Statistics* (Washington, DC: IMF).

Jaramillo, Juan C., Roberto Steiner, and Natalia Salazar, 2001, "A Long-Lasting Crawling Peg: Political Determinants of Exchange Rate Policy in Colombia," in *The Currency Game: Exchange Rate Politics in Latin America* ed. by Jeffry A. Frieden and Ernesto Stein (Washington DC: Inter-American Development Bank), pp. 199-247.

Kahler, Miles, 1998, "Introduction: Capital Flows and Financial Crises in the 1990s," in *Capital Flows and Financial Crises* ed. by Miles Kahler (Ithica, NY: Cornell University Press) pp. 1-22.

Kamas, Linda, 2001, "Monetary and Exchange Rate Policy in Colombia: Effects on the Real Exchange Rate in the 1990s," *Journal of Development Studies*, Vol. 38, No. 2, December, pp. 131-166.

Kaminsky, Graciela L., and Carmen Reinhart, 1999, "The Twin Crises: The Causes of Banking and Balance-of-Payments Problems," *American Economic Review*, Vol. 89, No. 2, June, pp. 473-500.

Kessler, Timothy P., 1999, *Global Capital and National Politics: Reforming Mexico's Financial System* (Westport, CT: Praeger).

Kessler, Timothy P., 2000, "The Mexican Peso Crash: Causes, Consequences, and Comeback," in *Exchange-Rate Politics in Latin America*, ed. by Carol Wise and Riordan Roett (Washington, DC: Brookings Institution Press) pp. 43-69.

Kindleberger, Charles P., 1981, "Dominance and Leadership in the International Economy: Exploitation, Public Goods, and Free Rides," *International Studies Quarterly*, Vol. 25, No. 2, June, pp. 242-254.

King, Robert G., and Ross Levine, 1993, "Finance and Growth: Schumpeter Might Be Right," *Quarterly Journal of Economics*, Vol. 108, No. 3, August, pp. 717-737.

Kootnikoff, Lawrence, 1995, "Free Fall in Mexico," *U.S./Latin Trade*, Vol. 3, No. 2, February, pp. 26-30.

Larrain, Felipe, and Jeffrey D. Sachs, 1991, "International Financial Relations," in *Peru's Path to Recovery: A Plan for Economic Stabilization and Growth*, ed. by Carlos E. Paredes and Jeffrey D. Sachs (Washington, DC: Brookings Institution) pp. 228-252.

Leblang, David, 2003, "To Devalue or Defend: The Political Economy of Exchange Rate Policy," *International Studies Quarterly*, vol. 47, no. 4, December, pp. 533-559.

Leightner, Jonathan E., and C. A. Knox Lovell, 1998, "The Impact of Financial Liberalization on the Performance of Thai Banks," *Journal of Economics and Business*, Vol. 50, pp. 115-131.

Levine, Ross, 1997, "Financial Development and Economic Growth: Views and Agenda," *Journal of Economic Literature*, Vol. 35, No. 2, June, pp. 688-726.

Lijphart, Arend, 1977, *Democracy in Plural Societies: A Comparative Exploration* (New Haven, CT: Yale University Press).

Lopez Portillo, Jose, 1988, *Mis Tiempos: Biografia y Testimonio Politico* (Mexico D. F.: Fernandez Editores).

Lora, Eduardo, 1994, "Colombia: Structural Reforms and Economic Performance," *CSIS Policy Papers on the Americas*, Vol. V, Report No. 1, 17 March (Washington, DC: Center for Strategic & International Studies).

Los Angeles Times, 1993, "Privatized Mexican Banks Get Ready for Foreign Competition," 8 September, p. D4.

Loser, Claudio, and Eliot Kalter, eds., 1992, *Mexico: The Strategy to Achieve Sustained Economic Growth*, Occasional Paper No. 99 (Washington, DC: International Monetary Fund).

Lustig, Nora, 1995, "The Mexican Peso Crisis: The Foreseeable and the Surprise," Brookings Discussion Papers in International Economics No. 114 (Washington, DC: Brookings Institution) June.

Lustig, Nora, 1998, *Mexico: The Remaking of an Economy* (Washington, DC: Brookings Institution Press) 2nd ed.

Machlup, F., W. Salant, and L. Tarshis, 1972, *International Mobility and Movement of Capital: A Conference of the Universities – National Bureau Committee for Economic Research* (New York: Columbia University Press).

MacIntyre, Andrew, 2003, *The Power of Institutions: Political Architecture and Governance*, (Ithica, NY: Cornell University Press).

Martz, John D., 1992, "Contemporary Colombian Politics: The Struggle Over Democratization," in *The Colombian Economy: Issues of Trade and Development*, ed. by Alvin Cohen and Frank R. Gunter (Boulder, CO: Westview Press).

Masson, Paul, 2001, "Exchange Rate Regime Transitions," *Journal of Development Economics*, Vol. 64, Issue 2, April, pp. 571-586.

Mauceri, Philip, 1996, *State Under Siege: Development and Policy Making in Peru* (Boulder, CO: Westview Press).

Maxfield, Sylvia, 1991, "Bankers' Alliances and Economic Policy Patterns: Evidence from Mexico and Brazil," *Comparative Political Studies*, Vol. 23, No. 4, January, pp. 419-458.

Maxfield, Sylvia, 1997, *Gatekeepers of Growth: The International Political Economy of Central Banking in Developing Countries* (Princeton, NJ: Princeton University Press).

McKinnon, Ronald, and Donald Mathieson, 1981, *How to Manage a Repressed Economy*, Princeton Studies in International Finance No. 145 (Princeton, NJ: International Finance Section, Department of Economics, Princeton University) December.

McNamara, Kathleen, 1998, *The Currency of Ideas: Monetary Politics in the European Union* (Ithica, NY: Cornell University Press).

Melvin, Michael, 1985, "The Choice of an Exchange Rate System and Macroeconomic Stability," *Journal of Money, Credit, and Banking*, Vol. 17, No. 4, November, pp. 467-478.

Mertens, Brian, 1997, "Thailand Floats Toward Uncertainty," *Asian Business*, August, pp. 22-23.

Mexican Bankers' Association, 1991, "La Banca Mexicana en Transicion: Retos y Perpectivos," *Comercio Exterior*, Vol. 41, No. 2, pp. 1-44.

Minushkin, Susan, 2002, "Banqueros and Bolseros: Structural Change and Financial Market Liberalization in Mexico," *Journal of Latin American Studies*, Vol. 34, November, pp. 915-944.

Mishkin, Fredric S., 1996, "Understanding Financial Crises: A Developing Country Perspective," in *Annual World Bank Conference of Development Economics*, ed. by Michael Bruno and Boris Pleskovic (Washington, DC: World Bank) pp. 29-62.

Mohar, Javier Gavito, Aaron Silva Nava, and Guillermo Zamarripa Escamilla, 1998, "Recovery After Crisis: Lessons for Mexico's Banks," in *Mexico's Private Sector: Recent History, Future Challenges*, ed. by Riordan Roett (Boulder, CO: Lynne Rienner Publishers).

Montes-Negret, Fernando, 1996, "Structural Weaknesses and Colombia's Banking Crisis, 1982-1988," in *Bank Restructuring: Lessons from the 1980's* ed. by Andrew Sheng (Washington, DC: World Bank) pp. 99-107.

Montiel, Peter J., 1993, "Capital Mobility in Developing Countries: Some Measurement Issues and Empirical Estimates," Policy Research Working Paper WPS 1103, (Washington, DC: World Bank).

Moreno, Ramon, 1995, "Macroeconomic Behavior During Periods of Speculative Pressure or Realignment: Evidence from Pacific Basin Economies," *Federal Reserve Bank of San Francisco Economic Review*, No. 3, pp. 3-16.

Morris, Felipe, Mark Dorfman, Jose Pedro Ortiz, and Maria Claudia Franco, 1990, *Latin America's Banking Systems in the 1980's: A Cross Country Comparison*, World Bank Discussion Papers No. 81 (Washington, DC: World Bank).

Mosley, Layna, 2000, "Room to Move: International Financial Markets and National Welfare States," *International Organization*, vol. 54, no. 4, Autumn, pp. 737-773.

Mundell, Robert A., 1962, "The Appropriate Use of Monetary and Fiscal Policy for Internal and External Stability," *IMF Staff Papers*, Vol. 9.

Mundell, Robert A., 1968, *International Economics* (New York: Macmillan).

Naim, Moises, 1995, "Mexico's Larger Story," *Foreign Policy*, Vol. 99, Summer, pp. 112-130.

Narongchai Akrasanee, Karel Jansen, Jeerasak Pongpisanupichit, 1993, *International Capital Flows and Economic Adjustment in Thailand* (Bangkok: Thailand Development Research Institute).

Nordlinger, Eric, 1987, "Taking the State Seriously" in *Understanding Political Development*, Myron Weiner and Samuel Huntingdon, eds. (Prospect Heights, IL: Waveland Press) pp. 353-390.

Nukul Commission, 1998, *Analysis and Evaluation on Facts behind Thailand's Economic Crisis*, English language ed. (Bangkok: Nation Publishers).

Obstfeld, Maurice, 1994, "The Logic of Currency Crises," *Cahiers Economiques et Monetaries*, vol. 43, pp. 189-213.

Obstfeld, Maurice, and Kenneth Rogoff, 1995, "The Mirage of Fixed Exchange Rates," *Journal of Economic Perspectives*, Vol. 9, No. 4, Fall, pp. 73-96.

Olson, Mancur, 1966, *The Logic of Collective Action: Public Goods and the Theory of Groups*, (Cambridge, MA: Harvard University Press).

Olson, Mancur, 1982, *The Rise and Decline of Nations: Economic Growth, Stagflation, and Social Rigidities* (New Haven, CT: Yale University Press).

Ozkan, F. Gulcin, and Alan Sutherland, 1994, "A Model of the ERM Crisis," CEPR Discussion Paper no. 879 (London: Center for Economic Policy Research) January.

Paiboon Kittisrikangwan, Mathee Supapongse, Jaturong Jantarangs, 1995, "Monetary Policy Management in Thailand," *Bank of Thailand Quarterly Bulletin*, Vol. 35, No. 1, March, pp. 37-50.

Paisal Sricharatchanya, 1981, "The 8.7% Solution," *Far Eastern Economic Review*, 24 July, pp. 49-50.

Paisal Sricharatchanya, 1984, "Floating to a Balance," *Far Eastern Economic Review*, 15 November, pp. 112-113.

Pasco-Font, Alberto, and Piero Ghezzi, "Exchange Rates and Interest Groups in Peru, 1950-1996," in *The Currency Game: Exchange Rate Politics in Latin America* ed. by Jeffry A. Frieden and Ernesto Stein (Washington DC: Inter-American Development Bank) pp. 249-277.

Pastor Jr., Manuel, 1992, *Inflation, Stabilization, and Debt: Macroeconomic Experiments in Peru and Bolivia* (Boulder, CO: Westview Press).

Pastor Jr., Manuel, 1998, "Pesos, Policies, and Predictions: Why the Crisis, Why the Surprise, and Why the Recovery?," in *The Post-NAFTA Political Economy: Mexico and the Western Hemisphere*, ed. by Carol Wise (University Park, PA: Pennsylvania State University Press) pp. 119-147.

Pastor Jr., Manuel, and Carol Wise, 1994, "The Origins and Sustainability of Mexico's Free Trade Policy," *International Organization*, Vol. 48, No. 3, Summer, pp. 459-489.

Poirson, Helene, 2001, "How Do Countries Choose Their Exchange Rate Regime?" IMF Working Paper WP/01/46 (Washington, DC: IMF).

Pomerleano, Michael, 1998, "East Asian Crisis and Corporate Finances: The Untold Story," *Emerging Markets Quarterly*, Vol. 2, Winter, pp. 14-27.

Precious Shipping, 1996, *Annual Report 1996* (Bangkok: Precious Shipping).

Quinn, Dennis P., 1997, "The Correlates of Change in International Financial Regulation," *American Political Science Review*, Vol. 91, No. 3, September, pp. 531-551.

Reinhart, Carmen M., 2000, "The Mirage of Floating Exchange Rates," *American Economic Association Papers and Proceedings*, May, pp. 65-70.

Reinhart, Carmen M., and Kenneth Rogoff, 2003(a), "The Modern History of Exchange Rate Arrangements: A Reinterpretation," NBER Working Paper 8963, revised version (Cambridge, MA: National Bureau of Economic Research) March.

Reinhart, Carmen M., and Kenneth Rogoff, 2003(b), "Background Material to the Modern History of Exchange Rate Arrangements: A Reinterpretation (Part I)," available at http://www.wam.umd.edu/~creinhar/Papers.html.

Rich, Andrew, and R. Kent Weaver, 1998, "Advocates and Analysts: Think Tanks and the Politicization of Expertise," in *Interest Group Politics*, 5th ed., ed. by Allan J. Cigler and Burdett A. Loomis (Washington DC: Congressional Quarterly Press).

Riner, Deborah L., 1982, "Private Banks and the Politics of Economic Policy-making in Peru and Chile," Presented at the 78th Annual Meeting of the American Political Science Association.

Rizzo, Jean-Marc, 1998, "The Economic Determinants of the Choice of an Exchange Rate Regime: A Probit Analysis," *Economics Letters*, Vol. 59, pp. 283-287.

Rodriguez, R. Hernandez, 1988, *Empresarios, Banca y Estado: El Conflicto Durante el Gobierno de Jose Lopez Portillo* (Mexico City: Publisher unknown).

Rodrik, Dani, 1997, *Has Globalization Gone Too Far?* (Washington, DC: Institute for International Economics).

Rojas-Suarez, Liliana, and Steven R. Weisbrod, 1995, *Financial Fragilities in Latin America: The 1980s and 1990s*, IMF Occasional Paper No. 132 (Washington, DC: International Monetary Fund).

Ros, Jaime, 1994, "Mercados Financieros y Flujos de Capital en Mexico," in *Los Capitales Externos en la Economias Latinoamericanas*, ed. by Jose A. Ocampo (Fedesarrollo and BID).

Rother, Phillipp C., 1999, "Explaining the Behavior of Financial Intermediation: Evidence from Transition Economies," IMF Working Paper WP/99/36 (Washington, DC: IMF) March.

Ruland, L. J., and J. M. Viaene, 1993, "The Political Choice of the Exchange-Rate Regime," *Economics and Politics*, Vol. 5, No. 3, November, pp. 271-284.

Sachs, Jeffrey, Aaron Tornell, and Andres Velasco, 1996, "The Collapse of the Mexican Peso: What Have We Learned?," *Economic Policy*, No. 22, April, pp. 15-63.

Sarmiento, Eduardo, 1991, "Economia del Narcotrafico," in *Narcotrafico en Colombia*, 2nd ed., by Carlos Gustavo Arrieta, Luis Javier Orjuela, Eduardo Sarmiento Palacio, and Juan Gabriel Tokatlian (Bogota: Universidad de los Andes).

Savvides, Andreas, 1990, "Real Exchange Rate Variablility and the Choice of Exchange Rate Regime by Developing Countries," *Journal of International Money and Finance*, Vol. 9, pp. 440-454.

Scherlen, Renee G., 1998, "Lessons to Build On: The 1994 Mexican Presidential Election," *Journal of Interamerican Studies and World Affairs*, Vol. 40, No. 1, Spring, pp. 19-38.

Sender, Henry, 1997(a), "The Devil to Pay," *Far Eastern Economic Review*, 5 June, pp. 50-53.

Sender, Henry, 1997(b), "Minder in a Bind," *Far Eastern Economic Review*, 5 June, pp. 53-54.

Shambaugh, George, 2004, "The Power of Money: Global Capital and Policy Choices in Developing Countries," *American Journal of Political Science* vol. 48, no. 2, April, pp. 281-295.

Simmons, Beth A., 1994, *Who Adjusts?: Domestic Sources of Foreign Economic Policy During the Interwar Years* (Princeton, NJ: Princeton University Press).

Smith, Geri, 1996, "Tossing a Lifeline to Mexico's Biggest Banks," *Business Week*, 22 January, p. 80.

Smith, Peter, 1997, "Political Dimensions of the Peso Crisis," in *Mexico 1994: Anatomy of an Emerging-Market Crash*, ed. by Sebastian Edwards and Moises Naim (Washington, DC: Carnegie Endowment for Peace) pp. 31-53.

Springer, Gary L., and Jorge L. Molina, 1995, "The Mexican Financial Crisis: Genesis, Impact, and Implications," *Journal of Interamerican Studies and World Affairs*, Vol. 37, No. 2, Summer, pp. 57-81.

Stallings, Barbara, 1992, "International Influence on Economic Policy: Debt, Stabilization, and Structural Reform," in *The Politics of Economic Adjustment: International Constraints, Distributive Conflicts and the State*, ed. by Stephan Haggard and Robert Kaufman (Princeton, NJ: Princeton University Press) pp. 41-88.

Starr, Pamela K., 1999(a), "Monetary Misalignment and Inadvertent Democratization in Technocratic Mexico," *Studies in Comparative International Development*, Vol. 33, Issue 4, Winter.

Starr, Pamela K., 1999(b), "Capital Flows, Fixed Exchange Rates, and Political Survival: Mexico and Argentina, 1994-1995," in *Markets and Democracy in Latin America*, ed. by Philip Okhorn and Pamela K. Starr (Boulder CO: Lynne Rienner) pp. 203-238.

Stein Velasco, Luis F., 1988, "Menor Carga Financiera," *Alto Nivel*, November.

Suehiro Akira, 1989, *Capital Accumulation in Thailand, 1855-1985* (Tokyo: The Centre for East Asian Cultural Studies).

Summers, Lawrence, 1999, testimony before the Senate Foreign Relations Subcommittee on International Economic Policy and Export/Trade Promotion, 27 January.

Supoj Rojpibulstit, 1976, "Bank Competition in Thailand," MA Thesis, Thammasat University.

Tanner, Evan, 1998, "Deviations from Uncovered Interest Parity: A Global Guide to Where the Action Is," IMF Working Paper 98/117 (Washington, DC: International Monetary Fund).

Tasker, Rodney, 1997, "State of Confusion," *Far Eastern Economic Review*, 24 July, p. 88.

Tavlas, George S., 1993, "The Theory of Optimum Currency Areas Revisited," *Finance and Development*, June, pp. 32-35.

Thorndike, Guillermo, 1988, *La Revolucion Imposible* (Lima: EMI Editores).

Torres, Craig, and Thomas T. Vogel, 1994, "Market Forces: Some Mutual Funds Wield Growing Clout in Developing Nations," *Wall Street Journal*, 14 June, pp. A1 & A6.

Turnovsky, Stephen J., 1976, "The Relative Stability of Alternative Exchange-rate Systems in the Presence of Random Disturbances," *Journal of Money, Credit, and Banking*, Vol. 8, No. 1, February.

Vatikiotis, Michael, 1997, "Free at Last," *Far Eastern Economic Review*, 10 July, pp. 70-71.

Vega Canovas, Gustavo, 1995, "NAFTA and Financial Services," in *The Politics of Free Trade in North America*, ed. by Gustavo del Castillo and Gustavo Vega Canovas (Ottawa: Centre for Trade and Policy Law) pp. 187-222.

Velarde, Julio, 1994, "Macroeconomic Stability and the Prospects for Growth: 1990-1993," in *Peru in Crisis: Dictatorship or Democracy?*, ed. by Joseph S. Tulchin and Gary Bland, Woodrow Wilson Center Current Studies in Latin America (Boulder, CO: Lynne Rienner) pp. 139-154.

Velasco, Andreas and Pablo Cabezas, 1998, "Alternative Responses to Capital Inflows: A Tale of Two Countries," in *Capital Flows and Financial Crises*, ed. by Miles Kahler (Ithica: NY, Cornell University Press) pp. 128-157.

Walter, Stefanie, 2005, "Speculative Currency Attacks and the Private Sector," Presented at the 63rd Midwest Political Science Association Annual National Conference, available at www.mwpsa.org.

Waltz, Kenneth N., 1979, *Theory of International Politics* (Reading, MA: Addison-Wesley).

Warr, Peter G., 1993, *The Thai Economy in Transition* (Cambridge: Cambridge University Press).

Warr, Peter G., and Bhanupong Nidhiprabha, 1996, *Thailand's Macroeconomic Miracle: Stable Adjustment and Sustained Growth* (Washington, DC: World Bank).

Weil, Gordon, 1984, *Exchange-Rate Regime Selection in Theory and Practice*, Monograph Series in Finance and Economics, Monograph 1983-2 (New York: New York University).

Weintraub, Sidney, 2000, *Financial Decision-Making in Mexico: To Bet a Nation*, (Pittsburgh: University of Pittsburgh).

Wessel, David, Paul B. Carroll, and Thomas T. Vogel, 1995, "Peso Surprise: How Mexico's Crisis Ambushed Top Minds in Officialdom, Finance," *Wall Street Journal*, 6 July, pp. A1 & A4.

Whynes, David K., 1992, "The Colombian Cocaine Trade and the War on Drugs," in *The Colombian Economy: Issues of Trade and Development*, ed. by Alvin Cohen and Frank R. Gunter (Boulder, CO: Westview Press).

Willett, Thomas, 1998, "Credibility and Discipline Effects of Exchange Rates as Nominal Anchors: The Need to Distinguish Temporary from Permanent Pegs," *The World Economy*, Vol. 21, No. 6, August, pp. 803-826.

Williamson, John, 2000, *Exchange Rate Regimes for Emerging Markets: Reviving the Intermediate Option*, Policy Analyses in International Economics No. 60 (Washington, DC: Institute for International Economics) September.

Williamson, John, and Molly Mahar, 1998, *A Survey of Financial Liberalization*, Essays in International Finance No. 211, (Princeton, NJ: International Finance Section, Department of Economics, Princeton University) November.

Wise, Carol, "Argentina's Currency Board: The Ties that Bind?" in *Exchange Rate Politics in Latin America*, ed. by Carol Wise and Riordan Roett (Washington, DC: Brookings Institution Press) pp. 93-122.

World Bank, 1989, "Peru: Policies to Stop Hyperinflation and Initiate Economic Recovery," World Bank Country Study PUB7460 (Washington, DC: World Bank).

World Bank, 1998, *Global Development Finance 1999* (Washington, DC: World Bank).

World Bank, 2000, *World Development Indicators 2000* (Washington, DC: World Bank).

World Bank, 2001, *Global Development Finance 2001* (Washington, DC: World Bank).

World Bank, 2001, *World Development Indicators 2001* (Washington, DC: World Bank).

World Bank, various years, *Global Development Finance* (Washington, DC: World Bank).

World Bank, various years, *World Development Indicators* (Washington, DC: World Bank).

Wright, John R., 1996, *Interest Groups and Congress: Lobbying, Contributions, and Influence* (Needham Heights, MA: Allyn & Bacon).

Yeyati, Eduardo Levy and Federico Sturzenegger, 2003, "Classifying Exchange Rate Regimes: Deeds vs. Words," unpublished manuscript, February.

Forthcoming in *European Economic Review*. Available at http://www.utdt.edu/~ely/papers.htm.

Zysman, John, 1983, *Governments, Markets, and Growth: Financial Systems and the Politics of Industrial Change* (Ithaca, NY: Cornell University Press).

Index

www.ingramcontent.com/pod-product-compliance
Lightning Source LLC
LaVergne TN
LVHW011128300926
849160LV00008B/562
* 9 7 8 1 1 3 8 6 1 9 6 4 7 *